THE
RESTLESS
SLEEP

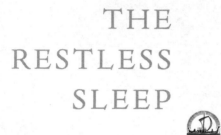

THE
RESTLESS
SLEEP

*Inside New York City's
Cold Case Squad*

STACY HORN

Viking

VIKING

Published by the Penguin Group

Penguin Group (USA) Inc., 375 Hudson Street, New York, New York 10014, U.S.A. •
Penguin Group (Canada), 90 Eglinton Avenue East, Suite 700, Toronto, Ontario, Canada
M4P 2Y3 (a division of Pearson Penguin Canada Inc.) • Penguin Books Ltd, 80 Strand,
London WC2R 0RL, England • Penguin Ireland, 25 St. Stephen's Green, Dublin 2,
Ireland (a division of Penguin Books Ltd) • Penguin Books Australia Ltd, 250
Camberwell Road, Camberwell, Victoria 3124, Australia (a division of Pearson Australia
Group Pty Ltd) • Penguin Books India Pvt Ltd, 11 Community Centre, Panchsheel
Park, New Delhi–110 017, India • Penguin Group (NZ), Cnr Airborne and Rosedale
Roads, Albany, Auckland 1310, New Zealand (a division of Pearson New Zealand Ltd) •
Penguin Books (South Africa) (Pty) Ltd, 24 Sturdee Avenue, Rosebank, Johannesburg
2196, South Africa

Penguin Books Ltd, Registered Offices: 80 Strand, London WC2R 0RL, England

First published in 2005 by Viking Penguin, a member of Penguin Group (USA) Inc.

10   9   8   7   6   5   4   3   2   1

LIBRARY OF CONGRESS CATALOGING IN PUBLICATION DATA
Horn, Stacy.
  The restless sleep : inside New York City's Cold Case Squad / Stacy Horn
    p. cm.
  ISBN 0-670-03419-3
  1. New York (N.Y.). Police Dept. Cold Case Squad. 2. Murder—Investigation—New
York (State)—New York—Case studies. 3. Murder—New York (State)—New York—
Case studies. 4. Detectives—New York (State)—New York. I. Title.
HV8079.H6H66 2005
363.25'9523'097471—dc22   2004061236

Printed in the United States of America
Designed by Carla Bolte   •   Set in Scala
Maps by Virginia Norey

To the Cold Case Squad and everyone in law enforcement—thank you.

Preface

The minute you die you start to fade from the world and from the memories of the people who knew you. In a generation or two you're an old picture your great-grandchildren can no longer identify. The value of a treasured object, the letter from your dead father, the first gift your child ever gave you, something she made that you placed proudly on a windowsill in the kitchen so you'd see it every day—all of that is lost. As sad as it might be, we all die, then disappear. That has to happen. But when you're murdered, that's something else.

When someone breaks open the skull of a young girl who still thought she could make all her dreams come true and ends her chances forever, the sadness added to the universe goes beyond what can be endured. People get sick, accidents happen, but we're still in the realm of what we have to swallow and can. We'll complain to the universe about it, but we don't expect an answer. But someone gunning for us? We have so little time to begin with, and must contend with so many other possible bad endings, and now this? A murderer has taken fate into his own hands, and the balance, which is bad enough, shifts unnecessarily into the unacceptable range. The loss he inflicts is intolerable. We want someone to answer for it.

But the universe is not fair, and justice is not always served. Sometimes the killer is never identified or caught. They're out there in the thousands, free. You may pass through the life of that killer for just a second: he's behind you in line as you order coffee from the deli, he cuts you off on the highway or doesn't hold open a door at Grand Central, and you stare for a moment at the person who seems indifferent to you and to small, everyday courtesies. Maybe he's exceedingly polite and you share a smile with someone who once shared a smile with someone else before forcing a knife inside of them. Murderers touch us. Their presence in the world makes all our lives, for moments, unbearable. And for others, an eternity.

■

I first heard of the existence of the Cold Case Squad while delivering cupcakes to a 9/11 command center at Pier 40, on West Street along the Hudson River, less than a mile uptown from the World Trade Center. A Cold Case detective was assigned there that night, and he explained what the squad did and what a cold case was. I've always been drawn to stories of the lost and forgotten, and I felt like I had the entire history of New York City death in front of me. I imagined questioning this Cold Case detective long into that disturbing night. But he got called to the site and I was left with questions. Who are these guys? What are they working on? How far back did the cases go? A couple of months later I scheduled a meeting at the Cold Case Squad headquarters in Brooklyn to discuss a possible book.

The squad's office is like most of the NYPD offices. Nineteen fifties–style drab. There's an open and exposed phone company punch-down block on the wall, along with an old suggestion box, which is now used for overtime slips. The arrest logbook sitting out on a table is the same style logbook the police department has been using since at least the 1930s. The conference room is referred to as the TV room, and sure enough, there's a TV going inside, some game show I've never seen. Pictures of the casts of *The Sopranos* and *The Three Stooges* are thumbtacked to the walls.

The commanding officer of the squad, Deputy Inspector Vito Spano, and his executive officer, Lieutenant Bob McHugh, are elegantly dressed. They don't really look like "cops," but of the two, Spano is the nearest to what I see in my head when I think law enforcement. Later a detective will explain that the closer you get to police headquarters (or higher up in rank), the nicer the suits.

Spano tells me his background in a gravelly, I-don't-have-time-for-this voice: "I came here from hostage negotiation, sex crimes, child abuse, gang investigation. . . ." Sex crimes, gangs, child abuse. I start to explain my interest, but Spano's expression while I talk seems to say, "And I should give a shit about this *why?*" My enthusiasm for the subject when confronted with men who deal with real, serious harm was starting to feel a little small. McHugh asks me some polite questions about my background, shakes my hand, and leaves. I turn back to Spano, who now looks bored. I try again. I ask him about his history with the police force and how he got assigned to the Cold Case Squad. Somehow the fact that he is divorced comes out. I'd just had a terrible date a few nights before. I see common ground and I pounce on it, not thinking.

"Don't you just hate dating?"

Now he looks incredulous. Why am I talking about dating? I keep going. "Don't you wish you could somehow find the person of your dreams while sitting on the couch, watching TV?" He's just staring now. My own expression is probably pained. Oh, please, I'm thinking. Yes, it's mundane next to murder. But we're both human. Is there nothing about you that is anything like me? Then his face changes. "Yeah," he says, full of relief, it seems. "I do. If I have to get dressed up one more time . . ." He drops the stony, professional facade. The mood in the room lightens. He walks over to a metal locker full of old photographs and mementos and pulls out scrapbooks of newspaper articles from his decades-long career with the NYPD. He's telling me stories, talking about cases they're working on. The gravelly, tough-cop attitude is gone, like that. He's out of his seat and talking nonstop, and for now he wants to tell me everything he knows. He's not scary. He's vulnerable and proud. "You remember that guy out in Queens?" he asks, telling me the story of a murderer they caught. I don't remember, actually, but I smile.

Cops and detectives are often portrayed the same way in books and in movies, and that is some version of the '50s noir, hard-boiled guy. They all may try to come off like that hard-boiled guy, and usually in the first five minutes of meeting any one of them they do. But you get to know them and they're nothing like the TV dicks. Most of them are trying to eat well and stay in shape. They worry if they are wearing the right outfit for a given occasion, or if they've said the wrong thing. Unlike characters from a pulp-fiction novel, they have a range of emotions and they get embarrassed and defensive, disappointed and petulant; they long for a better life, and they're trying to do a good job. But they can't always win. Sometimes they do something brilliant, which leads to an arrest, and sometimes someone makes a mistake and fails; sometimes a murderer will elude them no matter how much time, money, and heart they put into the case, and then not only will they be haunted, they must also face the bosses who need to produce numbers to climb to the top.

My interest in the Cold Case Squad is probably rooted in a lifelong interest in the subject of death and my own desire to not disappear. The likely possibility that the minute you die the meaning of your life immediately starts disintegrating until nothing remains has repeatedly left me frozen in an existential panic with absolutely no means of comfort. It shouldn't happen. If nothing else, I'm driven to slow that final vanishing down. I can't do anything about death, but I can try to affect memory. It is, perhaps, a futile quest, but like these detectives who want to provide some measure of relief to the families who have suffered the worst kind of loss, I want to resurrect the city's forgotten dead. I want to recover the lost stories, cases, files, and name as many names as I can. Who have we forgotten? What records are tucked away in the seventy-six precincts of the

New York Police Department? What are the oldest unsolved cases on the books, and how many are there? What kind of artifacts of murder are gathering dust in police department warehouses all over the city? What is left?

We don't have to disappear. At least, not so completely or so quickly.

Contents

THE
RESTLESS
SLEEP

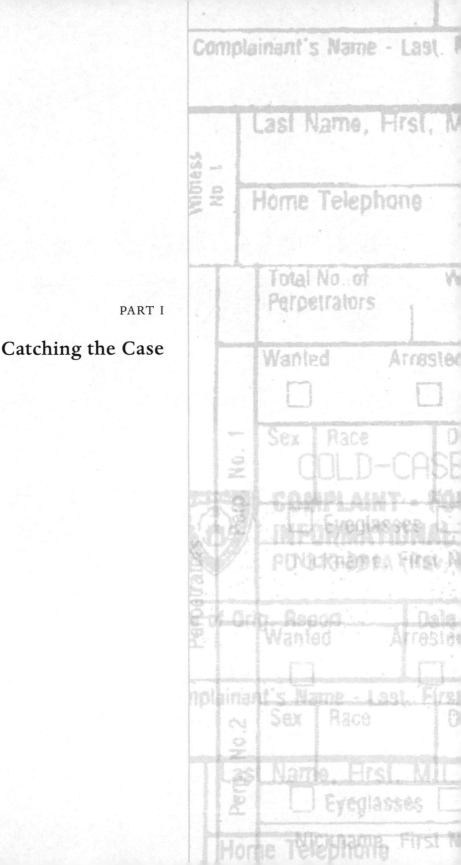

PART I

Catching the Case

1 Linda Leon and Esteban Martinez

December 15, 1996

Ten days before Christmas in 1996 a six-year-old boy calls 911. We don't know how long it takes him to work up the nerve to call, but it's just before eight o'clock at night. Speaking clearly, he tells the 911 operator, "You know, my father died." "What?" she asks. And he repeats, "My father died." The operator is all business. "What is your address?" When he tells her, the operator doesn't immediately respond. "Okay?" he asks, to prompt her. "I'm just trying to verify the address," she answers. "Where's your mother?" "Died. Died. I'm here on my own. My father and my mother died. Somebody killed my mother and my daddy." In the background, his two younger brothers don't even sound human. They make noises like animals grunting. It's an ugly sound, ugly because it's so not right. Then, it sounds like they are roaring. Finally, their voices resolve into something more human, and they sound like children again, children wailing and crying. Apparently, these are the sounds young children make when they come upon the remains of their tortured and murdered parents. The 911 operator asks the boy what apartment he's

3

in and how old he is, and he gets progressively more upset. He thinks she doesn't understand the problem. "My mother and my daddy died," he tells her again. And then he begs, "Please help me, okay?" The first officers on the scene find the boys in their underwear climbing over the bodies.

Linda Leon, twenty-three years old, and Esteban Martinez, twenty-nine years old, were tortured, then shot in the head while their three children listened from the next room. The kids were meant to die too, it was later learned, but the girlfriend of one of the killers argued—you got what you want, let's just get out of here—and the kids were left alone to cry. Leon and Martinez were drug dealers. So who cares, right? Pathetic lives, pathetic deaths.

Linda and Esteban were doomed. Limited by circumstance, talent, imagination, and character, dealing drugs was the best they could manage. They weren't going to get to do something fun or worthwhile in life. Instead they would live soul-destroying lives and die, scared, after being stabbed in the ear with a Sheetrock saw for perhaps an hour, according to the police estimate, before being shot, while the only things in the world they cared for listened to every word, every scream, every plea for their lives, reduced to animal noises. The wretched killing the wretched, the case goes "cold," who gives a fuck?

■

Since 1985, in New York City alone, the killers of 8,894 people remain free. That's 8,894 murderers among us. Even if you want to say some of these murders were committed by the same people, as if attributing the crimes to serial killers were a better way of looking at this, that's still a lot of murderers walking around who get to go see the new Steven Spielberg movie, eat their favorite dinner, and have sex. What could be uglier than a murderer transported by pleasure, living years and years and years, sometimes long enough to make it until a nice, relaxed old age?

Unsolved homicide cases are never closed, but some can go cold if enough evidence can't be found to convict anyone. Sometimes detectives find themselves overrun with murder. Whenever someone is killed in their precinct they have to drop what they're doing to investigate. The cases they were working on get pushed farther and farther back, some all the way into oblivion. And the fact is, most murder victims are people the general public cares little about. Middle-class people, people with lots of friends who never break any laws, famous people, wealthy people, sure, they're stabbed to death from time to time, but chances are you haven't heard of a single one of the 8,894. They had so little going for them to begin with, and now this. They've become nothing more than a cast-off case.

In the New York Police Department there's a unit called the Cold Case and Apprehension Squad. While the rest of the world has forgotten the cases that have gone cold, if they ever even noticed them in the first place, the Cold Case Squad reaches into our worst past and yanks these victims back from oblivion. Who were they? What happened to them? Who did this to them? Someone deliberately, knowingly took away whatever time in life they had left. They're supposed to answer for that. For the families who figure the world isn't going to give their son, daughter, husband, or wife another thought, the Cold Case Squad is their one shot to correct a terrible imbalance, however inadequately.

Cases find their way to the Cold Case Squad through a number of different channels. Sometimes the commanding officer is told, "Do something with this," when someone sends a letter to the mayor, or the police commissioner, or some other important person. A couple of years ago, the sister of a man who was killed with a meat cleaver in 1971 wrote, "This is the 28th year of this heinous crime and the injustice was terrible then and to this day is still quite overbearing. Are you still working on this case? Or have you decided that since 28 years have past [*sic*], we may as well let another murderer walk away free?" The Cold Case Squad soon discovered that her brother's killer had already been dead ten years when she mailed that letter. He died of smoke inhalation from a kitchen fire in his tiny, squalid one-bedroom apartment in Philadelphia. After three decades of waiting, it was a very unsatisfying ending for the victim's sister. She was sorry he didn't burn alive.

A record of every murder in New York, solved or unsolved, is kept at the Homicide Analysis Unit at 1PP, in homicide logbooks. (Police headquarters is always referred to as 1PP, short for One Police Plaza, the address for NYPD headquarters. It's pronounced OnePeePee. For months I'd look up to see if the grown man or woman saying OnePeePee was saying it with a straight face. Another name for OnePeePee: "the Puzzle Palace," except the people who work there don't like that name, so no one uses it to their face.)

The oldest remaining logbook in the NYPD's possession is from 1964. There were 697 homicides listed that year. Of the 697, 122 cases are cold. We'll probably never learn who killed 122 men, women, and babies that year. Most of these victims were stabbed. After that, they were killed by guns and cars. Fists and feet are listed as weapons in 21 cases. In 1964, abortions were officially considered homicides, and there were 12 of them in the logbook, including one "charred fetus." One person was killed by a pumpkin (no explanation was given). Other unusual weapons listed are a television stand, a bar stool, acid, a beer can opener, a candle. On October 6 of that year, in the 73 Precinct, Anni Malzen died of wounds made by a sledge-hammer. (Detectives don't say the "73rd" Precinct, they say the "seven three" Precinct. The "one two oh" Precinct, not the "120th." This is true for all the precincts above the 19th.) And while an arrest was made, someone later added, in parentheses, "suicide." How do you kill yourself with a sledgehammer?

Murders committed from 1985 on are now entered into an electronic database, but every entry from 1964 to the present bears exactly the same information: entry number, date of homicide, precinct number, name of victim, type of weapon, and whether an arrest has been made. That's it. A detective can't tell just by looking at these records if there is anything he can solve.

Sometimes the squad commanders themselves go out to the precincts and bring back a case. Perhaps they got a phone call from an old friend, "I got a tip about this case . . . ," or there's a case from their younger days in another precinct that they never quite forgot.

Every time the Cold Case Squad solves a case and it hits the local papers, they get calls about other murders and sometime manage to pick up a few leads. Now they get e-mail, too. Tips can come from anywhere.

In May 2004 a forty-four-year-old Queens man named Eddie Delmage called *Opie & Anthony,* a Howard Stern–like radio show that was on WNEW at the time, and confessed to the 1977 murder of two Colombian drug dealers during a segment called "Total Truth Tuesday." Eddie said he shot them during a drug deal, burned the bodies, then threw what was left away in the meat-packing district by the river in Manhattan. He was calling *Opie & Anthony,* he said, to offer his place to a homeless woman known on the show as Stalker Patty. He wanted to make up for his past mistake. "He didn't sound like the kind of guy to make this up," cohost Anthony Cumia said. Detectives from the squad couldn't find a case fitting his description, but they had to look into it nonetheless.

Anthony was wrong. Eddie was making it up. When detectives arrived to investigate he answered the door to his dark apartment in nothing but an undershirt and slippers. "I asked, would he like to get dressed before we start talking," Deputy Inspector Vito Spano, the commanding officer of the Cold Case Squad, said, "because he really wasn't a pretty sight standing there." Eddie was nervous. "It felt like a sad house that time had passed," Spano continued. "Something had happened here and Eddie was too devastated to pick up the pieces. Things were out of place or left out, not put away, a heavy dust over everything. He was like a man still waiting for his wife to come home." These are the glimpses the detectives get into our lives. "It wasn't nice to look at," Vito told me. "I felt depressed." Eddie had worked for a cargo-handling company at the airport, but he'd been on disability for the past twelve years. Eddie felt that Opie and Anthony hadn't appreciated his generous offer to Stalker Patty, and he took it as an insult to his manhood. The phony confession was a desperate shot at building himself up. He wanted to be the romantic, dangerous but reformed killer, looking for redemption by rescuing the damsel in distress, not the pale, paunchy, middle-aged man living downstairs from his mother, abandoned by life, who, if he had ever had any dramatic moments in his life, had few left now. "Defending his manhood" is a recurring theme in Cold Case Squad investigations.

More often, though, cold cases are picked up and brought back by detectives themselves. They say "I'm assuming a case" or, simply, "I'm working the case." There's also the more crude but popular "This is my bag of shit." The detectives have their own contacts and informants, their own resources, and their own ambitions. Sometimes they read about a case in the newspaper and think, *Okay, they did this, but I would have done that.* Assuming someone else's case can be a delicate matter, but not always.

When someone is murdered, the case belongs to the Homicide Squad in the precinct where the body is found. Back in the eighties and early nineties, when there were more than two thousand murders a year in the city, no one wanted to pick up yet another homicide in their precinct, especially if it looked like it was going to be "a loser," what they call cases that are difficult to solve. Precinct commanders literally fought over which side of the precinct lines a body fell. Spano remembers a 1987 murder committed in the 83 Precinct. The killer moved the body and it sat for a week in a Dumpster in the 72 Precinct, where at the time Vito Spano was a young and less experienced Detective Squad commander. Then the body was carted off, along with the trash, to the 94 Precinct. Thinking the case was a loser, the 94 Precinct Detective Squad commander, who was older and meaner, called Spano and made him take it, even though by rights the homicide should have been the 94's. Mistake. Spano's squad solved the case two days later. Fingerprints were lifted off the linoleum the body was wrapped in, and when Vito and his detectives went to the address listed on the suspect's record and peeked inside, there on the floor, with a large piece missing, was the same linoleum.

Assuming someone else's case once they've put some effort into it, however, is something else. You're saying, "I think I can solve the case you couldn't." The initial reaction is often "You think you're going to show me up? Piss off." Technically, if the precinct detective isn't actively working the case, the Cold Case Squad detective can simply say, "Fuck you. Give me the case." If the precinct detective balks, Vito can call the squad boss at the precinct, and now it's Vito's delicate matter. But no one wants the running-back-to-daddy stigma of that. And there are other reasons the cold case detectives would prefer to handle it themselves than go to Vito. People get transferred, special units are dissolved. The guy you screwed carelessly today could be your boss or partner tomorrow. The smartest detectives use a little diplomacy and make the precinct detective comfortable with handing over the case: "You've got all these other cases, and I have a little time on my hands, would you mind if I take a look?" Once the case is formally signed out with the Cold Case Squad it's got the Cold Case Squad detective's name on it. He's responsible now. The precinct detective is off the hook. The case is logged into the Cold Case Squad's database and given a brand-new case number. If it's never solved, now it's because the Cold Case Squad couldn't solve it.

■

In 1998, the Leon-Martinez double homicide was assumed by a detective in the Special Projects unit of the Cold Case Squad because he "knew a guy who knew a guy" who said the case could be solved. But he didn't get any further than the precinct detectives before he retired, and his partner, who had been helping him, was soon to be transferred to another office.

But the Cold Case Squad is still responsible for the case. Lieutenant Joseph Pollini, the commanding officer of the Special Projects unit of the Cold Case Squad, chooses Detective Wendell Stradford to take over the Leon-Martinez case. *Why me,* Stradford thinks. He has a lot of cases already, but more to the point, the detectives on the case before him were good, capable detectives, especially Felix Marquez, the first Cold Case detective to take a shot. *If Felix couldn't solve it, how am I going to solve it?* When he questions Pollini's assignment, Pollini shoots back, "You're more capable than anyone else here to solve this case. This case should have been solved. I want you to get on it. Drop everything else that you're doing and finish it."

There's an upside-down fish in the aquarium sitting on Lieutenant Pollini's desk the day I come to visit. He's swimming furiously but in one spot, upside down. He'll be dead the next day, I later learn. The office is large but packed with piles of papers and books and dead red and yellow roses. A month later, the same dead red and yellow roses will still be sitting there, in vases on the table in the middle of the room. More bunches are hanging upside down behind them. The commanding officer likes dried flowers. In the VCR is a tape called *The Best AB Exercises.*

Pollini walks in. Perfect tan, perfect hair, perfect clothes. He's a college professor in addition to being a commanding officer, but he has a movie-star look about him, if a bit dated. He has a *Saturday Night Fever* thing going, the first few buttons of his shirt open to expose several gold chains. When he later introduces me to a member of an organized-crime family, I see that Pollini's look makes perfect sense. He looks comfortable. He understands these guys. He can speak like an academic about them, and speak like a peer to them. And, more to the point, he knows how to catch them. We don't talk long. "I'm the boss," he explains. His detectives are the ones conducting the actual investigations.

All the detectives who work for Pollini sit together in one large open room. The Counter Terrorism Squad is right next door, and drywalls are halfway installed to separate them. "How long has construction been going on?" I ask them. "Forever." (A few months.) Everything else looks like it's been this way since the fifties, every year getting more and more worn and battered and bleak. Dirty windows look out onto old and new New York. Outdated wanted posters and a two-year-old calendar decorate the walls. Their furniture was made decades before anyone knew the word *ergonomic*. Every time I wait to speak to a detective in any of their offices, I mentally make over their dismal rooms. Lieutenant Pollini is the first of many to say to me, "You gotta talk to Stradford."

■

Detective Wendell Stradford is one of the original members of the Cold Case Squad. Before coming here he worked for Jack Maple, the deputy commissioner of Operations, in a special unit called the Police Commissioner's Investigation Squad, the PC Squad for short. If a precinct was having problems, someone from the PC Squad was sent to help. They were the cavalry. Maple had a hand in selecting detectives when the Cold Case Squad began, and Jack Maple did not fuck around. He only picked the best, and he picked Wendell twice.

When I first meet Wendell I think, *Denzel Washington will play him in the movie.* He'd prefer Laurence Fishburne, he tells me later, because "he's more street." I have no doubt that Wendell can be street when he has to be, but his manners are elegant when he's in the office. Definitely Denzel. Wendell is handsome, and he loves women. He's intoxicating to be around.

Stradford is directly, right-off-the-bat impressive. Smart, poised, gentle, with an understated self-possession. A few minutes after meeting him, he leads me out of the room because a criminal informant he doesn't like has just shown up. "I don't want him to get to know your face and then think he can come up to you on the street and say hello." Stradford has a degree in criminal justice. He's forty-four, and he will be turning forty-five on a day the NYPD and most of the rest of us hate most, September 11. But it doesn't matter. "I haven't celebrated my birthday since college," he tells me.

When the informant leaves, Stradford plays me the tape of the six-year-old calling 911, and I feel guilty because he looks more upset than I do, and he must have heard this tape of Linda and Esteban's children's cries a million times.

The detectives initially assigned to the case didn't get far. It didn't help that no one tells cops the truth during an investigation, if they talk to them at all, particularly in lower-income neighborhoods.

When the detectives from the 43 Squad questioned family, friends, acquaintances, and neighbors, no one knew a thing. (Every precinct has a Detective Squad, so the 43 Precinct has what they will refer to as the 43 Squad.) Cops aren't here to help you. You talk to a cop and someone gets into trouble, is the feeling. Now, even witnesses in high-income neighborhoods won't talk. They hire lawyers and PR agents.

Lack of cooperation was not the initial detectives' only problem. They were led further astray in their investigation by the feds. The DEA (Drug Enforcement Agency) sold the detectives on a drug cartel connection. The DEA was tracking Martinez's activities at the time of the murder and was sure they had been killed by the Colombians. It made sense. While there was never any evidence that Linda participated in the drug business, Esteban was a known drug dealer, selling powdered cocaine. But the detectives hit nothing but dead ends from that day on. There was a liquor store in Linda's name in the Bronx, where Linda and Esteban lived and died. They called it Linda's Liquors. The detectives were told it was a front for drug deals, but nothing was ever found to connect the drug dealing to the liquor store. To make matters worse, concentrating on Esteban's drug dealing further alienated Linda's and Esteban's already distrustful and grieving families. Access to the children was limited. The detectives didn't know much about what happened during Linda's and Esteban's last hours or who else might have been in that apartment.

The detectives didn't have much else to go on. The only physical evidence at the crime scene was a set of fingerprints on a soda can that weren't on file anywhere. It was a clean scene. This was not a crime of passion. No one said "Fuck you," then, "No, fuck you," and got carried away with rage, then blows and knives and guns and death. It was premeditated. Someone brought weapons. Someone purchased and brought the duct tape that was wrapped around Linda's and Esteban's mouths. The killers were careful not to leave any trace of themselves behind. There were no leads.

Time went by. Nothing happened. No one wants to sit with failure too long, but you need a reason to make it OK to let go, to give up. The detectives must have finally thought "Well, fuck it. The family doesn't seem to give a shit if we catch their killers or not, so screw it." Why knock themselves out? The family may have said to each other, "Fucking cops. One of them dies and they tear this city inside out. We die and it's screw you." Their perception of the cops' actions confirmed what they already believed and justified their lack of cooperation. Reasons were in place. More time went by. Everyone moved on.

And the children of the murdered started to grow up.

When Wendell Stradford was a kid, he had no desire whatsoever to become a police officer. He really wanted to play basketball. "I had one of those neighborhood dreams. I wanted to be an NBA star, but it just didn't work out that way. I'm only six feet tall, and I didn't have a very good jump shot," he admitted. "But I could jump into the sky and do a whole lot of other things." He stops for a second and thinks. "It was just a dream. Kids have dreams."

Linda and Esteban's six-year-old son's statement to the police: "I told them, you killed them, he said no, they're not dead. That when I touch them. They didn't answer me."

Here's the thing: cold cases are hard. Louis Eliopulos, who works on cold cases for the Naval Criminal Investigator's Service, is fond of saying, "If they were easy cases they would have been solved already." Deputy Inspector Spano agrees. "So forget going on about how difficult they are; that's a given." All the detectives tell me the same thing. You've got to settle yourself in for the long haul, because the only thing that's going to help you now is patience, intelligence and imagination.

In 2000, Detective Wendell Stradford becomes the fifth detective to take on the Leon-Martinez case. Wendell looks at the same scene, the same evidence, the same lives, only he sees a whole other world.

2 A Brief History of the Cold Case Squad

Nobody can agree on who came up with the idea for the Cold Case Squad. The guy whose name comes up the most, Jack Maple, is dead. He died on August 4, 2001, from colon cancer. Whenever people describe Jack Maple they invariably talk about what an amazing dresser he was. But I've seen pictures. The man dressed like a pimp, for God's sake. Outlandish, inelegant, it's just plain embarrassing how badly he dressed. Didn't the man have friends? The kind of friends to pull him aside and say, "Jack, dude. Look in the mirror." Someone told me he smelled. Then someone else told me this: "If Jack Maple didn't know about something on Friday, he read every book he could get his hands on over the weekend, and he was an expert by Monday." It turns out, this incredibly bad dresser might be the reason thousands of us aren't dead right now.

Maple started out as an ordinary transit cop in the 1980s. I remember wondering if transit cops were "real cops." On the subway, I'd always check to see if their guns were fake. Not only were they not fake, they were deadlier than what the NYPD carried. Maple's boss, Police Commissioner William Bratton, then chief of the New York City Transit Police, got his men the frighteningly effective

9mm Glock sidearms long before they became standard issue for the NYPD. "Revolvers don't stop anyone," it was explained to me. You shoot a guy with a revolver and he'll keep coming at you and coming at you. Hit him with a Glock loaded with hollow-point bullets and a "large channel wound" opens up so immediately that the guy never moves another inch. His blood pressure drops and he goes straight down. A revolver is also comically awkward to reload during a gunfight. (When Bratton became the police commissioner in Los Angeles in 2002, he switched the LAPD to Glocks his first year.)

Under the effective transit-cop-arming chief Bratton, Maple worked his way up to lieutenant, and in a condominium on Vestry and Hudson, Jack and his "condo cops" developed a method of policing that cut felonies and robberies in the subways 27 percent. It included what they called their Charts of the Future. They stuck pins in maps, enabling them to track crime in the subways. Big deal, but no one had done it before. When Mayor Rudolph Giuliani appointed Bratton police commissioner in 1994, Bratton brought Maple along as his deputy commissioner of Operations. What the new guys had started over in Transit evolved into something called CompStat at the NYPD, and CompStat is credited with cutting crime in New York more than 60 percent between 1994 and 2004.

"The dirty little secret in policing back then was, we really weren't that good," admits Lou Anemone, Maple's boss and cohort at the time. Anemone was the chief of Patrol in 1994. In 1995 he became the chief of Department, when John Timoney became the first deputy commissioner. After the police commissioner and first deputy commissioner, the chief of Department is the most powerful person within the NYPD. As the deputy commissioner of Operations, Maple was just below Anemone.

"There really weren't a lot of people doing everything that they should have been doing," Anemone continued. "There was very little accountability. The whole reason for CompStat was the fact that nobody above the rank of cop was talking about crime or doing any planning about crime."

"Detectives were great when the media put a little spotlight on a case; if it was a high-profile case, if it was a Manhattan case, or anywhere in the Diamond District or Midtown, those cases got solved. Jack had the view that, if they could do it for those cases, don't you think they could do a better job for the run-of-the-mill cases?"

So they set up the CompStat process. First, they went after petty crimes like spray-painting names on subway cars, or harassing drivers with squeegees. The theory was that these small crimes created an atmosphere of lawlessness that fostered bigger crimes. Then they put together a database of all the crimes committed in New York, and started holding meetings twice a month where all precinct and operational commanders in a patrol borough got together and, apparently, humiliated each other into action. "Why were there so many murders (or rapes or robberies) in your precinct, and what exactly are you doing about it, hmmm?" And they'd better have an answer for every one-, two-, and three-star chief who is now turned in their direction, waiting for one.

For the first time in NYPD history, incredibly, the NYPD was precisely targeting patterns of crime, and commanders were being held accountable. With eight patrol boroughs in New York (Manhattan North and South, Brooklyn North and South, Queens North and South, the Bronx, and Staten Island), every commander could look forward to a CompStat grilling at least once every two months. Other people attended. Pretty much any legitimate law enforcement agency or special unit, people from the DA's office, for example, could wrangle a position inside this testosterone-packed room. CompStat was an updated Charts of the Future.

It worked. However, you don't change the rules and turn something as big and entrenched as the NYPD around without a battle, and these guys knew how to fight. "You had to fucking kill people," someone high up in the NYPD explained. In a 1999 interview with a magazine called *Government Technology,* Jack Maple was asked how he dealt with the turf issues within the department. "Law enforcement professionals are well known for drawing turf lines and protecting them at all costs," the interviewer began. Maple responded. "If you have turf issues like that, you murder who is in command of that division and you don't have the turf issues anymore. It is right out of Sun Tsu (*The Art of War*). Sun Tsu wants to be the general, so he goes before the emperor with a battalion of concubines. Sun Tsu says, 'Forward march,' and they giggle at him. So he beheads the squad leaders and puts new ones in charge. When he says, 'Forward march' again, they do it."

A retired detective told me about one CompStat meeting where they had an animation of Pinocchio with his nose growing up on a screen behind a commanding officer the entire time they were questioning him. When he was done answering they said, "Turn around." They gave him a minute to fully grasp his complete and total humiliation. "Now tell us the truth."

I guess you could say that in Jack Maple's time, heads rolled. They had to. People tend to resist change, even when it's positive. It's not just the NYPD and law enforcement; every large institution is like this. In 1986, I encountered the same resistance introducing the Internet and on-line communication to the Mobil Corporation, my employer at the time. Perhaps the NYPD is worse. Who is more hardheaded, a cop or a chemist? So while CompStat was ultimately very effective, anyone with allegiance to Bratton, Maple, Anemone, and Edward Norris—a young deputy inspector who helped push CompStat along—was alienated. To this day people complain about how ruthless some of them were, but theirs was likely the only way to get CompStat in place. Perhaps the very process of instituting change attracted a particular kind of person to help—lone wolves, black sheep, people with enormous egos and axes to grind, who must have been complete assholes at times. At least they were brutal and effective as opposed to just plain brutal, which some cops who opposed CompStat were. Anyone who stood in the way of CompStat or was revealed as ineffective quit, took early retirement, or transferred out as far away as they could. And New York's crime rate started to plummet.

In 1993 there were 1,927 murders. In 1995, a year after instituting CompStat, there were 1,181. In 2003 there were 596. New York hasn't seen numbers like that since 1964. How many people would be dead right now if it weren't for CompStat? Using the number of people murdered the year before CompStat was implemented—1,927— let's say 1,927 New Yorkers would have been killed every year since 1994. After subtracting the actual number of people killed each year, that comes to a total of 9,598 people walking around who would have otherwise died horribly between 1994 and 2003.

But it wasn't just about punishing guys who weren't doing jack, former first deputy commissioner John Timoney explained. It was about figuring out who was and rewarding them. Everyone always said the Patrol Bureau was "the backbone of the police department," but it was the guys outside Patrol, the political favorites closer to 1PP, who got the promotions. When he was chief of Department, John Timoney did two things. He eliminated the middle layers of command. The guys at the top now had to get down and involve themselves with crime on a day-to-day basis. At the same time, he reorganized the command structure of the seventy-six precincts. He got rid of the existing divisions, then took the ten worst precincts and called them "A houses." The next thirty became "B houses," and the remaining thirty-six were "Cs." Captains just starting out were put in C houses. If they did a good job, they were promoted to deputy inspector and put in charge of a B house, and so on. Not only were they in the thick of it for the first time in their NYPD-boss lives, but for the first time commanders in the Patrol Bureau had an honest-to-God career path.

There is still some debate about how much CompStat alone had to do with the decline in murder in New York City. With so many other people and countless community groups working toward the same goal, it wouldn't be fair to say that CompStat is the only explanation. But the NYPD finally had the power and numbers to go after the bad guys in a real way. It's hard to understand why something like CompStat wasn't in place long before, but it's not surprising that the murder rate dropped so dramatically once it was.

In 1995, the year following the implementation of CompStat, Jack Maple and Edward Norris came up with the idea for the Cold Case Squad. They knew what they were in for. Oh great. Another new idea. It was going to be CompStat all over again. Maple, Norris, and Anemone didn't respect the chief of Detectives at the time, Charles Reuther. "An obstructionist," they called him. Norris and Reuther couldn't have hated each other more. At Maple's suggestion, Norris was transferred out of the Detective Bureau, and out from under Reuther's thumb, to the more amenable Chief Anemone and the office of the chief of Department.

Anemone approved the new Cold Case Squad, Police Commissioner William Bratton approved his approval, and in the first months of 1996, Anemone, Maple, and Norris, who became the first commanding officer of the Cold Case Squad, gave some thought to whom they wanted for their new unit.

Norris said, "Not every detective is a superstar. It's true in every business or corporation; it's the same at IBM or Mrs. Field's Cookies, and the police department is no different. In the Detective Squad you've got one or two guys who are real warriors, one or two lunkheads who shouldn't be there, and the rest of the guys who do what they're told to do. You assign them a case and they'll do a decent job. That's all they're going to do for you. They're not going to knock themselves out."

Anemone, Maple, and Norris wanted the warriors. "We took the best that we had, a mixture of good hunters and good case guys, and we set them loose."

What personality traits make up a warrior? They were the best detectives, but they were also all the people who, for one reason or another, pissed people off and were OK about that. Some of them weren't liked. Some of them didn't get along with their commanders. It really was CompStat all over again. Lone wolves, black sheep.

Talented, brilliant misfits. Detective geeks who like to kick ass. And right from the start, that is exactly what they did with cold cases. This peculiar combination of personality strengths and flaws worked. Some of them had problems getting along with others, and perhaps they had something to prove. So they did. In the eight-year history of the Cold Case Squad, of the 2,136 cases they've adopted, they've arrested 1,332 people in connection with the crimes, successfully cleared 629 cases, and got exceptional clearances on 71 more. (Although they don't like to do it, a case can be "exceptionally" cleared when the murderer has been identified definitively—by a substantiated confession, for example—but the murderer has since died, or is in a country that refuses to extradite him. They don't like to do it because it's not as satisfying as taking someone off the streets and putting him in jail. Furthermore, exceptional clearances don't show up in the NYPD's monthly stats for cases cleared. They don't officially "count," and since it's all about the numbers, they want to clear cases that are going to make the police department look good.) That's 629 murderers, more or less, who are not among us, making our lives miserable or worse. ("Or less" because they find some of the guys they're looking for in prisons or in graveyards.)

When the announcement for the squad was made, people went nuts. Again, the newly formed Cold Case Squad was running under the office of the chief of Department and not under the Detective Bureau, the natural place for a special unit of detectives. It was the only way they were going to get that squad up and running. The political ramifications were explosive.

And there was another issue that made an already explosive situation worse. Jack Maple came out of the New York City Transit Police, which was a separate police department until Mayor Giuliani merged them with the NYPD in 1995. A lot of people in the police department thought they were better than the Transit guys. To this day, there are members of the police department who look down on the Transit guys, and Jack Maple, a former Transit guy, filled the Cold Case Squad with men from Transit (among others, including guys from Housing, who are considered by some to be even lower than Transit). So not only had this elite squad been created right under the nose—but not under the command—of the chief of Detectives, here's a bunch of Transit guys whose very job was to take over and clear cases other "real" detectives hadn't. It's amazing people didn't spontaneously combust or keel over from heart attacks right there on the spot. "They're going to go in and try to find something we didn't do," someone within the NYPD complained to the *Daily News*. Once more, "every single bit of it was a battle," Anemone complained.

Well, no one wants to look bad. The Cold Case Squad was created to look at cases that had gone cold, cases no one was looking at. Presumably, it wasn't the detectives' fault that they weren't looking at them. They had to solve the current cases first, and then, when they had time, they were to go back and look at the older unsolved cases. Except no one ever gave them the time, and new cases were always coming in. "In the eighties, when we had twenty-two hundred murders a year, guys were just racing," as Eddie Norris describes it. "You solved the ones you could, but then another one was coming through the door, and then another one was coming in the door. Nothing was wrong with what they were doing, but you multiply that over fifteen years—that's a lot of cases that are sitting there. You multiply that by seventy-six precincts, that's a whole lot of people out there killing people." And a lot of cold cases. Whose fault was that?

"There was a lot for them to be embarrassed about, initially," Anemone admits. "Eddie would go out with his team, with five or six or ten or twelve different cold cases. He'd come back after a weekend, only a weekend mind you, with nine or ten of these cases put to rest. He'd find five or six of these people already in jail on other charges, he'd hunt the other people down and find them in their homes, at their workplaces, indicating to me and to Jack that the detectives weren't doing their jobs."

And the not-having-the-time thing? "These were not low-level cases that they were going after, these were the worst of the worst, these were homicides, shootings. We had declining crime during those years. You may have been able to make the case that there wasn't enough time earlier on, but it was my position that the chief of Detectives had the resources under his control to do exactly what we were doing."

When questioned about his opposition to the formation of the Cold Case Squad, Charles Reuther said it was because it created an adversarial relationship between the precinct detectives and the Cold Case Squad detectives, which was initially true. "They also took some of the best investigators and diluted the precinct squads," he said. Yes, they were some of the best, but their comparatively small number could not have impacted the squads too much, and besides, these were murder investigations. What better area to put your best investigators? Reuther also brought up a memo he wrote in the beginning about twenty cases the Cold Case Squad poached and how they exaggerated some of their early results, sometimes with organized-crime cases, which typically involve a lot of arrests. "Prove it," William Bratton responds. "Jack Maple did not play games with numbers." Wendell Stradford, who has been there from the beginning, agrees. "All the early arrests were live arrests, not paper arrests [exceptional clearances, i.e., arrests of people already in jail]."

"There were never, ever, any reports that made the case Reuther is talking about," Lou Anemone, the former chief of Department, responds. "He wrote a report that took days to compose to try and attack the unit. Yes, there was some differences of opinion about clearances, but there was never any doubt about who found the known perps or who got the old ones solved. It was about turf—they didn't report to him—they made his detectives look bad, they proved that the 'detective mystique' was nothing more than proper supervision and tremendous motivation and initiative." It's still harder to find a basis for the poaching claim. There was nothing stopping the precinct squads from taking another look at cases they hadn't worked on in months or years, or participating in an organized-crime investigation, and accomplishing all that the Cold Case Squad had. "It sounds like sour grapes," Bratton added, when told of Reuther's comments.

■

There are three reasons a case goes cold. Either they couldn't solve it (no evidence or witnesses), they didn't want to solve it, or someone screwed up.

Anemone and Norris's feeling at the time was, if the detectives really weren't doing their jobs and clearing these cases, fuck 'em.

In the detectives' defense, the Cold Case Squad gave, and continues to give, their detectives all the time they need. It takes a long time to solve a cold case. The Cold Case commanders know this. The Cold Case Squad is not under the same pressure the detectives in the precincts are under. They handpick their cases and decide their own caseload. They can take more time to track down these killers. They can take advantage of the fact that ten and twenty years later friends are now enemies, wives and husbands are now ex-wives and ex-husbands, and are willing to talk. And they can do DNA testing.

The Cold Case Squad tried to work with the detectives in the homicide squads. "It wasn't about, 'Hey, see how stupid you are? How lazy you are?' It wasn't about that," Norris explained. "We offered sharing the arrest with the original detectives. We had no problem with taking the prisoner to be debriefed by the original detective. You had to walk on eggshells with this. Police chiefs are not a nice bunch. At that time you had a bunch of crotchety older guys who got there by stepping on each other's throats their whole careers and not making mistakes. The whole culture that the FBI is being criticized for now, that was the NYPD back then."

They got it going and they were doing well, but they weren't getting any help from anyone, and the chief of Detectives wanted them torn limb from limb.

At the CompStat meetings, Anemone says, "the Cold Case Squad and Eddie Norris were probably grilled more, and tougher, by Jack and by me than anyone else because we didn't want anyone to get the sense that, well, you know, they were favorite sons, look at the way they're taking it easy on them."

"'Are you sure these are cold cases and not just warm cases?'" Norris remembers being asked. "The feeling was, we were just trying to take slam dunks on cases that were simply hanging, and humiliate the detectives. It wasn't true. If there's no DD5 in six months or a year or something, what are you doing with this?"

DD5 stands for Detective Division 5. Every time something is done on a case, it's written up on their standard follow-up form, a DD5, and added to the case records. A typical cold case file consists of a 61 (the first form that is filled out whenever a crime is committed) and one big fat pile of DD5s, stacked one on top of the other. "Filler 5s," they're sometimes called. Each says some version of "This case was reviewed on," then a date, and ending with "and no new developments have occurred." Usually because everyone stopped trying.

"If it's not actively being worked," Norris explained, "give it up."

Three months after the Cold Case Squad was formed, Police Commissioner Bratton tangled one time too many with the famously not-to-be-tangled-with Mayor Rudolph Giuliani, and guess who won? Bratton was history. His friend Jack Maple soon followed by resigning. Norris was now fair game. The chiefs could barely contain their glee. *Payback.* Reuther taunted Norris with the name "Dead Man Walking" in the hallways. He called a meeting with Norris and the new police commissioner, Howard Safir, and laid into Norris. The Cold Case Squad is doing a bad job, he says. They're stealing cases. "I'm a midlevel person at this time," Norris tells me. "This is the chief of Detectives. I thought, Fuck it, I'm dead anyway; if I don't fight for myself he's going to kill me, so at least I can try to save my reputation. I talk about what my vision was, what the plan was, and why we're doing this." Safir listened for a while, then he pushed his chair back from the table and said, "I understand the issue completely," and left.

At the elevator with Anemone, Norris figured this was it. "Just do me a favor, give me some decent assignment. I'll go anywhere, I'll work hard for you. Just get me away from this nut."

Soon after, Safir called Norris in for a meeting. "What would you do if you could fix the department?" Norris started by saying the police department was doing a good job. "Cut the bullshit." "You really want to know?" Safir did. Norris didn't take a breath for a half hour. Two weeks later Norris was invited to Safir's daily staff meeting. Seconds before the meeting began, Safir brought Norris into his office and told him he'd like to make him deputy commissioner of Operations, Jack Maple's old job. The boss of Charlie Reuther, is the point, and the boss of all the rest of them.

They walked into the conference room. Reuther was there, chiefs were there, deputy commissioners were there, all waiting for the daily staff meeting, and all wondering what this asshole deputy inspector was doing there. Norris remembers Safir announcing, "If you're wondering why Eddie Norris is here, I just made him deputy commissioner of Operations. I'd like him to look over all the operations of this department. I expect him to be extremely critical. When he speaks he speaks for me, and he begins immediately." Safir turned to the chief on his left. "Okay! What do you have?" Dead Chiefs Sitting.

In a matter of weeks, at least two people in that room were gone. The Cold Case Squad made out like bandits because their guy was now the deputy commissioner of Operations. "The two people most important to them were myself and the chief of Department," Norris explains. "As long as it was me and Anemone, and it was for those few years, they got whatever they wanted. They got the people they wanted, the equipment they wanted, they were protected against all this nonsense."

Two months after that meeting, Chief Reuther was out as chief of Detectives and Patrick Kelleher was in, and the newly established Cold Case Squad was transferred from the office of the chief of Department to the Detective Bureau. Deputy Inspector Ray Ferrari, someone who was known and trusted by Chief Kelleher and apparently well liked by everyone else, was now in charge of the Cold Case Squad. Ray Ferrari is a calm and easygoing guy. When Ferrari was promoted to head of the Fugitive Enforcement Division (which the Cold Case Squad operates under), Vinnie Ferrara took over Ferrari's position for less than a year. He left in the summer of 2001, and in his place came the alternatively craggy and sweet Deputy Inspector Vito Spano, who seemed to have allegiances to both the new and old guard within the NYPD—you could almost see the two sides, tough guy–sensitive guy, battle for control of expression on his face. William Allee, the former chief of Detectives, says, "Vito Spano makes coffee nervous." When describing Vito, people invariably laugh and say, "What a character" or "He's colorful."

Spano was one of the people in charge on the ground when American Airlines Flight 587 crashed in a neighborhood in Queens one month after 9/11, killing all 260 on board. The plane had dug into the ground. Vito jumped inside the wreck and starting throwing bodies and body parts up to the men lined up around the plane. He was like a recovery-operation machine, his arms pumping up and down like pistons. A detective who was there described him as a maniacal Arnold Schwarzenegger rescue worker. Vito said he was moving as fast as he could because it was one big fucking horrifying mess, and so soon after 9/11, and he wanted the job finished quickly and his men out of there.

■

Shortly after we met, Spano told me about a twenty-one-year-old girl from West Virginia who was shot in the back of the head in 1997. She had come to New York to start a new life, but any hope for that new life was taken away from her the second she stepped off the bus. There are particular kinds of predators who, at a glance, can spot the girl so desperate to be loved and accepted she'll do anything. They wait for the buses to roll in and pick them off—just like they picked off this girl. They befriended her and then they killed her. Life goes on. The world barely notices the existence or passing of the desperately sad, clueless, and overweight girl from West Virginia.

"How does a girl end up in such a terrible mess?" Vito asked aloud. How did she get from a pretty farm in "almost Heaven" to a crappy room in Brooklyn, where she had sex with men she thought were the only people who truly cared about her, only to have them fuck her, send a bullet exploding through her skull, and then leave her sprawled out on a chair, exposed and undignified, dead and unloved. In a matter of seconds he worked himself up into such a state talking about her we both had to look away. Pictures of his two sons sat on his desk. Was he thinking of his own children, his boys? He's a conservative fifty-year-old Catholic who grew up in Queens. A man like Deputy Inspector Spano might perceive a daughter as more vulnerable. Maybe he got so upset wondering, *How do you protect a daughter?*

Vito Spano took command of the Cold Case Squad in the summer of 2001, one month before September 11. As did many within the NYPD, the Cold Case Squad had to put some of their workload aside for almost a year to perform duties related to the World Trade Center attack. For some that meant interviewing the relatives of the dead and collecting DNA at the Family Center in order to file missing-person reports and death certificates. The detectives assigned there still have trouble talking about it. Others were assigned to the crime scene—the entire World Trade Center site. For most, however, it meant morgue duty. Each body, and, in most cases, each body part, was assigned to a detective. They had to follow that body part through the cataloging and identification process: fingerprinting, dental inspection, body search, photographs, and X-rays.

Deputy Inspector Spano was put in charge of compiling the lists of the dead, the missing, and the injured. Vito is proud that while the newspapers kept wondering if there were people sitting unidentified in hospitals who were, in fact, World Trade Center survivors, he was able to quickly confirm that there wasn't a single one.

3 Police Officer Ronald Stapleton

December 18, 1977

According to DD5s in the original case files, on December 18, 1977, an off-duty cop named Ronald Stapleton is at the scene of a robbery in progress in Sheepshead Bay in Brooklyn. So many crimes happen around Christmas. The poor guy is shot with his own gun, his eye is torn from its socket with a meat hook, and he's beaten so badly he can't move his legs. When Helen Minneci finds him lying in the parking lot as she leaves the Trade Winds Bar, which she owns with her husband, Nicholas, Stapleton asks her to please turn him on his side so he can throw up. "Those guys beat me up bad," he tells her. "I'm going to die." But he doesn't die right away. He hangs on through Christmas and he hangs on through New Year's—every additional day of life gives his family reason to hope. The doctors try everything but everything goes wrong, sepsis sets in, and he finally dies on January 3, 1978.

This is a cop. All the might and influence of the NYPD doesn't help. They can't find the guy who did it. The case goes cold.

A few years later, on November 2, 1982, a pharmacist named Jan

28

Schenley is killed during a burglary. The killer ties up Schenley and covers his face from chin to forehead with duct tape, then steals art and antiques from his home while Schenley slowly dies of asphyxiation. Jan Schenley is fighting for his life, and the killer is walking around his home thinking, "How am I going to carry all this?" They never find that guy, either.

Five years after that, a seventy-eight-year-old judge named George Aronwald is shot to death in Queens. No one can figure out why. He's a retired civil lawyer working for the Parking Violations Bureau at the time. Just some old guy. Three months after that, two mob brothers, Vincent and Enrico Carini, are shot to death. No mystery here. Just some more mob guys. This time, all the detectives have to figure out is, who did they piss off? Three more months go by and two more mob guys are shot to death, Carmine Variale and Frank Santora. Okay. Who did *they* piss off? The detectives never find out. They never find Police Officer Ronald Stapleton's killer, or pharmacist Jan Schenley's, or Judge George Aronwald's, and they never find the killers of the mob guys Vincent and Enrico Carini or Carmine Variale and Frank Santora. All seven cases, seemingly unrelated, go cold.

Then, twenty years after Stapleton was shot and meat-hooked, an FBI agent named Steve Byrne calls Detective Steve Kaplan of the Cold Case Squad. They'd worked together before. They like each other. Byrne tells Kaplan, "We've got an informant who says he knows who killed a cop in Sheepshead Bay."

The Cold Case Squad finally catches a break in a case that will lead to several arrests, linking all the murders described and uncovering a plot to kill a then unknown federal mob prosecutor.

In the meantime, the bodies continue to fall. Enrico Carini's widow moves in with Colombo family boss Joel Cacace (pronounced Ka-CASE), who also goes by the name Joe Waverly. She later leaves him for—of all people—a police officer named Ralph Dols. Maybe she is finally going straight. Police Officer Dols is shot on the corner of Avenue U and East 19th Street, in Sheepshead Bay, on August 25, 1997. He dies at Coney Island Hospital, the same hospital where Police Officer Stapleton succumbed twenty years before. We're up to eight.

■

Like Wendell Stradford, Detective Steve Kaplan was invited by Jack Maple to join the Cold Case Squad when the squad was formed, except Kaplan never actually met Maple. At the time, Steve was working for the Career Criminals Apprehension Unit (CCAU), a federally funded, Keystone Kops–like group of misfit detectives with "over a thousand years on the job," Kaplan explains. With only six or seven years himself when he joined the CCAU, Steve was the youngest member of an otherwise gray and gritty team of vets. "We sucked," Kaplan admits. According to Kaplan, the men in CCAU were once the best, but they were old now. The job beat them down, they lost heart, and they didn't care as much as they once had. Edward Norris didn't want the CCAU guys, but Maple wanted the money that went into CCAU, so he moved everyone from CCAU into Cold Case, got the money, and got the seasoned detectives plus one relative newcomer, Steve Kaplan.

Steve Kaplan is a big, beefy ex–high school football player who's combative but turns shy if you confront him head-on. "As big as he is, he's very timid. He's not a flashy guy," says Chuck Harrison, another Cold Case detective. Kaplan has tiny blue eyes set in a large face that is at times irresistibly friendly but also capable of menace— if he can stop himself from cracking up. "Everyone likes him," Harrison continues, while watching Kaplan disarm yet another New Yorker, this time a flower vendor near the squad's headquarters. An eighteen-year veteran on the force, the forty-six-year-old Kaplan, who grew up on Long Island, thinks he needs to lose some weight. Unlike everyone else in the Manhattan office, he doesn't dress up. He doesn't wear a suit. He wears khaki pants and casual button-down shirts. Like Wendell, Steve's name comes up frequently around the Cold Case Squad offices. All the commanding officers rave about them both.

Still, when asked what he's working on, Kaplan cringes. The detectives like attention but not too much attention. A call from a commanding officer is on par with a call from a journalist—rarely good. Someone's in trouble.

Detectives on the squad also don't want to be glamorized. Much of their day-to-day work is absolutely mundane. They call police departments around the country to get background information on people, then sit on hold. They fill out forms. They follow dead leads and wait months for DNA results. Seven detectives in Queens must share two cars, and they fight over who is going to use them. After all that, they use those cars to drive hours to prisons to talk to inmates who don't know anything. Finally, and invariably, they spend some part of their day fighting for a few lousy hours of overtime. After crime, the most frequent topic of conversation in the NYPD is money.

A cop's base pay is determined by rank. The NYPD hierarchy:

Chief of Department (4 Stars)
Chief (3 Stars)
Assistant Chief (2 Stars)
Deputy Chief (1 Star)
Inspector: *Ferrari*
Deputy Inspector: *Spano*
Captain
Lieutenant: *Pollini, Wray, Panzarella*
Sergeant
Detective 1st Grade: *Stradford and Kaplan*
Detective 2nd Grade
Detective 3rd Grade
Patrol cop (Technically, cops and detectives are the same rank, but detectives have more prestige and they make more money.)

A 1st-grade detective makes $79,547.00 a year. Not bad, really. But the average Cold Case detective can increase that by $20,000 or

$25,000 or more in overtime. Not a trivial amount. Overtime is broken down into three categories: investigative overtime, arrest-related overtime, and "other." Other could mean standing at a barricade at the Thanksgiving or Gay Pride parades or escorting and protecting dignitaries at the UN. Arrest-related overtime is easy to explain and easy to get. We've found the bad guy and we have to get him *now* before he gets away. No problem. When an arrest is made, crime goes down and that generates impressive statistics for the police department. Everyone wins. "Sure, stay late." Investigative overtime is the hardest of all to get, even harder within the Cold Case Squad, where homicides are anywhere from six months to more than twenty years old. "Why can't you do that computer work or make those phone calls during regular working hours?" a commanding officer might reasonably ask. With older cases it's hard to explain why something can't wait another day. It's different for detectives working in precincts, when someone is murdered right then. The imperative is clear: find that murderer NOW. On top of that, precinct detectives have to investigate all the cases that come into their precinct, not just homicides, and they end up carrying anywhere from 100 to 150 cases a year. A Cold Case detective usually has no more than five to twenty cases at any one time. So precinct detective squads are always allotted more overtime than the Cold Case Squad. Detectives who are in it strictly for the money stay far, far away from the Cold Case Squad because there is only so much overtime to be had. And whenever you have a limited resource, you have endless battles.

For the detectives in the Cold Case Squad, it feels as though not a day goes by without a small, slightly humbling struggle for overtime. "They're constantly after you," Pollini complains. "Could we stay today?" "How about today?" Detectives gossip about who got how many hours and how can I get more? Once, during a Cold Case status meeting, where it took only twenty minutes for the subject of overtime to come up, the meeting was interrupted by voices from another floor, which came on over the loudspeakers in every room in the building. Someone had unknowingly hit the intercom button on their phone. Naturally, everyone in the building stopped what they were doing to listen to the conversation. The topic? Overtime.

■

The only other way to make more money is through a promotion. "When the Cold Case Squad started, the upper regime decided that the squad would be the pinnacle of your career as a detective," Lieutenant Pollini explains. "If you worked your way into the Cold Case Squad, this was where you were going to get promoted. And people within the Cold Case Squad got promoted at a much higher rate than anywhere else." But that was a lot of chiefs ago. Anemone and his friends are long gone. The Cold Case Squad and its commanders no longer have the power and connections they once had. Or, as they put it, they don't have the juice. When detectives and commanders retire, they can't replace them. There are only so many detectives and commanders to go around and now other, more powerful units, like Counter Terrorism, get all the people they feel they need. The Cold Case Squad has shrunk from fifty-two members to thirty-two. Promotions are more scarce than overtime, and the Cold Case Squad now has to battle it out for them along with the rest of the NYPD. Like anywhere else in the world, the criteria for promotion are based partly on merit and partly on politics. Make more arrests than anyone else and you'll get promoted. Probably. Hopefully. However, drink or golf regularly with the right people, do them a favor from time to time, stay out of trouble, and you might get promoted just as quickly. Someone owes someone else a favor and their girlfriend gets promoted from 3rd- to 2nd-grade detective above other, perhaps more deserving detectives. It happens. Which is not to say that someone who gets to 1st grade by making the right friends isn't also a great detective. Those same skills— making friends, ingratiating yourself with the people who hold the power in different groups—can be used effectively in investigative work. Still, Pollini points out that "Police Commissioner Ray Kelly has made it tougher to schmooze your way to the top. Maybe now 50 percent of the promotions are fair, as opposed to 10 percent."

So wrangling for more money, steaming about someone else's promotion, sitting on hold, reading, filling out forms, and every once in a while arresting a bad guy, that's what they do. That's their job. "I'm no fucking hero," Kaplan says if anyone gets the least bit starry-eyed about what they perceive as an exciting and dangerous job.

Steve Kaplan works in the Special Projects office, the same office as Wendell Stradford. There's a twin-sized mattress leaning against the wall by his desk and it's still wrapped in plastic. His case, the Stapleton case, is the most complicated one I've heard yet.

For a change, time is actually on Steve Kaplan's side. Usually, when too much time goes by it hurts a homicide investigation. Memories fade, people disappear. But sometimes it helps. For example, in 1979, with the help of her sixteen-year-old son, Madeline Carmichael beat her two-year-old daughter, Latanesha, to death, then walled her up first in one closet, then in another, where her body remained for the next twenty years. Mother and brother murdered Latanesha because she threw up after being forced to eat. Madeline's nine-year-old daughter, Sabrina, saw the whole thing, but it took twenty years for Sabrina to feel safe enough to talk about it. Madeline routinely abused all her children, including Latanesha's twin brother, Andre, and even though Andre and Sabrina were placed in separate foster homes when they were ten and sixteen, Sabrina was so frightened by her mother she never talked about the murder with anyone until she was reunited with Andre in October 1999, when they both were in their twenties.

One month later, Cold Case detectives found Latanesha's black, mummified remains still clothed in a shockingly clean, bright white diaper and red T-shirt, and with a yellow, gellike substance covering parts of her shriveled body. The trunk they found her in was wrapped in twelve layers of garbage bags and mothballs and sealed inside a closet filled with incense sticks, baking soda, used air fresheners, and exhausted camphor sticks. Upon arrest, Madeline Carmichael rambled, "I can't remember the name, but I remember the picture, all I can remember is the force. It's a night-mare, it's a dream. I can't remember faces or eyes."

▪

In Steve Kaplan's case, which began with the murder of a single off-duty cop, Frank Gioia Jr., a Luchese mob family soldier, or "made man," is also finally ready to talk. But not because he feels safe. While doing time in jail Gioia learns of a plot to kill his father. He figures he'll talk, and in exchange his whole family will go into the Witness Protection Program. So in 1997, Gioia "proffers."

When someone in organized crime is out of options they'll turn to law enforcement. If law enforcement thinks the guy might have enough information to help them catch an even bigger bad guy, they will arrange for a proffer session. In a proffer session, the guy who is there to talk must come clean about everything he's ever done, every crime, and every crime he knows about. It's the start of nego-tiations for a written plea or cooperation agreement, which will then be brought before a judge. While the cooperation arrangement is being worked out, the prosecution won't go after the guy for any-thing new he admits to in the proffer session, although the guy prof-fering usually has to agree to plead guilty to *something* in the end. Information isn't always enough. If law enforcement finds out later that he didn't come completely clean, or he lied, all bets are off. They can come after him for anything that came up during the proffer. And, even if an agreement is never reached, law enforcement is free to pursue any leads about other crimes picked up during the proffer.

FBI Special Agent Steve Byrne arranges for a proffer with Frank Gioia Jr., but Gioia doesn't come completely clean. He doesn't imme-diately give up someone named Frank Smith, a guy who will ulti-mately help the FBI and the NYPD catch the biggest bad guy of all. He doesn't tell them because Gioia is dating Smith's sister at the time. A man has his limits. But he does give them information about two other killers, Manny Gonzalez and Vinnie Cilone. One killer leads to another, and pretty soon guys can't give up other guys fast enough.

This never would have happened in Al Capone's day. Currently, organized crime is unraveling, in large part due to RICO, the Racketeer Influenced and Corrupt Organizations Act. RICO is part of the Organized Crime Control Act enacted in 1970. It's a complicated piece of legislation that gives prosecutors increased power when going after criminal enterprises that operate as businesses, as the mob does. The prosecution can bring together seemingly unconnected criminal acts like murder, kidnapping, extortion, gambling, robbery, and so on, and try them all together in one case instead of separately, if they can demonstrate that they were done in order to help the enterprise, or "family." It all falls under a pattern of criminal activity referred to as racketeering. Not only can members of organized crime be fined on top of being imprisoned, they can lose any property gained through racketeering. Restraining orders and injunctions are allowed before anyone is even convicted, so a mob boss can't start selling his house or businesses if he thinks the government might try to seize them.

RICO changed everything. Law enforcement gained power and the mob lost a lot. When everything's going great and there's a lot to be gained, people play by the rules, even in the mob. When an organization starts to lose power, however, people start scrambling. And for fewer and fewer scraps. Unbendable rules become bendable. There was once a strict code of conduct within the mob. Don't raise your hand to a made member. Don't kill made men without first getting sanction. Don't kill cops. Don't mess with wives or goomahs (mistresses). And never cooperate with the government. Ever. They cooperate now.

Kaplan and the FBI simply follow the pointing fingers until they get to Frank Smith Jr. Kaplan admits he likes Smith, and he describes him with affection. "He's a regular guy. If you went out to a bar and sat and talked to him, and didn't know his background, you'd think he was okay. He talks sports, he's a guy's guy. He's not disrespectful."

Detectives don't necessarily hate all murderers, it turns out. Their feelings toward the people they hunt and arrest are complex. Cops and organized-crime guys actually used to hang out together back in the day, although now it's no longer done, at least not out in the open. "We came from the same neighborhoods," Kaplan explains. They grew up together. "We're from the same mold. Same personality." One guy chooses crime, one guy chooses law enforcement. Mark Feldman, the section chief of Organized Crime in the United States Attorney's Office, Eastern District, says, "With good cops, that was a good thing. They could understand the organized guys and talk to them."

"They're not all bad guys," Kaplan insists. Not bad? How not bad? "Would you live next door to Frank Smith?" Kaplan thinks for a minute, and smiles. "Yes. I'd live next door to the guy. He doesn't kill out of passion. It's just business."

But before the FBI and Kaplan get to Frank Smith, Kaplan begins with two murderers, Manny Gonzalez and Vinnie Cilone. Frank Gioia, turned informant, now tells the NYPD and the FBI that twenty years ago, Manny and Vinnie killed "some cop" in Brooklyn with a meat hook and the cop's own gun. Vinnie always carried a meat hook, Kaplan later learns. "It was his weapon." He worked as a delivery guy at a seltzer factory and used the meat hook to pull down cases of soda. But that's all Gioia gave them. He didn't have the cop's name or an exact date. Usually, you begin with a body, then you find the perps. Kaplan had the perps and no body. Who did they kill?

Kaplan talks to a friend of his in the Major Case Squad, Captain George Duke. "I got a meat hook and a dead cop," Duke tells him. Duke leads him to the Stapleton case, which has been sitting untouched for fourteen years in the offices of the Brooklyn South Detective Task Force. It's an informal place. "The CO didn't care who solved it, as long as it got solved. That precinct will give you whatever you want." Kaplan simply goes over and signs the case out.

4 Christine Diefenbach

February 7, 1988

Early in the morning, on Sunday, February 7, 1988, fourteen-year-old Christine Ann Diefenbach goes out to indulge her happy, childish obsessions with singer Wayne Newton and TV star David Hasselhoff from the popular television show *Knight Rider.* While all the other girls in America are taping pictures of Kirk Cameron, River Phoenix, or Jon Bon Jovi to their walls, Christine gazes up at Wayne Newton. Her family needs milk, she needs the latest about Wayne and David, so Christine leaves her house in Queens at 7:30, headed for a newsstand on Lefferts Boulevard and Jamaica Avenue to see if there is anything new in the Sunday papers about her heart-throbs. Four hours later her body is found twenty feet from the Long Island Rail Road tracks, at the top of a small wooded hill. Christine either walks up or is dragged up the hill, and disappears from her future.

Some man who is not Wayne or David or any girl's dream come true, and who cannot understand or protect the delicate feelings in a young girl's anxious heart, wants simply to fuck her. And when he can't, he beats her so badly he tears off one of her ears, breaks up her skull, and rips into her brain. Even though Christine's killer manages to get her pants almost all of the way off, and her underwear is gone and she is completely exposed, he isn't able to rape her. She fights him. Deputy Inspector Vito Spano explains again and again, "In your average, run-of-the-mill homicides, not robbery-homicides, murder always come down to saving face or proving your manhood." Maybe her killer can't keep his erection during the struggle. It's a matter of pride. The big man has to show the little girl.

In cases involving children, investigators start with family members and their friends first. But everyone in Christine's circle has solid alibis. Vagrants in the area are also quickly ruled out. The Long Island Railroad, which conducts their own extensive investigation, provides the NYPD with information about transit workers in the area, who are also cleared. Detectives are not able to recover DNA or prints from the scene. Leads are followed that go nowhere. Plus, it's 1988. That year, 1,896 murders are committed. And 1,905 will be committed the next. There will be 2,245 the year after that. It's fucking nuts. When a detective is assigned a case, they say "he caught the case." Detectives at the 102 Precinct in Christine's area of Queens, like detectives all over New York, are catching cases left and right, and they are running out of options on Diefenbach.

No one wants a case involving a child to go cold. An unsolved child murder never lets you go. It ruins sleep and taints the future for parents and siblings and any detective whose heart isn't already wrecked by one dream-destroying homicide after another. People who once looked to the future with optimism live the rest of their lives as if slightly drugged.

The reward is the first sign that it's nearing the end of the line in an investigation that's going nowhere. Transport Workers Union Local 100 puts up five thousand dollars "For any information leading to the arrest and conviction of the person(s) responsible for the murder of Christine Diefenbach." It doesn't help. Filler 5s start piling up. The thing that no one wants to happen happens. The Christine Diefenbach case goes cold.

■

A dozen years go by. Lou Anemone and his buddies Jack Maple and Eddie Norris put Lieutenant Philip Panzarella in charge of the Queens unit of the newly formed Cold Case Squad. There was never really any question about who'd be running the show in Queens. Panzarella had been working homicide there since 1984, and he was the best homicide man in the borough. But it was also a rescue. Panzarella had just been transferred to the Robbery Squad. Larry Loesch, the head of the Queens Detectives Squad at the time, was at war with Lou Anemone and Panzarella was Anemone's guy. Nothing personal. It was a political thing, according to Panzarella. (Others suggested that it might be because Panzarella is a bit of a maverick and difficult to manage. He doesn't always respect the chain of command. One detective said it was simply because Loesch and Panzarella hated each other.) Loesch needed someone he could control, so he had to get Panzarella out of the way. He went to his friend Charlie Reuther, the chief of Detectives, who was not a friend of Anemone's, and arranged for the transfer. "I took the hit," Panzarella says. But Panzarella was strictly a homicide man and he was lost in robbery. Phone calls were made. Anemone told him, "We're putting together a new unit called Cold Case and you're going to have it in Queens." A few months later Panzarella was out of robbery and back working homicides, except now he was working the most difficult cases. Reuther was transferred to the Criminal Justice Bureau, and Loesch went to Brooklyn as an executive officer. Balance was restored, friends were rewarded, and enemies vanquished. Panzarella has no hard feelings, he says, and Loesch later apologized to him. It was just office politics.

The first detective Panzarella invited to join him in the Cold Case Squad was Jimmy Annunziata, the detective at the 102 who had caught the Diefenbach case. "Bring the Diefenbach case with

you," Panzarella tells him. It had always bugged him. Of all the unsolved murders in Queens crowding his head—and he had memo-
rized every one of them—he wanted this one solved. When a girl is
murdered it gets to the detectives, who are almost all male, even
more. In this conservative, masculine culture, a female victim is per-
ceived as being more innocent than a male victim. When a man is
murdered, detectives ask, "Well, what the fuck did he do?" With girls
they wonder, "What mistake did she make?" Perhaps a little girl hit
particularly too close to home for Panzarella.

Phil Panzarella is about as close as you get to that grizzled detective we've been raised on in the movies and on TV. He's an old-
fashioned, "don't give me any bullshit," policeman. You can't even
go near him on Mondays, the guy can be such a crank. Everyone
knows not to ask Panzarella for any overtime on a Monday. That is,
unless he spent the weekend with his daughter. Then, everything is
all sunshine and bliss. Get Panzarella talking about his daughter and
it's like watching someone with multiple personalities shift personas
midsentence. Kill a young girl and tracking you down moves to the
front of his file-cabinet-for-a-brain and stays there, sometimes for
years, until his men find you and are rewarded for all their hard
work with that one heroic moment, when they get to whisper those
sweet words of payback, "You're under arrest." Ultimate satisfaction. Lieutenant Philip Panzarella couldn't forget a murdered daughter. The Diefenbach case became one of the first unsolved homicides
assumed by the Queens unit of the Cold Case Squad.

The Queens unit is one of five separate units within the Cold
Case Squad, but they don't call them units; they confusingly call
them squads. "I work out of the Queens squad of the Cold Case
Squad." Awkward phrasing, but it's correct. The other four squads
are Brooklyn, Special Projects, Manhattan, and the Bronx. Every
squad has its own personality. The Bronx squad is far away and
ghostlike. Even within its own precinct it's tucked away, and you
have to walk through the Warrant Squad to get there. While all the
Cold Case Squad offices are battered and worn, the Special Projects

Squad office has at least some fancy touches because of its proximity to 1PP. The office of Lieutenant Pollini, the commanding officer of Special Projects, is almost grand. The Manhattan and Brooklyn squads, which are both housed in the Brooklyn office, are less fancy, but they have a certain formality and tension because this is Cold Case Squad headquarters and the headquarters for the Fugitive Enforcement Division under which it operates. Spano and Ferrari, the commanding officers, are here. Detectives outside Brooklyn complain that the guys in Brooklyn get everything they want because they're in Spano's face every day. The Brooklyn detectives complain *because* they're in Spano's face every day.

The offices of the Queens squad are down and dirty. They are the darkest and bleakest of all the dark and bleak Cold Case Squads offices. More than any NYPD office, the Queens Cold Case office has the most schizophrenic mix of hard-nosed, 1950s, we-don't-talk-about-our-feelings attitude, and twenty-first-century angst because sometimes they do. It's Mickey Spillane on Prozac. It's "motherfucker" this and "motherfucker" that, and held-back emotion and tears. There are as many typewriters here as there are computers because the DD5s are not computer-ready. The detectives have to turn away from their PCs and the Internet and the databases they use and stick a form with carbon copies into a typewriter and *thwack, thwack, thwack* away. The smell and perpetual fog from Panzarella's cigars evoke images of dames with legs up to there and detectives in trench coats downing shots of whiskey from the bottles in their desk drawers. In reality, the detectives in this borough are the boys next door. I can imagine a Special Projects guy at a cocktail party holding a martini, but I can only see the Queens guys at a little league game with a beer.

And that all comes down from Phil Panzarella, the quintessential New York City policeman, what Steve Kaplan calls a "cop's cop," a blue-collar tough guy, but a tough guy with a lot of health problems. Nothing too serious, but since I've met him he's been in the hospital twice. Once was to remove polyps in his nose. "What are polyps?"

I ask. "Groats." "What?" "Groats." (Growths.) Another time was for kidney stones. He has an enlarged prostate and he suffers from gout. He epitomizes the old world–new world mix: he doesn't want to deal with bullshit, but he'll consider his men's feelings. When detectives aren't having any success with a difficult case, Panzarella is quick to give them something new. "You can see it bothers them. I give them another case. To get them away from it for a little while, because they can become too emotional."

The men who work for Panzarella are devoted to him. Part of it has to be because he's the only commanding officer in the Cold Case Squad who gets to handpick the detectives who work for him. Everyone else has to take who they're assigned. And Panzarella gets his men more overtime than any other squad in Squad. Pollini from Special Projects describes him as "one of those non-compliance-type guys. Most of the other teams comply with what they are directed to do. He just does whatever he wants to do." How does he get away with it? "That's Spano's problem."

In the Cold Case Squad there's a hierarchy of tension. It begins with the constant tension between the different squads, followed by the tension between the detectives *within* each squad, then between detectives and their commanding officers, and finally between the commanding officers and Spano. It's particularly painful to watch the war of wills between Panzarella and Spano. Panzarella rants to his men one afternoon about how he doesn't give a fuck what Vito has to say. Vito walks into the room mid-rant. He may even have caught Panzarella's last words. Every man shifts in his seat and Panzarella suddenly fades into the background as if he's stepped off a platform after giving a speech. Vito immediately starts making jokes. He looks around and smiles at everyone in the room and acts as if the lieutenant is doing him a favor by being polite to him at all. He compliments Panzarella. The men let out the breath they'd been holding, the moment passes, everyone's dignity is preserved.

Spano is the boss. The Cold Case Squad attracts independent personalities, but they're still working for a paramilitary organization with a very strict chain of command. Spano has the command. They all know it, and, ultimately, they all bow to it. It's one thing to not give a fuck, it's another to say it to the commanding officer's face. Panzarella and his men actually do go their own way pretty much. But in that one horrible instant they were reminded that it's partly because Vito lets them, and all of that can change at any moment.

It's very easy to lose ground in the NYPD. Panzarella has powerful friends, but alliances shift. He's getting older and a lot of his powerful friends have retired. Like the Cold Case Squad, Panzarella himself is running out of juice. Spano is a decent manager, however, and he doesn't want to weaken an effective commander. He doesn't want Panzarella to lose face. And, while Panzarella may not like having to answer to anyone, ultimately he's a cop and a professional, and at times seems to like Spano personally. They've known each other since 1992, when Vito was in charge of the 105 Precinct in Queens, and Panzarella was in charge of Queens Homicide Squad. Besides, things change. Panzarella could get some power back, Vito could lose some. In any case, Vito has not had any better luck getting Panzarella to toe the line than any other Cold Case commander before him.

■

Detective Tommy Wray picks up the still-unsolved Diefenbach case when Annunziata retires in the summer of 2001. Wray's a 1st-grade detective, one of an elite group of 202, as of this writing. He was promoted on Christmas Eve the year he took over the Diefenbach case, twenty-seven years after he first joined the force. He is very tan the day I meet him, which in New York looks downright strange and unhealthy, but everything else about him, his hair, his eyes, is light. He's the Long Island boy-next-door. His eyes are generous and kind. He looks at you with the sweetness that you would find in the eyes of men you've known since childhood. He's not sophisticated. He's polite and vulnerable. He doesn't need to go to therapy to sort out his feelings; they're right there on the surface.

Minutes after I meet him, Tommy leaves the office to go out for a walk because he's that upset. Assistant District Attorney Richard Schaeffer has just called. Jack and Robert Rotger, two murder suspects that Tommy had found and arrested in 1998, have been handed their sentences. Back in 1992, three days before Christmas, Salvatore Lopis was stabbed seventy-eight times and shot in the head while in his apartment. Tommy believes his killers tortured Lopis in order to find his stash of drugs. Schaeffer has called to tell Tommy that he just accepted a plea. Robert pleaded guilty to a weapon possession charge and got three to six years, and Jack pleaded guilty to attempted manslaughter and got five to ten. The sentences defeat Wray. He wanted more. He can't talk, he needs to regroup. With a cigar in his mouth altering his words as they come out, Panzarella shrugs and says, "He's like that."

Wray is the most religious man in the squad. The Cold Case Squad is a conservative bunch, and that usually means religious—but Tommy Wray is the real deal. It's one thing to announce that anyone who believes that we should take the words "under God" out of the Pledge of Allegiance should fucking leave the country, as one Cold Case detective recently declared, but it's quite another to get your butt into a pew practically every single Sunday, year after year, as Tommy Wray has for almost all of his fifty-one years. He even goes to nine o'clock mass during the week sometimes. "I need that. That hour that I'm there takes my mind off all the other stuff that's going on." Wray's a Roman Catholic, and his views on capital punishment do not coincide with those of most of the NYPD. "It's a tough position for a cop to be in," he says with an apologetic expression. "When you see someone kill fourteen people, don't you expect that person to die? Shouldn't that person die? People that have no remorse?" He stops for a second, like he might get an answer. "But I've come a long way since I first came on. Now I kinda realize that it's not our job. It's easy to say that's what we should do, but I've gone past that."

Like Wendell Stradford, Tommy didn't grow up wanting to be a cop. He was into sports. He wanted to be a baseball player. He played in high school, but instead of going into the minor leagues or playing in college, where he spent three months before dropping out, Tommy was surfing at Rockaway Beach in Brooklyn and partying. "I let that opportunity pass me by," he admits. "I guess I wasn't good enough." Not good enough at baseball and not good enough at college, he believes. "Then it came time to put all the fun aside. It was time to start thinking about making a living." This was a year after high school. Wray went into the army reserves, worked for a while at Citibank, then took the test for the Transit Police. But instead of getting a call from the Transit Police, he got a call from the NYPD. They were short on officers and would he consider working for them instead of Transit?

Wray has only two regrets in life. One is not going to Vietnam. "It bothers me. Guys I know went there and died and I didn't go." The other is not finishing college. "Maybe if I did go to college, and I had that college attitude when I came on this job about studying and applying yourself, maybe I'd be higher than just a 1st-grade detective now. Maybe I could be a deputy inspector or an inspector. I'm happy I'm a detective, I really am, but sometimes I feel I am because you put lower expectations on yourself. Maybe if I would have put a higher expectation on myself and worked hard in college and studied, I could have a college education and still be a detective, but at least I'd feel better that I applied myself. I can apply myself on these cases, and I never give up on a case, so why couldn't I have done that? Because you know why? I was stupid at the time."

Tommy Wray spent eleven years, from 1979 to 1990, in the 9th Precinct in the East Village, a tough precinct at the time. Tiny brown crack vials used to pile up on the curbs and in doorways. "There were probably more drugs being sold in that precinct than anywhere else in the United States." He met his wife, a nurse at Bellevue, while working at the 9th. He was in uniform for only a year before he went into the Anti-Crime Unit. From there he went into RIP (Robbery Identification Program), then to the Detective Squad, then to Manhattan North Homicide in 1990. In 1992 he was transferred to Queens Homicide, where he met Phil Panzarella, who was the commanding officer at the time. Panzarella asked Wray to join the Cold Case Squad in 1996, the year it was formed. It was a lateral move, but Wray couldn't resist. "I worked for Panzarella before, and I liked the idea of going after guys who thought they had gotten away with it."

Right away, Wray asks to assist on the Diefenbach case. He has three daughters who at the time are nine, eleven, and thirteen years old. When Jimmy Annunziata retires and types up his last DD5 in June 2001, the case naturally falls to Wray. The first thing he does is take the two brown cartons full of case files into the kitchen in back of the Queens office, read through the 466 DD5s, and make to-do lists out of problems he finds—things that were left off, tips that weren't pursued. "They didn't call this guy back." "They never found this witness."

One name stuck out. "Trucker [not his real name*]." Two years after Christine was murdered, an anonymous drunk called the 102 from Finnegan's Bar, an old bikers' bar located two blocks from where Christine was found. The caller had been drinking next to this guy Trucker, who said he killed Christine after a fight with his girlfriend, Carolyn. Instead of taking his anger out on his girlfriend, Trucker said he decided to take it out on a young girl he saw walking along the railroad tracks. Trucker bragged that he "fucked her up pretty good," the caller said. The detectives talked to Trucker on the phone a couple of times, and they had one conversation with Carolyn, who said that she and Trucker had broken up long before 1988. Trucker was supposed to come to the precinct on May 3, 1991, but he didn't show. The detectives never spoke to Trucker again.

Some mistakes are so close to being right it almost doesn't seem fair to call them mistakes. There should be a better word, one that

---

* Some names and details have been changed, as this remains an open investigation.

concedes at least some credit, and acknowledges that they almost had it, that they were that close, but still, they failed. It's impossible to eliminate mistakes entirely. No matter what a detective does, there is always the chance that one day someone might be hurt, either directly or indirectly, because he did something as small as not make the right phone call. A murderer could remain free, and more people could be killed.

The police department gets a lot of tips, some more promising than others, and information from some nameless drunk in a bar doesn't usually carry a lot of weight. According to the drunken caller, Trucker was proud to take all the credit for bashing in the head of a fourteen-year-old girl, except he said he killed Christine around Easter, and Christine was murdered in early February, two months before Easter. Trucker's ex-girlfriend told detectives that their fight couldn't possibly have happened that morning, or even that year. As a result, his claim wasn't given a lot of credit. Tommy Wray figures the detectives must have back-burnered Trucker. Years went by, thousands of murders were committed, and no one ever got around to calling Trucker again. When Tommy takes the case over, however, he learns that in the mid-'90s Trucker had been arrested twice for beating up women. The second time was in a bar in Queens located a quarter of a mile from Finnegan's Bar, where the original lead about him had come from. Trucker punched, kicked, and threw the woman to the ground, then hit her with a stool. "Find that guy now," Tommy writes on his to-do list.

■

Christine Ann Diefenbach was a little thing—five feet one inch, according to the autopsy report, and eighty-four pounds. She was an average student at Intermediate School 217 in Jamaica whose best subjects were music and art. Her teachers and few friends invariably described Christine as shy and nice, and the principal even called her a loner, but Christine's parents were said to be on the strict side, and her mother was a Jehovah's Witness. Christine had a loner-in-training childhood.

Jehovah's Witnesses don't celebrate holidays. That doesn't just mean Christmas, but Halloween and, more painfully, birthdays. Even if a child learns to understand and accept this for her own birthdays (and certainly an engaged and loving parent could find ways to fill the birthday void), imagine being a kid and having to say "I can't go to your party." The children of Jehovah's Witnesses also frequently have to accompany their parents as they proselytize door-to-door. If any kids from school ever caught Christine at the door with her mother, pushing copies of the *Watchtower*, you can be sure they made her life miserable the next day in the hallways, if only with a significant look. Dating is not allowed unless you intend to marry the person, and who knows their marital intentions at age fourteen? The list of things that alienate children from their peers at this particularly sensitive age is long. Christine was never going to sing the solo in the chorus because she wouldn't be allowed to join the school choir. She'd never score a goal in field hockey because she wouldn't be allowed to play on the team. School clubs, sports, politics, all the places where children develop their interests and learn about themselves are forbidden. To make matters worse, Christine wore corrective footwear as a child, which made her walk pigeon-toed, and that alone would have been enough to have immediately and irrevocably singled her out as a freak and taken her out of the popular-girl running.

Lonely kids look for sanctuary. For some it's in books. For Christine it was at the movies. There's a song called "Vivien Leigh" that goes, "Only the lonely live for the cinema," and Christine rented movies twice a week. Three days before she died she rented the movies *Nothing in Common*, starring Tom Hanks and Jackie Gleason, and *Puff the Magic Dragon*. She told her brother she wanted to be either a movie star or a director for Wayne Newton. Of all the fourteen-year-old girls in the world, Christine Diefenbach was likely the only one in 1988 to have a crush on Wayne Newton.

The other savior of the lonely child is the imaginary friend. While the other girls her age were starting to date, Christine began a relationship with a character inspired by the movie called *The Dark Crystal*. Child psychologists believe that most children stop having imaginary friends at around six or seven years old. Yet, one study found that 55 percent of the fourteen- and fifteen-year-olds who kept diaries wrote about imaginary friends.

Christine named her imaginary friend Cyren Careen. "If you've seen this movie," she wrote in her diary, "you'd probably say it was just too deep and you haven't the slightest idea what's going on. Don't worry cause that's just how I felt the first time around. I was just 9 back then.

"But as time went by & I began learning a little more about it I really began to like it. In fact now that I'm 14 I'm obsessed with the movie." Her character Cyren "started off as just an imaginary friend and began to become something very different & very special to me."

Christine had a few real friends. Yuri Forbin, who knew Christine from school, remembers what she was like. They shared what was called a Resource Period, where they were tutored in math. Forbin, like everyone else, says, "Christine was very shy. We were in the class together for months before she cracked a joke." She was also very insecure about her appearance. She was short and thin and pale, and this was the eighties. Everyone in their school had big hair, and was very flashy, and Christine was just the opposite. "She was the kind of person where if you didn't look for her you wouldn't know she was there." But she noticed others. And she was kind. She could tell before the teacher could when Yuri was lost and frustrated. She'd say, "Calm down," and then go through the problem step-by-step, and explain it in a way that he could understand.

When the students were told that Christine had been murdered, Yuri felt bad, "but it was like it didn't register," Forbin remembers. It wasn't real. "We talked about it that day and then we blocked it out. Isn't that weird?" He was fifteen years old then. Years later, after he joined the army, he thought about Christine for the first time in years, and he cried. "That's when it finally hit me. She was my friend." Now, whenever someone dies, Yuri remembers Christine. Some unanswered-for murders reverberate forever.

■

Christine was buried in a white dress with blue flowers. Her mother didn't go to the funeral because she was too distraught, and her five-year-old sister didn't go because she was too young. Had she lived, Christine would be twenty-eight at this writing.

■

Tommy Wray doesn't contact Trucker immediately because you never contact the suspect first. Once you confront a suspect, he can deny everything and never say another word. He doesn't have to speak to anyone. "Very few perpetrators cooperate with us," Wray explains. "They're never like, 'Oh! I've been wanting to talk to you!'" Worse, now he's on to you. So you begin with his friends and associates. You build a case. Everyone Tommy talks to says that around the time of Christine's death, Trucker was hanging out with a guy named Russell Burns (not his real name). Russell Burns tells Tommy he's never heard of Trucker. "So," Tommy naturally wonders, "why is he lying to me?"

5 Jean Sanseverino

March 8, 1951

Sitting in a closet in the 76 Precinct, in a box that hadn't been opened for twenty years, is the 1951 Jean Sanseverino case. On March 8, 1951, when Jean was twenty-six years old, she had sex with someone, then was strangled to death. Her autopsy report notes that she was brought in wearing a black brassiere labeled "Forever Yours," Style 500, size 32B, and a pale blue slipover sweater with short sleeves. "Human excretion," the DD5 states, was found on her lower body, on her white anklets, on her underpants, on the couch, and on the floor in front of the couch. If it had been blood, the detective would have just said so. According to a list of questions the detectives had drawn up, each suspect was asked, "Did you have a bowel movement in Jean's room?" In a description that presumably only NYPD personnel and lawyers would read, it's touching that the detective who wrote up the DD5 tried to be sensitive. A DD5 may be a record of the investigation, but it also reflects the personality of the detective who wrote it, and the culture of the NYPD at the time. Wendell Stradford says the bowel movement was a "fuck you" gesture. Except the excrement was everywhere. Experts at the Office of the Chief Medical Examiner confirm that the presence of excrement at a crime scene is not unusual. "Sometimes they're overcome by the excitement of the strangulation," Spano adds. "They have to go." But the fact that the man who strangled Jean and smeared his excrement on her clean white socks took time to cover her partially naked and soiled body with her decorative print bedspread indicates he knew her—the gesture is viewed as protective. "Or territorial," Spano counters.

A month before she died, Jean split from her husband, who might have been a "transient," according to one of the DD5s. Even though it had only been a month, the police found a bunch of what looked like love notes written on various scraps of paper in her pocketbook found at the scene. Penciled on the back of a restaurant check are the words *I love you.* Lipstick imprints and the address of a man named Bill are found on a different piece of paper. Still another note says, *Come to 318 State St 2nd floor, front, the door will be open and I'll be waiting for you. Signed, Joe Moore. P.S. The front door will be open.* Three days after she was murdered a letter postmarked from Queens arrives. It was mailed just hours after she died.

Dear Jean,

I just can't go through with it. I know it looks to [sic] dangerous for me to try it maybe during the summer I might take a crack at it things are getting to [sic] tough now. I know my wife is having me watched day and night she knows to [sic] much already so thats now [sic] I can't do it now. We cannot see other for a long time but I will try to see you next Monday night at 9 P.M. on the corner of Myrtle and Gates Ave. by the drug store please have some hope I will try my best darling hoping you are in good health until we meet again please wear a white carnasion [sic].

Johnny
xxxxx

Sometimes having a lot of boyfriends makes you feel more alone than having none at all. At 12:30 in the morning, just hours before she died, Jean was sitting by herself in a booth at the Sheridan Restaurant. Two of Jean's friends were at the restaurant at the same time; her roommate, Sylvia Krumholz, and a mutual friend named David Poole sat together in another booth. In a little while, David would walk Sylvia over to her boyfriend Joe Bernard's apartment. So, her marriage over, married men letting her down, and her friends having a good time without her in another booth, Jean went drinking from bar to bar.

She was only twenty-six. Before she was murdered she spent the last month of her life making the same stupid mistakes young women everywhere make in their twenties, especially at the end of a marriage that wasn't everything a young girl dreams. Jean never got the chance to stop, grow up, and pull her life together. She wasn't around long enough to discover there are things a lot worse than loneliness.

The medical examiner estimated that Jean died at roughly 5:30 that morning. A little while later, the sun rose. It was chilly that morning, 38 degrees, and it felt like it was going to rain.

There were 243 murders committed in New York in 1951, and 65 of them took place in Brooklyn, where Jean was murdered. The 1951 NYPD Annual Report said there were 66, but one was later declared "unfounded." Some murders don't count, according to the police department. "Justifiable homicides," such as one committed in self-defense, or when a member of the police department kills someone in the line of duty, will not be included in the final tally. The Office of the Chief Medical Examiner counts everything, so their numbers never match the NYPD's.

Sixty-five is not a lot of murders. When the 82 Precinct (the 76 was the 82 in 1951) caught the Jean Sanseverino homicide it must have been a big deal, but the investigation was over quickly. The last DD5 where someone actually did something on the case was 1956, but significant activity ended within a month. A month. "If you don't have the God damn thing solved in a couple of days you've got a problem," Deputy Inspector Vito Spano explains. "In most cases, if you don't have viable leads within a couple of days, this thing isn't going to go. You're going to get stuck with a cold case." In Jean's file, every DD5 after 1956 until 1984 says, "No new developments." Proof that a detective touched the file, nothing more. After 1984 no one in the 82 bothered to even claim that. Today, everyone involved, the detectives, Jean's friends and family, and any suspects are all most likely dead. The Cold Case Squad isn't interested in picking up the case. "I don't have time to look for ghosts," Lieutenant Panzarella snapped. He wants to catch the murderers who are still alive. The ones who might beat someone to death *again*. Understandably, the detectives want to save lives, so they don't care about murderers who are dead. No one anywhere in the NYPD is trying to solve her murder. Her relatives aren't writing the mayor or police commissioner. It's over.

Fifty-two years later, the scant information about Jean's life is fading on the aging DD5s, which are still kept together with straight pins. She came to New York from somewhere in Alabama. Several towns are mentioned, but it's not clear which one was hers. Her maiden name was Bessie Jean East, but she dropped the Bessie when she moved to New York, presumably because Jean sounded more cosmopolitan. There are a few Alabama residents named in the case files, along with three relatives—her mother and two sisters. The list of people she knew in New York is longer and includes the name of her maybe itinerant husband, Raymond Sanseverino. If they're still alive, the youngest people recorded in the case files would be in their seventies today. There's a slim chance someone can still be found.

June Pruitt is one of the youngest people named in the case files. He'd be seventy-four now if he's alive. Calls to every Pruitt in the Gadsden, Alabama, phone book yielded Shirley Pruitt after the twentieth try. "I'm looking for June Pruitt, who was a friend of Bessie Jean East," I start to explain. "I knowed her! I knowed Bessie," Shirley tells me excitedly. "She was purty. Her sister Blanche married my third cousin Fuzzy. I don't know his real name. We always called him Fuzzy."

Shirley was just thirteen when Jean died. When they brought Jean's body back from New York, Shirley was playing with a bunch of other children on a huge mound of sawdust behind Jean's sister Blanche's house, where Jean's body was laid out in the living room. "We used to take a piece of tin, like what you put on the top of a house, tie a rope to it, and sleigh down the sawdust pile."

■

Jean Sanseverino, the former Bessie Jean East, was born at home on September 4, 1924. She was the second daughter of Lillie and Lawrence C. East. Sometimes they called her Bessie Jean, sometimes just Bessie. Everyone in New York thought she was twenty-five when she died. The ME's report says twenty-five, all the newspapers say twenty-five, but she was actually going to turn twenty-seven that year. Her husband, Raymond, was two years younger, so she became two years younger.

Bessie was raised on Webster's Chapel Road in Calhoun County, Alabama. It's not in a city or a town or even a village. It's just "the country," people in the area explain. A farming community. Some records say that Bessie Jean grew up in Wellington, but Wellington was just the place they went to get their mail. It's amazing that someone can live in this country and be, technically, nowhere. In 1920 there were 537 people living in Wellington, the closest town that was included in the local census. When Bessie and Ray moved to New York in 1950, it was up to 1,026. As of 2002, they had grown to 2,137.

The house where Bessie Jean was raised didn't have running water, plumbing, or electricity. Electricity was added in 1951, when her youngest sister, Joann, married Bobby Ray Jones, an electrician. Plumbing was never added. They used an outhouse thirty feet from the house, in a field. There were two holes inside the small wood structure, Joann, the only living member of Bessie's immediate family, remembers. "One for big butts and one for little ones. Daddy kept toilet paper in there for us, when they started making toilet paper." The East house was painted cream on the outside, the only house in the area to be painted at all, but on the inside the wood in the few rooms was left raw. Bessie shared a linoleum-floored bedroom with her sisters Blanche and Doris.

Bessie Jean's mother, Lillie, had a flower garden by a pear tree near the front of the house, by the road, where the mailbox would have been if they'd had a mailbox. She grew verbena, daises, and dahlias. Two big oak trees stood on one side of the house, pear trees on the other, and there was a large pecan tree in front, which still stands today. The house is gone now. All that remains are the pecan tree, a well and a pump, and the name L. C. East, still written in green paint on the cement culvert, right where Bessie Jean's father painted it years ago.

Until she reached the ninth grade, Bessie and her sisters, Blanche, Doris, and Joann, and their brother, Sherman, rode two miles down the road in a wagon drawn by mules to Webster's Chapel School. The school didn't have bathrooms either, and in the winter the children kept warm next to wood heaters. The community was too small for a high school, so all the kids went to the nearby Alexandria High School. Bessie Jean declared to her youngest sister that she was going to be a "world traveler" when she grew up. She said maybe she'd go into politics, but she stopped going to school after the eleventh grade.

Bessie's father, Lawrence, served in the army in World War I. He was stationed in Germany, and he was thirty-three years old when he came home and married Bessie Jean's mom, Lillie. He was listed as a farmer in Bessie's high school records, but he also worked for a while in the rock quarry owned by his brother Charlie. Bessie Jean's father worked in the crusher. He was the one who made sure the rocks went down and were crushed into very fine rocks that they'd use to build roads. The quarry has since closed, and the little town built by the company for the workers is gone, but some of the tenant houses and the commissary still stand, empty and caving in. Like most of the families in the area, the Easts ate what they farmed—things like tomatoes, lettuce, corn, and potatoes. Bessie Jean's father also farmed cotton and hay. He sold the cotton when they had cotton to sell, until the thirties and forties, when he was paid by the government to stop.

According to Jean's sister Joann, Christmas was a big deal in the East household. Lillie baked chocolate, coconut, and lemon cakes and stored them in a wood hutch in the kitchen. During the holidays, the two shelves with glass doors were always filled with her baking. If their father was working, it would fall to Bessie and Doris to cut down the tree they'd later decorate with glass balls and foil garlands and tinsel. They didn't have Christmas lights because they didn't have electricity.

"We were all poor back then," Shirley Pruitt told me. They didn't have money for store-bought clothes, so all the girls wore handmade dresses. And there were not a lot of things to do for fun. Their father didn't let them play cards—cards were considered gambling. Bessie Jean and her sisters would sometimes walk four miles to the town of Glencoe for entertainment. There was something courageous about that. Bessie, this young country girl, with her hair washed from a pump, setting out with nothing but anticipation for all the possibilities a "city" offered. Everyone would congregate at their cousins the Sims, where there were five girls, and more cousins who came over from nearby, and they'd all go into town for restaurants, movies, or dances. But mostly, in the evenings back on Webster's Chapel Road, the family would sit on their porch with the Morris girls from across the road, Dorothy and Mary, and sing. Hymns mostly. "What a Friend We Have in Jesus." "When the Morning Comes." But Bessie Jean also loved the big band hit "A String of Pearls."

Bessie Jean's first love, Wade Chapman, used to visit her on that porch. Wade operated a steam shovel at her uncle Charlie's rock quarry. He later joined the army, and during World War II Wade served as a technical sergeant with the combat engineers in Germany and France. A handsome man, with dark skin and dark hair, Wade was nicknamed "Blackie." By the time Wade came home in 1946 and went back to the quarries, Bessie's heart was elsewhere.

There wasn't a lot of formal dating in the Webster's Chapel area. At school, the boys and girls used to have what were called "box suppers." The girls would fix a box supper with sandwiches or chicken, and maybe a piece of cake or pie, and they'd sit with the boy who bought their supper, usually for a quarter. There were also dances at the Fort McClellan army base in Anniston. Bessie Jean, her sister Doris, her cousin Sue, and Dorothy Morris would meet on the highway to catch the bus to Anniston to go to the USO and NCO clubs at the base. Then they'd ride the bus back at midnight and walk the two and a half miles back home. Bessie Jean was a pretty girl. She was five foot five, had blue eyes and long black hair. One night at Fort McClellan, while still a teenager, she met Raymond Sanseverino. Ray was born and raised in Brooklyn, New York. Ray and Bessie must have seemed so exotic to each other—the boy from one of the biggest cities in the world and the girl who grew up without Christmas lights.

In the case files is a letter from Ray's mother, Eleanor, to Bessie's mother, Lillie, dated July 4, 1945, which said, "I beg you please if you love your daughter don't let Raymond marry her." He'd proposed to another girl in January, she continued, and had given her a ring. He had proposed to four girls in New York, it turned out. One of them received a letter from Ray's friends saying that Ray had been killed in action. Eleanor wrote that he drifted from job to job, got drunk every night, and slept in gutters. She had taken him to a priest to straighten him out, but it didn't work. Eleanor was afraid that Ray would marry Bessie, bring her to New York, and then leave her alone and possibly pregnant, with no friends. "New York is not exciting or glamorous," she wrote. "It is just a struggle for existence unless you have plenty of money."

But Bessie Jean's family adored Ray. He made Bessie Jean happy. He loved to play the harmonica, and they loved to listen. He was kind to the children. He sent Bessie's sister Joann an accordion from Germany when Joann was thirteen, and she learned one song, "Tea for Two," which everyone made her play again and again. Ray loved Bessie Jean's family as much as they loved him. He never had much of a family himself, he told them. Ray's mother, Eleanor, who would marry four times in her life, left Raymond and his five brothers and sisters in an orphanage for over five years after her second husband, John Sanseverino, died. There was talk that John was not dead but in jail. She retrieved the children when she married husband number three, but the damage was done. Ray never felt connected to her or to his brothers and sisters.

Ray and Bessie Jean married on September 1, 1945, just a few days before Bessie's twenty-first birthday, and a couple of weeks after Ray's nineteenth, when Ray was home on furlough. Army records show that Ray went AWOL for twenty-three days in 1945, when he returned from overseas, so perhaps he didn't marry her during a "furlough." The army later granted him an honorable discharge nonetheless.

Like many young couples in the area, Ray and Bessie Jean lived with Bessie's parents when they first got married. The first place of their own was in an apartment complex in East Gadsden. There, they made friends with F. C. Elrod and his wife, Martha, and Claude and Mary Smart. Claude had a small hamburger joint at Burn's Park, and Bessie Jean worked for him for a while. She loved ice cream and burgers, and she played songs on the jukebox there whenever she had extra change. Later, Bessie Jean went to work for Nell and Guy Alford at the Frosty Parlor, and she became close to them, too. Bessie was never much of a drinker in those days. Her friends would beg her to have a beer because of the way it made her laugh. They called it "giggle water." Pretty much everyone who met Bessie loved her.

For the most part, they all liked Ray, too. He had an engaging personality, but they had a problem with his laziness. Eleanor was right. He worked inconsistently. Worse, he became involved with one of the waitresses at Roy's restaurant, where he worked as a cook. He and Bessie had a huge fight about it. It was only the first. There would be many more fights about women.

Still, Bessie's sister Joann liked to stay with Bessie and Ray in Gadsden. Like her sisters before her, Joann liked to get out of the country. There were things to do in Gadsden. One night, when she was fourteen years old, Joann and her friend Doris visited Bessie Jean and Ray. Bessie was working at the Frosty Parlor that night, but Ray was home. Joann went into the bathroom to take a bath, and Doris followed her to do her hair. There was a hole in the wall. Joann and Doris stuffed it up with toilet paper, and minutes later they watched as the paper was pushed out of the hole and fell to the floor. Doris put her eye up to the hole and another eye looked back. The girls screamed. Ray was looking through. Joann ran out of the bathroom and confronted him. "I'm going to tell Bessie Jean," she yelled. Ray got mad, put his hands around her throat, and said he would kill her. He took his hands away quickly, and while Joann wasn't hurt, she was badly frightened. Ray had made suggestive re- marks to her from time to time. He once told Joann that he'd snapped pictures of her naked and that she had a lovely body. He'd recently finished a photography course at a local trade school, paid for by the GI Bill, so Joann believed him. But after that night, Ray never threatened or made suggestive remarks to Joann again. From that moment on he treated her like a little sister. Perhaps the en- counter frightened him, too.

One day in February 1949, Bessie came home and found a note from Ray. He was gone. He said he was on his way to New York and didn't want her with him. Bessie was devastated. A year later, when she was just beginning to get over him, Ray called and told her to sell everything she had and follow him to New York. He loved her and wanted her back. Bessie Jean didn't hesitate. She sold what she could, gave everything else away, and left for New York two days later. Before she left, Bessie's mother placed her own wedding ring on Bessie's finger. Lillie East used to let each daughter take turns wearing it, and it was Bessie's turn. With a little over a hundred dollars in her pocket Bessie Jean was gone, just like that. She got on the bus with curlers in her hair because she wanted to be pretty for Ray when she got there. She waved good-bye to her little sister Joann, and no one in her family ever saw her alive again.

PART II

Banging on Doors

6 Detective Wendell Stradford

The Leon-Martinez Double Homicide

In the Leon-Martinez case, the DEA saw drug connections, because that's what they do. That is their area of expertise. They believed Linda Leon and Esteban Martinez were murdered by members of a Colombian drug cartel, and that's who everyone focused on. The killers were probably Hispanic, possibly Dominican, because Linda and Esteban were both Dominican. Case closed. On a list of names of people to investigate, it was as if the Hispanic names were floating inches off the page, in large bold type, and any other names were far, far away, almost unreadable, and they would be investigated last, if at all. One detective after another followed the DEA's Colombian lead without results for four years. Once a theory in any investigation is developed it's hard to let it go, especially when you have facts to support that theory, and the DEA had a lot of facts. Also, with so many people to investigate, and countless other cases that needed their attention, the detectives naturally went after the most viable suspects first. But after four years and nothing to show for it, how hard would it have been to start looking elsewhere?

How badly do you want to keep your job? The NYPD is not the place to go out on a limb. "If I push something and it doesn't work, my fucking career is over," Lieutenant Panzarella barked. It's a practical matter, in part. The police department is not in a position to absorb loss like Microsoft. They're in perpetual financial ruin. No one in the NYPD could ever conceivably utter these words: "We just spent a million dollars and it didn't work." To make sure that never happens, a culture has evolved that is openly and effectively hostile to risk and gleefully punishes failure. Few commanders are willing to try anything that hasn't already been clearly demonstrated—by someone else—to work. And while CompStat helped by forcing commanders to consider trying something new, anything at all, to bring down crime, Anemone, Maple, and the people who helped them are gone. CompStat meetings are tame now, by comparison. The period of innovation CompStat created is winding down, and the police department is curling back up inside itself again. Tradition has resumed its grip, and traditionally, careers in the NYPD are not made by trying new things. Careers are made by never making mistakes. Keep your head down and do your job.

It's not like the police department doesn't make mistakes. But on an individual level, between their own culture and an unsympathetic public and press, they can't seem to win. When they're aggressive they're doing too much, but when crime goes up they're not doing enough. It discourages trying and fosters insularity, discontent, and bickering. The result is that cops do things the way they always have, and that change, which is hard enough to bring about as it is, is so violently resisted and so slow within the NYPD that some police department annual reports from a hundred years ago read as if they were written today.

For instance, the NYPD's enemies have remained constant: the press, the public, and the FDNY. "Judging from past experience," Police Commissioner Richard E. Enright wrote in 1921, "it is quite useless to expect the press to publish anything about the Police Department except sensational nonsense and scandalous falsehoods, unless it serves some ulterior motive of the management to tell the truth." They must have been getting killed in the papers that year. And the public just eats that stuff up. "The general run of Americans are always ready to criticize the government in its entirety, or any of its departments," Enright continues, "regardless of the justification of their criticisms." Freedom of speech has always bugged the police department. The NYPD has been complaining about the fire department even longer. Perhaps if the members of the fire department were paid, the 1864 Annual Report suggests, firemen wouldn't be so violent and rowdy. That and the fact that too many of them live in the firehouse and not at home. "Such a course of life is fatal to the men and fearfully mischievous to society."

The annual reports also indicate that the NYPD has been catching bad guys at pretty much the same rate and in the same way for the past century. Like any other risk, scientific innovation is a possible source of ruin and failure, and the NYPD has rarely ever been the first to embrace scientific innovations. The first bullet comparisons were done by Scotland Yard. Using fingerprints in criminal cases was first suggested by a microscopist in the U.S. Department of Agriculture in 1877, but he was ignored. Tokyo was the first to give it a try in 1880. The list goes on. The Sorbonne produced the first truly serious study of hairs in 1910, and the first police crime lab was established in France. DNA was first used forensically in England, the lifting of trace evidence with tape was developed by a Swiss criminalist lab, and superglue fuming was developed by the National Police Agency in Japan (blowing fumes of superglue over a surface makes latent prints visible).

There are exceptions, however. The New York Police Department has experimented occasionally. A chart under the heading Scientific Police Techniques from 1948 lists things like blood examinations, gas analysis, and photomicrography alongside more quaint technologies such as retrieving magnets (presumably used to recover guns from the river) and "etching deleted numbers." A device informally called the imagemaker and officially known as the Variable

Image Reflector was developed in 1963 for producing pictures of suspects based on eyewitness descriptions. But the annual reports never refer to it again. In 1967, the police department tried to speed up the process of latent print comparisons by photographing fingerprints with a modified Polaroid camera that was originally developed for the medical and dental fields. Cops used it to photograph fragile prints, like blood prints, which might be destroyed when detectives tried to lift them. But the camera eventually ended up being mostly used as a photocopier. Called a "one on one," it was a quick way for precinct detectives to make copies of mug shots when they needed extras. The police department had some firsts. In 1905 Detective Joseph Faurot went to Scotland Yard to learn about fingerprinting, and while his newfound skills were initially treated with the usual skepticism, in 1911 the first conviction in the United States based solely on fingerprint evidence was gained through evidence and testimony supplied by Faurot. The NYPD also had the first airborne unit in the world, which was put into place in 1929. And then there is, of course, CompStat.

Still, detectives are a conservative bunch, and any cop who welcomes new methods of scientific analysis is treated with disdain. It doesn't help that the relationship between the NYPD and the people at the Office of the Chief Medical Examiner (OCME), which conducts all the forensic DNA and serological testing in New York, is sometimes strained. Detectives say scientists routinely balk when they ask for DNA tests. The people at the OCME don't see it that way. "The police and DAs want you to do everything on everything, and you can't," Dr. Robert Shaler, the head of Forensic Biology, explains. "If you have a trail of blood leading away from a crime scene, you really only have to test one at the beginning, one at the end, maybe one in the middle to make sure it's all the same one. I had a DA in Queens who wanted me to do all fifty droplets. I had to tell him that it was a waste of time and money." A senior medical examiner says, "The detectives don't adequately understand the science."

The detectives feel the scientists don't appreciate the urgency of their investigations. "They're not criminal detectives," Wendell Stradford counters. "They're scientists and doctors. We want to prosecute. We want to have enough to arrest this person. What we ask for might not be important to them, but it could be important to us. A defense attorney might later ask, 'Well, detective, why didn't you find out if my client's semen was in this person?' My job is to get every piece of evidence I can." The detectives want to make their cases as strong as possible. The OCME wants to curtail unnecessary and expensive procedures. A DNA test can cost anywhere from roughly thirty dollars, to analyze a pristine sample taken from a convicted offender under the best possible circumstances, to five hundred to two thousand dollars, to test evidence gathered from a crime scene. In New York, those tests come out of the OCME's budget, not the NYPD's, which is why scientists at the OCME don't like to test DNA unless the detectives have a suspect. Their position is, why spend the money and time, which are considerable, when we're so backed up, and you don't have a suspect to compare the results with? "That's what we have the DNA database for," the detectives respond.

Finally, the detectives complain about the wait. As of this writing the turnaround time at the OCME for a DNA test is fifty-four days, faster than every large forensic lab in the country, which typically takes three to six months to come back with a report, Shaler says. Small, private labs have short intervals because they're not analyzing as many samples. "We can turn it around in three or four days if someone says they need it," Shaler continues. "We can make it as fast as necessary, but you can't make all the cases that fast." They are currently building a new lab that will allow them to process more tests more quickly.

With an organization resistant to change, and a delicate, sometimes-at-odds relationship with science and scientists, it is not surprising then that so many cases go cold. When CompStat was first instituted the police department quite rightly focused on bringing the number of homicides down. There were 1,946 murders in 1993, the year before CompStat. In 2003 there were 596. That's the lowest the number has been for forty years. At the same time, the average percentage of unsolved murders, which hovered around 35 percent for decades, began climbing. Right now you have an almost 50 percent chance of getting away with murder in New York: 49.3 percent of the murders committed in 2003 remain unsolved. That figure will drop in 2004, but not by much. An unsolved murder has up to 5 to 10 percent chance of being cleared within one year after it goes cold. After two years, that chance decreases to less than 1 percent. If you murdered someone in 2000 and you're not in jail already, you're in the clear. You got away with it. Congratulations.

Detectives have fewer homicides to investigate and therefore more time, and more tools to solve them with, and yet the percentage of unsolved homicides is creeping up. When it comes to solving murder, CompStat has had no effect whatsoever. Murder clearance rates were lower in the eighties, before CompStat.

The most conservative possible estimate of the number of unsolved murders in New York, from 1900 to the present, and giving the police department every possible benefit of the doubt, is 23,091 out of 72,328 known and reported murders. That's not such a big number. It's also nowhere near correct. Earlier reporting practices and clearance rates were not standardized. Other possible homicides are listed as CUPPIs (Circumstances Undetermined Pending Police Investigation) because the ME needs more information before classifying them as homicides, although Dr. Shaler says few deaths are classified as CUPPIs anymore. "We're better at determining what the cause and manner of death is." (Cause and manner of death. Cause is a medical distinction, i.e., blunt force trauma or strangulation, for example. Manner is a legal one, like homicide or suicide or accidental.) Also, some percentage of missing persons are actually homicides, and finally, there are victims we'll never know about because their bodies will never be found. The true number over the past century is unknowable and surely a great deal higher than

23,091. However, since the NYPD has standardized their reporting practices over the years and has made their clearance rates less creative, the number of known, unsolved homicides since 1985, when the NYPD started a computer database, is closer to reality: 8,894.

Other telling facts are contained within the homicide database. Don't live in Morrisania (Bronx), East New York (Brooklyn), or Inwood (Manhattan), for instance. Those neighborhoods have the highest number of unsolved murders. Three hundred seventy-three of the 8,894 victims of unsolved murders have never been identified, including eight skeletons, two skulls, two sets of body parts, three torsos, and thirty abandoned newborns. The 373 bodies were found in the street, in the water, and scattered about in alleyways, subways, school playgrounds, the garbage, motels, hotels, abandoned buildings, parks, parking lots, sewers, and construction sites. Fifty-nine of the murders that went cold happened on Christmas Eve and Christmas, and eighteen occurred on New Year's Eve.

Normally, when a particular area of the city shows an increase in crime, the NYPD sends in reinforcements. The fastest growing category of crime in New York is unsolved crimes. Since 1996, the year the Cold Case Squad was formed, an estimated 1,250 precinct detectives have cleared 3,400 homicide cases through 2003, or 2.72 cases per detective. (Note: this number is the total homicide cases the precinct detectives cleared. The precinct detectives are not just working homicide cases, however, and while they were clearing those homicides, they were working and clearing burglaries, robberies, rapes, and so on.)

In the same time period, 35 Cold Case Squad detectives have cleared 519 homicides, or 14.8 cases per detective. The cases they cleared were by definition the hardest cases, the ones the precinct detectives couldn't solve in the first place. The Transit guys weren't doing too badly, it turns out. And yet, as members of the Cold Case Squad retire they are not replaced. And while the police department now does a better job of gathering information about crime in the city, much of that information is hoarded. It sometimes takes months for the Homicide Analysis Unit to provide reports about unsolved homicides to the Cold Case Squad.

To makes things even more difficult, criminals are getting sophisticated—they watch TV, too. They've learned to keep their mouths shut and demand an attorney. "What are you going to do now?" Spano asks. "You're left holding your dick. The days of beating someone up or threatening them or any other bullshit are long gone. If you need this guy to make your case, and he says he wants an attorney, you're screwed. And the attachment is forever. If a Cold Case detective comes back five years later and tries to talk to him, it still applies. His attorney must be present."

Also, new technologies, like the use of alternate light sources for finding evidence at crime scenes, superglue fuming for exposing latent fingerprints, and DNA analysis—all the stuff of cop shows—are not having as big an impact as expected. The truth is, detectives are not using them to the extent that's portrayed every night on TV. To date, DNA has been used in less than 2 percent of the cases the Cold Case Squad clears. In fact, the grand total of forensic DNA hits in all of New York to date is only 1,529. Only 7 percent of those were murder cases (72 percent were for sex crimes). Most crimes are not currently being solved with DNA evidence because there are just not that many profiles to compare to yet.

We've been hearing the term *DNA* for so many years now it feels like the science has been around long enough to stop calling it "new," but practical applications are still surprisingly recent. "You used to need buckets of blood to do a freaking DNA test," Spano explains. But now a process called PCR (polymerase chain reaction) allows scientists to develop DNA profiles from a couple of skin cells. PCR was introduced to the scientific community in 1985, but it wasn't used forensically in New York until 1992, when they built the lab and filled it with the necessary equipment. That doesn't always help the Cold Case Squad detectives, who are working on cases going back as far as 1965. The crime scenes are long gone. Either a bucket of blood or a few skin cells were collected and saved or they weren't.

Also, DNA databases like the FBI's CODIS (Combined DNA Index System) need time to accumulate samples or profiles. While the FBI started collecting DNA test results in 1990, and Congress passed the DNA Identification Act in 1994, allowing them to formally begin a national database, the database didn't become operational until 1998. New York State's DNA database didn't go live until March of 2000. The OCME in New York City, which began collecting profiles in 1990, and started its own local database in 1996, joined CODIS in January 2000. Just a few years ago. By comparison, New York's collection of fingerprint cards has been growing since 1910. It's immense. They passed the billion mark several years ago. And every year of accumulation counts. Fingerprints from crimes committed in the 1970s that had no matches then sometimes get hits when resubmitted now.

That said, the technology for DNA comparison is obviously more sophisticated than fingerprint comparison. On TV, fingerprints shoot by until two match up, always within seconds. In reality you enter a print. Nothing. You try again. Nothing. The process can take as little as ten minutes, but generally it takes hours, and the software is incapable of finding matches. It brings back possible candidates (if they exist), and then a person has to sit down and manually compare each possible fingerprint candidate. Sometimes the computer doesn't come back with any likely candidates, but detectives learn later that the perp's prints were in the database all along.

DNA comparisons are done by computer, and they are quick and exact and even more mundane. No exciting graphics, just an ordinary spreadsheet. There are thirteen fields for each DNA profile; each field corresponds with thirteen regions (or loci) along a strand of DNA— the current FBI standard for mapping DNA. All labs in the United States look at the same thirteen locations and therefore can compare DNA profiles. To find out if DNA at a crime scene matches someone's DNA in the database, a criminalist sits down at his computer, hits control-z to enter a value in the first field, and then he checks the profiles that come up to see if any match all the remaining fields.

There are two databases, or indexes, of samples: one for convicted offenders and one for any DNA recovered from a crime scene. Storage of these samples is divided into three tiers: the city's database, or LDIS (Local DNA Index System), the DNA tests performed and stored at the OCME; the state's, or SDIS (State DNA Index System), kept at the New York State Police Forensic Investigation Center; and finally the national level, or NDIS (National DNA Index System), the highest level of CODIS, managed by the FBI. As of August 2004, there were 12,460 total DNA profiles in New York City's database; 139,344 in the New York State collection; and 1,945,163 combined profiles at the national level.

The local samples are uploaded to the state monthly, and the state samples are uploaded to the national level every week. The OCME generates 1,500 DNA profiles a month, and because not all 1,500 tests produce unique profiles, they end up uploading around 500 of those to the state. Individual state laws, which limit whose DNA can be collected, stored, and shared, are preventing CODIS from growing as quickly as law enforcement would prefer.

The reality of the cold case statistics is more subtle than the numbers might indicate. The truth is, the percentage of cold cases continues to climb not because the precinct detectives are incompetent (although the NYPD, like any organization, has its share of losers) but because these are the cases without leads. Fifty-four percent of the cases that went cold happened in the street, in the subway, in a park, or in an abandoned building—places where a witness, if there was one, most likely didn't know or recognize the murderer or the victim. And depending on when the body was found, hundreds of people could have walked through and contaminated the crime scene—meaning no DNA. A 1994 doctoral thesis about unsolved murder found that "murder in residences not only accounted for the most frequent murder location but stood the greatest chance of being solved when compared to other locations." The author of this thesis also found that while more murders are committed with handguns, a case is less likely to go cold if a victim was stabbed to death. Basically, go outside, wear gloves, don't get anywhere near your victim, shoot them from a distance if you can, and keep your mouth shut. Follow these simple steps and you will get away with murder.

"Also, it's a numbers game," Vito Spano explains. The police department emphasizes arrests. "I've got twenty major crimes which I can solve and one homicide. Where am I going to focus my energy?

"And the sharpest guys are retiring." The NYPD hired a lot of people in the early eighties, while almost no one was hired in the seventies, due to the fiscal crisis New York was having at the time. Officers' pensions used to be based on an average of their three highest years of income, whenever that was. As of 2000, pensions are based on whatever officers made their last year. At the same time, the police department began giving out more overtime through programs like Operation Condor, which specifically paid people overtime in order to make more arrests. Arrest overtime generates court overtime. Then, 9/11. Still more overtime.

The people with twenty years of experience were never going to make money like this again. They had to leave. "Who the hell is going to stay around here?" Spano asks. "Are you crazy?" In 2002, a large number of detectives retired.

The detectives left in the Detective Bureau are not experienced homicide investigators. "It's not the same as doing narcotics, for instance. It's not a vertical investigation, it's fluid," Spano explains. "When I'm doing narcotics, and a kite [a complaint] comes in, I start by making observations. I arrest the people buying the drugs. 'Who sold you the drugs?' Then, you send in undercover, or a CI [confidential informant] and you buy drugs until you make a case." That's a vertical investigation. "When you do this shit, homicide, I got a body, now you gotta tell me who did it. The victim can't talk. You gotta work with nothing. You have to be able to do a number of different things, gather witnesses, forensics, you have to be a relationship builder, you have to be a good interrogator, you have to be articulate on the stand in court, you need to gather evidence, all the forensic bullshit, you can't be a dickhead. It takes time to learn all that shit."

The percentage of cold cases is growing because experienced Cold Case detectives like Wendell Stradford have to do their job with fewer and fewer guys covering their backs, while periodically stopping their murder investigations to put on a uniform and watch over a parade. At the same time they have to fight for every second of overtime they can to continue their investigations, while waiting days and weeks for information and test results, all in an environment that sometimes makes you feel like a jerk for wanting to try something new.

Vito Spano once brought several DNA experts from the FBI and the OCME to the Cold Case Squad headquarters to give presentations about DNA analysis. Seasoned detectives and commanders who genuinely cared about solving these crimes sat in the back smirking. The same guys who say motherfucker a hundred times in a row without taking a breath when the DA won't proceed without more evidence leaned back in their chairs, making a big show of not listening, as if being made to sit through these lectures was an insult to their detective manhood. Some of the information was, in fact, painfully basic for a group that has been working homicides for ten to twenty years, but some of the detectives didn't even listen while Julie Pasquini from the Department of Criminal Justice Services explained one key way to navigate the DNA system. If a detective has a suspect, and he needs his DNA but he doesn't want to tip the suspect off that he's investigating him, Pasquini can search to see if the suspect has an earlier assault or drug conviction, which would allow her to collect DNA instead. If she finds one, she can call the suspect's parole officer and say, "I just discovered that we don't have Joe's DNA, and he is required by law to provide it." The detective can now quietly compare the suspect's DNA against the DNA recovered from their crime scene.

It's impossible to know everything. But would any of these gun-toting cowboys who routinely face their own mortality have the guts to face down their disapproving peers, raise their hands, and ask Pasquini or the other presenters a question? Three members of the squad did. Wendell Stradford was one of them.

You can hold onto your job by keeping your head down, but you make it into the special squads by taking a risk every once in a while, and in a place like the NYPD, sometimes the biggest gamble is not what you're going to find on the other side of a door but admitting what you don't know in order to learn. An enduring complaint about "New York's Finest" is their absolute dedication to the belief that they are, in fact, the best. "When it is assumed that this is true, then improvements are harder to come by," the International Association of Chiefs of Police wrote in a study of the New York Police Department in 1967.

If anyone was going to put up their hand and chance public humiliation, however, it was the detectives in the Cold Case Squad. They're older, and somewhat beaten down and jaded by a lifetime in the NYPD, but the only way to solve a case that no one else before you could is to do something, anything at all, differently. All the usual methods have already been tried and they didn't work. Detectives are a complicated bunch. The flip side of the arrogance that made them act like a bunch of babies and all "above it all" in the back of the room at the DNA lecture is another characteristic that's needed to take on these difficult, loser cases: balls. When Wendell addressed the speaker to outline one of his cases and ask if it applied to what had just been explained about finding another way to collect a suspect's DNA, not one guy in the back of the room dared say a word.

■

In August 2000, Lieutenant Joe Pollini tells Detective Stradford to start working with Detective Steven Berger on the Leon-Martinez case because Detective Berger is about to be transferred from Special Projects in Manhattan to the Cold Case Squad in the Bronx. The Colombian drug cartel connection had been pursued for four years. Wendell goes back through the case files and finally asks, "Who else we got to look at here? Who did we miss?" He focuses on a name they had two months into the investigation: Robert Mitchell. "We had the name," Stradford explains, "but we didn't know who he was."

Standard procedure in every investigation is to pull the phone records. Linda and Esteban were murdered in the midst of an ongoing DEA investigation into their drug business, and the DEA had a wire going at Linda's liquor store, the center of all the drug activity, they believed. They'd collected tons of names. Not among them was the not very Hispanic name Robert Mitchell.

But the phone records for their home, not the liquor store, showed that Robert Mitchell called Esteban Martinez from his cell phone on the day of the homicide and left a message. Esteban tried to call Mitchell back twice, once to Mitchell's cell phone, and once to his pager. The cell phone and pager traces came back with addresses in Virginia and Maryland. Well, fuck this guy, everyone thinks. If he's making a call from Virginia or Maryland on the day of the homicide, he's not the guy. Plus, he didn't have a NYSID number. When you're arrested in New York for most felonies, and some misdemeanors, you're fingerprinted and you get a NYSID number (New York State Identification number, pronounced nigh-sid). This is entered into a database that is maintained by the state police in Albany. There were a lot of names to check in the beginning. So they ignored the home phone records. They ignored Robert Mitchell.

Next, Stradford rereads the children's statements. Investigators in the DA's office tried to gently prompt the children about who killed their parents. At one point, the oldest boy pointed to a black investigator and said, "He looked like him." Everyone turned to the investigator. "Tío Rob [Uncle Rob]," the little boy continued. "He came to my house all the time, he played with me . . . we went to McDonald's with them." That's when they thought for the first time, maybe we're looking for black people here and not Hispanic people. Still, they weren't ready to truly embrace that possibility. There was nothing on the wires about any guy named Rob. "But it was unexplained, you can't discount it," Wendell remembers. "You have to get an answer for it."

"It was Robert," Linda and Esteban's oldest son insisted. So Wendell goes back through the DD5s, and asks, "How many Robs do we have in this case?"

Wendell Stradford has eight CIs, five he actually uses with any regularity. It's a formal arrangement. Detectives must register their informants using a Confidential Informant Request form, which is three pages long and thorough to the point of tediousness. After exhaustively pumping the detective for information about the CI, the form references eight other forms that may or may not need to be attached. The detective must then submit an authentic signature card in duplicate and collect five signatures, ranging from his immediate superior officer up to the Borough Enforcement Deputy Inspector. It takes a day to fill out and a few days to process. A CI and drug associate of Esteban's had confided, "There's a guy named Rob, who came to New York with his girlfriend, and we took them to a hotel." Also in the car with Rob, the CI, and Rob's girlfriend were Esteban and his three children. The CI wasn't talking about the day of the murders, but it establishes that there's a guy named Rob from out of town who's connected to Esteban.

Normally, Esteban never brought anyone he was doing business with to the house. Only one person ever came to his home and met the children. Tío Rob. The CI mentioned that the children were hungry that day and that they stopped the car and ate at McDonald's. The kids also talked about going to McDonald's. The other detectives thought it was just a coincidence, but Wendell is thinking, Esteban's oldest boy didn't say it was some Spanish guy who did this, he pointed to a black man. And he called him Uncle Rob. "I'm just putting it together, Rob, Tío Rob, Uncle Rob, it's got to be the same one," Wendell remembers. The only Rob they had, the Robert Mitchell from the phone records, had an address in Virginia and Maryland. Yeah, there was nothing on the wires about Mitchell, Wendell sees, but he notices that the phone records at the home show constant contact. He was using a cell phone, Wendell thinks. How do we know he was really in Virginia or Maryland when this call was made? Wendell finishes reading the DD5s and wonders, how come we're not looking for him?

It's August 1. Another Cold Case detective in their office happens to be going down to Maryland to drop off some DNA for analysis. "Let's go down to Baltimore and see what we can find out," Wendell suggests. They have friends there. Their old commanding officer Eddie Norris is now the Baltimore police commissioner.

They haven't seen him for a year. Wendell, Steve Berger, and another Cold Case detective, Margie Yee, show up at his office and identify themselves. "Send them right in," Norris almost shouts into the phone. They're shown into the office, and Norris comes out from behind his desk and gives Stradford a hug, Yee a kiss, and shakes the hand of Detective Berger, whom he is meeting for the first time. "What brings you down here?" They tell him they need some help with a case that might have a Baltimore connection. Norris responds, "Absolutely. Whatever you need." He arranges a meeting with Major Robert Stanton (the Baltimore Police equivalent of deputy inspector, the same rank as Vito Spano) and members of the homicide and narcotics units Stanton commands, maybe eight guys altogether. "You tell them what you have and what you want to do."

They didn't have much. They had Mitchell's name, a phone number, and two addresses. That was it. The Maryland guys go to their computers. With Stradford and Berger sitting close by, they run through every Robert Mitchell that has ever been arrested in Baltimore. A Robert Mitchell who had been arrested in 1998 comes up with the same address from the phone records. Wendell points at the screen. "This is the Robert Mitchell we want."

They put together a list of Robert Mitchell's co-defendants. Maybe one of them went with Mitchell to New York that day to torture, murder, and rob Linda and Esteban. One name stands out, Tavon Blackmon. "He hit us in the face," Wendell remembers. Tavon was wanted for murder in Maryland. It's the perfect setup for a possible plea. He has the most to lose, so he'll be the most anxious person on that list to make a deal. "This is the guy we want to talk to."

But they have to find him first. "We have an idea where he is," the Maryland homicide guys tell them. "When we have him in custody, we'll call you."

They do an AutoTrack search on Robert Mitchell next. AutoTrack is a database of information about people run by an outfit called ChoicePoint Asset Company. The detectives sometimes refer to Auto-Track as the Faces of the Nation. Faces of the Nation is a search tool within AutoTrack used by law enforcement and insurance companies, among others to find people. You put in someone's name and it may have their date of birth, Social Security number, their current address, and other places they've lived, sometimes going back decades. It may also list cars registered in their name, any homes they may own, their arrest history, job history, the people living with them, and possible relatives. If they've died, it may have the date of their death. It costs twenty-five dollars per report, and some detectives rack up bills in the thousands, making Vito Spano scream at Lieutenant McHugh and his commanders, "What the motherfucking fuck is this?" To Spano it's an indication that the case is going nowhere. "What am I getting for my three thousand dollars? Are they bringing the ball over the goal line? We're supposed to hit the ball in the God damn hole. If the damn thing is hopeless, go get something else. As a manager, I have to be fiscally conscious." ChoicePoint reports can also include financial information, but that costs more and the NYPD doesn't have that kind of account. The FBI does. If Cold Case detectives really need that information, they call their buddies at Quantico.

When detectives complete the search on Robert Mitchell they have a name they've seen before—Keisha Washington. Keisha came up on a DMV check because she once lived with Mitchell.

Steven Berger, however, wants to continue to pursue the drug cartel–Hispanic connection. He interviews Juan Serriano, an inmate at Metropolitan Correctional Center, a federal jail at 500 Pearl Street. Berger shows him a photograph of Julio Garcia, an associate of Esteban's, and Serriano says yeah, he knows Garcia, and Garcia and Martinez were involved in the drug business together.

Meanwhile, back in Baltimore, Major Stanton assigns Detective Robert Snead to the case. Normally the commander from an out-of-state police department would have said, "Sure, do what you can to help them today, but get back to your own work tomorrow." Assigning Snead in particular is even more unusual, given that Snead is on the Achilles Task Force, a joint effort of the Baltimore Police Department and the Bureau of Alcohol, Tobacco and Firearms (ATF) focused on guns and drugs. But his participation is crucial. "He was there," Wendell explains. "In New York, I would know who to talk to and where to go. I'm a fish out of water in Baltimore. I had to follow his lead." Police Commissioner Eddie Norris gets on the phone and smooths the way. Shortly after, they have an official joint investigation between the New York and Baltimore police departments.

In New York, the investigation still hasn't exclusively zeroed in on Mitchell. They're holding on to the Colombian-Dominican drug connection, and Juan Serriano has given them someone new to check. Julio Garcia. They contact law enforcement agencies in Florida. Garcia doesn't have a record, they're told, but they're given an address. They also get the current address for Leo Everth, another associate of Esteban's they've been looking for.

Wendell and Berger do an AutoTrack check on Everth, then head down to Florida to interview him. With his lawyer participating via conference call, Everth confirms that he was friends with Linda and Esteban, and a co-owner of Linda's Liquors, the liquor store the DEA had been watching. But he insists Linda and Esteban were never involved with drugs. He's a drug dealer and he's lying, Stradford thinks at the time. He could have been involved in the murder.

The next month, in October, they go back down to Florida to talk to Julio Garcia. No one answers the door at the large high-rise condominium where he lives, but Wendell isn't too frustrated. He's not buying the Julio Garcia connection. There was nothing on the wires about him, the DEA hadn't even bothered to arrest him. He doesn't want to spend too much time on Garcia. He's got a feeling about Mitchell.

Reluctantly, they decide to talk to the kids again. "They're children. How many times are you going to make them relive this?" Wendell asks. On November 14, with two social workers present, and without Wendell, Margie Yee and Steve Berger meet with the children one last time. Cold Case detectives carry anywhere from seven to twenty cases, and whenever one of them has to be in court, or sit on a location (surveil), another detective they trust steps in. Wendell can't be there, so Margie Yee takes his place. But that day she and Berger come back with nothing.

A few weeks later, Stradford and Berger return to Maryland and meet with Mitchell's parole officer, who gives them an address where Mitchell lives with his wife and child. Stradford wants to talk to Mitchell, but he's not at the absolute he's-the-one point yet. He needs more information.

Then they catch a break. The Baltimore police have Tavon Blackmon in custody. On November 30, Berger and Snead question Tavon Blackmon. Thin, wiry, definitely a drug dealer and possibly a murderer, Blackmon is a tough guy. "Yeah, I know Robert Mitchell," he tells them. Mitchell was his supplier. He knew Robert Mitchell (who Blackmon called Bookie) and Keisha Washington, Mitchell's girlfriend at the time, and Keisha's brother, Kevin Washington. And, he tells them, he knows all about the murder of Linda Leon and Esteban Martinez.

Mitchell had told Blackmon that four years ago, around Christmastime, he, Keisha, Kevin, and Kevin's girlfriend, Nisey (pronounced Neesy), went to New York and "smoked" a guy and his wife. Linda was screaming, Mitchell had added. They got a kilo and a half of cocaine and crack, Mitchell had bragged, and thousands of dollars, which Mitchell used to buy a new Acura Legend.

The Tavon Blackmon interview is brief. Tavon doesn't want to talk too much because he thinks he is going to beat his own murder case. Why risk the payback of snitching? he's thinking. It doesn't matter—he says enough. "This is the guy we want," Wendell says. Robert Mitchell is now the one. Plans to go to the Dominican Republic to find Julio Garcia are immediately scrapped. It is also Detective Berger's last day in the Cold Case Squad office in Manhattan. On January 16, 2001, the Leon-Martinez double homicide formally becomes Detective Wendell Stradford's case.

A few weeks later Stradford fractures his finger playing basketball with his church fellowship and is put on restricted duty through February. It must drive the strapping, athletic workaholic detective nuts to have to cool his heels all because of a mere finger, but those are the rules. Wendell Stradford works so obsessively he frequently doesn't stop to eat. When you ride along with Wendell, you starve. Most people know to eat beforehand or to bring something with them. He's "in the hunt," he explains, using the phrase detectives have for investigating. "Who has time?"

Stradford and Snead keep in contact daily by telephone. Stradford likes Snead. A streetwise former marine from New Jersey, Snead sometimes does things unconventionally to get what he needs. Snead was regularly calling Keisha Washington at this time, pretending to be a social worker. "We're allowed to use deception to get information," Wendell says. Referred to as a ruse, the Supreme Court has generally found that it doesn't violate the witness's constitutional rights. Keisha has a son with Robert Mitchell, and Snead gains her confidence by explaining that Mitchell owes Keisha child support. "Help me find him," he tells her, and "I'll get you the money." Keisha agrees to meet with Snead. She tells him she doesn't want Mitchell in her life. She talks about an awful time, long ago, when he caused her a lot of problems. She and her brother Kevin are currently estranged because of something Mitchell had involved them in. "Something that I can never make up for," Keisha, who is now a born-again Christian, explains regretfully.

They know she is talking about the murder of Linda Leon and Esteban Martinez. She has also confirmed that her brother Kevin was involved. Kevin is in jail in Maryland for attempted murder, they learn, and is due for parole in less than a month. "We decided to make a go at Keisha," Wendell says. She trusts Snead. She is born again. "She was the one most likely to talk to us." So Wendell and fellow Cold Case detective Steve Kaplan head back to Maryland. With Snead and Snead's sergeant, they drive over to the hospital where Keisha works. "No one wants to create a scene at their job. They're more cooperative. They just want to get it done and get us out of there."

Keisha comes out to talk to Snead. She glances at Wendell and Steve, who are sitting over in the hospital lounge, but she doesn't know yet that they are all together. Snead introduces his sergeant as an associate. "Is this about my case? Am I going to be getting my money?" "There's a couple of gentlemen who need to speak to you first," Snead answers, and gestures to Wendell and Steve to come over. Wendell begins gently. "We need you to help us out. Mr. Snead said you're a pretty nice person. You're a mother, you work, you're taking care of the things you need to take care of. But now it's time for you to take care of something else." Keisha freezes. "You're not from here, are you," she says warily. "No." "You're not even with HRA [Human Resources Administration]?" "No, we're not." "Where are you from?" "We're from New York," they answer simply. She turns to Snead. "And you're not a social worker." "No. I'm BPD." (Baltimore Police Department.) "Please, what is this about?" she pleads. "Have you ever been to New York?" Wendell asks. "A couple of times with my baby's father," she answers. "But that was a long time ago."

Wendell takes out a picture of Linda and Esteban's three children and puts it on the counter in front of Keisha. "Do you know these kids?" Keisha picks up the photograph. "No, I've never seen these kids before." Then Wendell pulls out a photograph of the entire family. "Do you know them?" She puts her hand to her mouth.

"This is about that thing that happened in New York?" "Yeah." "Oh my God. Am I under arrest?" "No. But we're going to talk to you now," Wendell responds, fully in command. "You help us out and we'll decide what's going to happen after that." She starts to panic. "I knew this day was going to come, I knew this day was going to come," she repeats, something Wendell says she does when she gets upset. She'll stop on one sentence and say it over and over. Snead calms her down. She can meet them at the police station, he explains. They don't have to haul her away in handcuffs. "We don't want you to lose your job. We'll tell your boss that this is about an old burglary." She agrees to take a cab to the Baltimore Police Department. Except for fellow investigators, no one, not even captains, sits in on interrogations. Outsiders inhibit everyone. "There's stuff going on there that no one should see," Wendell explains. "Not the rubber hose," he quickly adds, "but what goes on psychologically." For the detective, it's an intensely private performance, a co-performance, really, between the detective, the other investigators, and their suspect, and it can't be pulled off with an audience.

"You probably already know that when a district attorney takes a statement from a defendant that whole process is taped," Spano explains. "But how do they get to that station? It usually takes hours of interaction between a detective and his partner and the defendant. I never like to let them know I'm watching, it impedes the process. The detective has to get the defendant to agree that it is in his interest to make a statement to the district attorney. They help them rationalize what they did. To make it seem not as bad. That somehow, between the two of them, they're going to make it all right. You're not judging them, you're not bigger or better, you're going to do this as a team. We have this thing going on between us." The perp has to feel sufficiently fucked and alone, and here's this guy who seems to know the deal and can help. "There is a degree of intimacy that goes on in the room that is nothing illegal or violent. There has to be a real connection with the suspect. Why would someone reveal themselves to you if you don't have, at least in their mind, a real connection? While the process is going on it is not faked. No matter how vile the defendant is or the crime is, in order to connect you have to have that bond. Of course you feel weird or icky afterward—you're bonding and having a relationship with a person that committed murder.

"The heavier, more threatening stuff, the shouting, is a last last resort. When the person isn't talking, when it's not working.

"The more people that are witnesses to an interrogation the more witnesses a defense attorney can now call to the stand and examine and cross-examine and make potential mischief with the prosecution's case."

Steve Kaplan listens as Wendell questions Keisha Washington on March 12, 2001, in Baltimore's Cold Case Squad office. She's a big girl, quiet, soft-spoken, and nervous. She's twenty-eight years old now, but she was twenty-two at the time of the murder. She asks if she can call her mother, to check on her baby. "I want to tell her I'll be a little late." She turns to Wendell, her anxiety starting to peak again. "I am going home, aren't I?" "Yeah, I told you," Wendell assures her. "We're not going to arrest you." Wendell and the others are surprised when she proceeds to tell them everything.

Robert Mitchell said he was losing money because of Esteban, she explains. So, they got on a Peter Pan bus to New York to address the matter. "My duty was to maintain the children," she tells them. After they tied up Linda and Esteban, she and Kevin's girlfriend, Denise, sat on the bed with the kids in their bedroom and watched TV. "The children asked, 'What's going on with Mommy and Daddy?' They kept asking over and over." Robert and Kevin came into the room. "'Shut 'em up,'" they said. The children cried while they looked for money in the bedrooms. "They were asking what was going on with their mom and dad. That's what they kept asking us. And we said, 'Oh, nothing.' They kept asking over and over again, they asked us several times what was going on. 'We want to go out there and see what's going on with Mom and Dad.'

"We tried to play. They had the TV on. So we tried to play and watch TV."

When they couldn't find all the money and drugs, Kevin stabbed Linda to get her to tell them where everything was hidden. "He dug something in her ear," Keisha describes. Then Kevin shot Linda. "I believe the kids heard because they kept trying to come out the room."

"We did have to basically hold them, hold their mouths, me and Denise. Once they heard the gunshots that was it. It was like the children, they knew something wasn't right. So they started like going off, they started screaming."

There was a final frantic search for more money. "Then Robert said, 'Come on let's go, we got enough. They dead. We got enough. They dead.' Then my brother Kevin said, 'No man, I want more than this, I'm risking my life. I want more than this.'"

Keisha turned around and looked inside the apartment one more time before running out. "The children ran out the room, they started crying, they scream."

The first time Keisha cries during the interview is when Wendell asks her about her brother Kevin, who is in jail for attempted murder and due to be paroled the next month. Then she cries at the end, when Wendell questions her about what Kevin had done to Linda's ear. During the interview, Keisha gives them one new important piece of information, a name. Denise. Tavon Blackmon only knew Kevin Washington's girlfriend as Nisey. After the interview, Keisha allows them to take her fingerprints. Wendell arranges to have Keisha and Kevin Washington's prints compared to latent prints from the scene.

The next day, Wendell and Steve Kaplan go back to the Federal Building to show photographs to Tavon Blackmon. Wendell pulls out Robert Mitchell's photograph and shows it to Tavon. "I sold drugs for him, we used to get high together," he responds. Then, Keisha Washington's. "That's Rob's girl." And finally, Kevin Washington. "That's Keisha's brother, he used to go out with this girl named Niece."

Snead calls Wendell the following day to say he has identified Denise as Denise Ann Henderson. She doesn't have a record in Baltimore, he tells him. Born in 1967, Denise was the oldest of the murderers, they learn. She'd be thirty-four now. Wendell checks everywhere else for any record of her, the NYPD's databases, Social Security, the IRS, HRA, AutoTrack. He has someone from the FBI check for financial records through ChoicePoint. Nothing. Snead, amazingly, gets ahold of her fingerprints and overnights them to Wendell in New York. They were taken as part of a job application she once filled out, and the Maryland State Police has a copy on file.

Wendell hand delivers the prints to the Latent Print Section, on the fifth floor at 1PP, for comparison. This is where they will be entered into the database to see if they match any prints on file. If the prints had needed to be lifted, they would have first gone to the Police Laboratory in Queens. Aside from serology and DNA tests, which are done at the OCME, anything else that needs to be tested—ballistics, narcotics, and fingerprint lifting—are done in the Police Laboratory. (The Cold Case Squad does occasionally go elsewhere for special tests. Vito Spano likes to use the Royal Canadian Mounted Police, for instance, for vacuum metal deposition testing, which is a method of lifting fingerprints from nonporous surfaces.) The result of the print comparison: Kevin, negative; Denise, negative; Keisha, positive. Two of her prints match two that were lifted from a soda can from Linda and Esteban's apartment. Five years after the murders they have their first solid piece of physical evidence. Wendell is not a hoot and holler kind of guy, he's reserved. He probably does little more than smile. But finding a piece of physical evidence to connect a killer to a crime scene is about as good as it gets, short of a confession, and Wendell already has one of those, too. He is getting it all.

Whether he shows it or not, Detective Wendell Stradford is exultant. Steve Kaplan, who's been helping, smiles and says, "Holy shit, can you believe that?" Wendell tells Lieutenant Pollini, then Bob Snead in Baltimore, then calls Nancy Borko, the ADA from the Bronx DA's office assigned to the case. A very thorough prosecutor, Borko wants every possible question addressed before she'll go to trial. Like all DAs, she wants to win. If she thinks she can get it, she won't budge on a case until detectives deliver the smoking gun. Wendell believes he's brought her the ammo she needs. Borko wants more. She wants statements from everyone. "Talk to Kevin Washington, talk to Denise Henderson, and talk to Robert Mitchell." She won't get a warrant for Keisha's arrest until they do all of this. Her response must have had a dampening effect on an otherwise exciting day.

For the next two months, Stradford joined Operation Condor and helped to execute old arrest warrants that had been sitting untouched, for years in some cases. They had no choice but to put a lot of their casework down. By June, Wendell and a thousand other detectives had gone through over forty-nine thousand warrants. The column for their case numbers in the arrest logs for the Cold Case Squad for a time instead said, "Condor, Condor, Condor, Condor," over and over.

That same month Keisha tells her brother Kevin, now out on parole, that she's talked to the police and told them everything. "You're not my sister," he says, and threatens to kill her. He's a big man—6' 3" and 230 pounds. Keisha's not exactly a little thing. She's 5' 9" and weighs 200, but she calls Snead, and they put her in a hotel for a couple of weeks until they can arrest her brother. She's their only viable witness at this point. On June 13, Snead has Kevin arrested on a domestic violence charge. Now Snead and a sergeant from the Baltimore Police Department can question him.

Kevin Washington is Keisha's fraternal twin, so he was also twenty-two at the time of the murders. The year before the murder he earned his GED. Kevin claims that Robert Mitchell told him that they were going to rob the couple and leave.

They purchased the duct tape, gloves, and knife from a Caldors, he begins. When they arrived at the apartment in New York, Keisha went to the bathroom. "When she come out Robert pulled out a gun." Kevin thought it was a joke at first. Esteban and Robert went back and forth a few times, like it wasn't serious. Then the girls duct taped Linda and Esteban and together they all looked for money and drugs.

Kevin admits that he had a knife and that he tried to cut Linda's neck, but the "wood knife" he had wouldn't cut. Linda and Esteban's oldest boy had said, "That bad man had a ugly knife." He described the knife as having "little teeth." Simple but horribly accurate. It was a Sheetrock knife with a serrated edge. He then made a hand motion— fist to chest—and said, "He was doing this to my mommy."

Kevin tells them he saw Robert shoot Linda in the bedroom, and then "Tone." (They called Esteban Tony, Tone for short.) Later, the women cried, Kevin remembers. "I'm like, why are you all crying?" But then he says, with regret, "Even though they was drug buddies, they was friends." When they got back to Maryland, Robert threw the gun into an empty lot. "We were supposed to be da brothers, man. He was going to marry my sister." He concludes by saying, "I'm sorry this had to happen and I wish Robert would be a man and admit to killing those people. Because he started this and it's time for him to end it."

Wendell calls the jail and arranges to have an official detainer placed on Kevin Washington, pending his arrest for the murder of Linda Leon and Esteban Martinez. Then, a process that has been evolving for more than a century kicks in quickly and efficiently. Snead sends the tape and associated paperwork up to Wendell, Wendell goes to court with Nancy Borko to get a warrant. This is transmitted back to Snead, and Kevin Washington is subsequently arrested and charged with murder two and robbery. They don't charge him with murder one because they can't prove he knew about and planned the murders beforehand. (Murder two is the standard murder charge. Murder one is used less frequently, and there are three pages in the penal code outlining its use.)

Shortly after Kevin's arrest, Keisha runs into Denise Henderson, who tells her where she is living with her children. Keisha gives the address to Snead, who immediately calls Wendell. They do a check on the address. "We jumped into a car and started looking for her the next day," Wendell says.

Stradford, Snead, and Chuck Harrison park nearby the address and watch. It turns out to be Denise's mother's address. They spend a couple of days watching, going back at different times to see who goes in and out. When they decide it's time to knock on the door, Denise's teenage daughter answers. "I don't know where she is," she tells them. They give her a phone number. "Could you ask her to please call us?" They don't want to scare the child, so they tell her it's about an accident. Then they sit on another address for Denise and watch some more. This time they only sit for an hour or two, because now that they've been to her mother's house, people are going to start tipping other people off.

They go to the door. Denise's cousin answers this time. They talk for a while, then they get aggressive. "Listen, talk to us or you're going to wind up having a lot of problems," they say. She gives them an address across the street. Across the street they're given still another address. Snead knocks on the door. Denise doesn't currently have an arrest record, so they've never seen a picture of her. Keisha said she was light-skinned, mixed race, black and Indian, medium height, and about two hundred pounds. That describes the woman standing in the door. It is Denise. Someone has clearly tipped her off. She is acting both confident and evasive.

"We want to speak to Denise Henderson. Nisey." "She's not here right now." "Oh no?" Wendell says, and they stand for a minute, looking at each other. Face off. Wendell's sure it's her, but he can't be positive. "Well, we need to speak to her. Who are you?" he demands. Almost instinctively, Denise backs away from the door. And Wendell, Chuck, and Snead walk in. They look around. Not a bad place. Denise had been in the middle of cleaning. "What do you need to speak to her about, she's not here," Denise says, as she continues to back away. "What's your date of birth?" Wendell asks quickly. "Why do you need to know my date of birth?" Denise shoots back, just as quickly. Now Wendell knows it's her. He takes command. "We know who you are, you need to come with us." Denise breaks down and starts crying. "What is this all about?" "Just come with us." Wendell speaks without sympathy.

Wendell doesn't give Denise Henderson's feelings a second thought. "I didn't really care. The chick murdered somebody." Denise agrees to get in the car and go with them to the Baltimore City Police Department headquarters. On June 25, 2001, they get their third statement.

Denise describes walking up the stairs to Linda and Esteban's apartment. "As we're going up we put gloves on," she tells them. In Denise's version, Mitchell is the one who went into the bathroom. When he came out "he pulls the gun out, and he's like all right, man, you know what's up, you know what this is about, and the man was like, 'Wait a minute, what are you doing?' And that's when Keisha put the handcuffs on the man, and Kevin grabs the girl and I puts the tape on her mouth and then when I turned around, that's when Keisha and Bookie had him on the floor. So, I just ran on back to where the kids were in the room." When the kids asked Denise who she was she didn't say anything. "And I was like petting on him," she says, describing the oldest boy, "because he started crying, and then he stopped crying."

She looked for money. "Every few seconds Keisha would come back in the room and she was like, 'Denise, did you find anything,' and I'm like, 'No I can't find anything.'" So Keisha helped her look. Then Kevin. "And the little boy was like, 'What are you doing, why are you looking, why are you all in my mom's stuff?' and I was like, 'I'm just looking for something.' Then he got scared and started crying and I'm like, 'Shhh, be quiet, don't cry. Everything's all right.'"

"Keisha found money and I found some money, and then Kevin put it in the bag and that's when I heard Bookie holler, 'Let's go!' I could see the man was still laying on the floor and I just jumped over him, and just went on out the door." Denise tells them that she stopped short on the first floor when she saw someone there watching them. Robert, Keisha, and Kevin bumped into each other and piled up behind her. "We all act like we were laughing and joking around and just walked out."

They went back to the Port Authority to wait for a bus. It was as if they didn't immediately grasp what money could buy and arrange for more comfortable transportation. Back in Maryland, they picked up Denise's two children, and Keisha and Mitchell's son, and spent the night in a hotel—the children in one room, the two couples together in another. Again, it never occurred to them that they could now afford separate rooms. Detectives estimate that they found fifty-five thousand dollars that night.

That evening, they split the money and drugs, although the women didn't get any of the drugs. The next morning, Denise remembers, "I went home, took a bath, got dressed, got the kids dressed, and then me and Keisha, we went to the stores shopping. We bought stuff for the kids. It was around Christmastime." Wendell asks, "Did you wonder what happened to the other kids in New York?" "Yes." "For their Christmas?" No answer. "Did you think about them at all?" Very softly she answers, "Yes, I did." "Did you make any inquiries about them at all?" No answer. "Did you see anything in the newspaper about it? Or, on the news?" "No." "While you and Keisha were out there shopping, spending all the money from there, did you talk to each other about—" "No."

The detectives now have three confessions. Wendell puts a copy of the taped interview on an Amtrak train to New York, with an Amtrak cop, who meets Lieutenant Pollini at Pennsylvania Station. Pollini drives the tape up to the Bronx DA's office, where they listen and make a decision. ADA Nancy Borko doesn't want to move forward until she listens to the tape herself. The Baltimore homicide sergeant, amazed at the DA's delay, arranges to have Denise held overnight.

The Cold Case detectives love the Manhattan DAs. They're fearless. They want to get into court and try the bad guys, and they're not afraid of losing. The DAs in Queens, Brooklyn, and the Bronx are more cautious. This is not always the wrong approach—they want to win. As Dr. Shaler puts it, "They have a batting average, too." Vito Spano agrees. "If they get ahold of a case that's going to be a loser, they'd rather not bring it to the grand jury. New York is a tough place to bring a case forward. We have very tough admission-of-evidence rules. Juries are tough, as well." Panzarella complains that not every witness will do. "The DAs want a former nun, a mother of five, and a priest as witnesses," he fumes. "At four o'clock in the morning, when a lot of these murders happen, you've got only junkies, drug dealers, and cops." There's also a long-standing adversarial relationship between the public and the NYPD. Juries in New York don't always believe what detectives say on the stand. And they don't always follow the judge's instructions.

"But they've got to take a risk sometime," Wendell Stradford argues. "You're a trial attorney. Get up and do your job. Convince the jury. Not every case is going to be a slam dunk. You're not always going to get all the evidence you'd like. Sometimes, it's not going to get any better than this, and if you know in your heart he's guilty, you've got to take a chance. You might lose, but you have to try."

Wendell's still in Baltimore, so Margie Yee goes to court with Borko, and twelve hours later the warrants are faxed to Maryland. On June 26, Wendell arrests Denise Ann Henderson and charges her with two counts of murder two and robbery. Keisha is still staying at the hotel. The next day, they go to where she works. No one wants a scene. "Just come back with us," they said to her quietly. Keisha accompanies them back to the Baltimore Police Department headquarters, where they process her arrest.

Later, Denise takes Wendell, Chuck, and Snead to the Cambridge Iron and Metal Company in Baltimore, where they disposed of the gun. "Fuck," they all say when they get there. They're never going to recover any evidence from here. It's a scrapyard. For five years people have been dumping metal, then clearing it out and putting it in a smelter and melting it. "Has anyone ever found a gun here?" they ask the general manager. Not that he knows of.

Now they have Kevin, Keisha, and Denise arrested and in custody. It is going to be a whole other thing getting them back to New York. Cold Case detectives can grab people in other states if they have a warrant, but unless the person is willing to go voluntarily, they can't throw them in a car and bring them back to New York. Instead, they work with local law enforcement.

Out-of-state arrest warrants are usually honored when the crime is a felony. The prisoners are processed in the local jail, then brought before a local judge for a fugitive hearing. In this case, the Maryland judge has to decide if there is enough evidence to hold Kevin, Keisha, and Denise on the New York charges. He decides there is. Next, each of the prisoners has the right to fight the extradition. Keisha waives her rights first. She knows she would have to sit for a minimum of thirty days in a Maryland county jail while Wendell gets a governor's warrant to bring her to New York.

Governors may demand extradition from other states by issuing a governor's warrant. However, honoring them is a matter of courtesy. Some states won't extradite prisoners, for instance, if it means the person might face the death penalty if they do. Most states work well together, however, and Keisha would not be facing the death penalty. One way or another, she was going back to New York.

So Keisha goes to court to let the judge know she is waiving her rights. After signing some papers, she is taken back to the jail, where they process her and hand over all the paperwork to Wendell, who signs some more papers accepting her. On July 3, Wendell walks her out of the jail, in handcuffs, and into a car and back to New York. Keisha is in cuffs the entire time. "She's a murderer," Wendell explains. They bring Denise Henderson back on July 27, and one month later, on August 23, they return with Kevin.

Wendell Stradford is doing a lot of traveling for the Leon-Martinez case, but this is not out of the ordinary for Cold Case detectives. New York's murderers are all around the country and the world, and sometimes cases go cold precisely because killers and witnesses leave the state and disappear. For Wendell, who has been coaching his son Tyler's basketball practices since 1997, every trip back and forth to Baltimore means a missed practice. Locking up Keisha, Denise, and Kevin has added up to just under a dozen missed games, and it's not over yet. Robert Mitchell is still at large.

A few weeks after bringing Kevin Washington back to New York, on 9/11 everyone in the Cold Case Squad, like all police department personnel, goes on various special assignments. Wendell is at the site on the first day, before the second plane hit. Everyone in the Cold Case Squad is told to go back and put on their uniforms to do perimeter security. Only emergency workers are to be allowed into the site. For the next couple of days, Wendell Stradford and Steve Kaplan stand guard at various locations around the World Trade Center site. They don't have masks, and everyone coughs continually, and when they blow their noses, it comes out black. "It's like when we were transit cops," Wendell tells Kaplan. Down in the subway, the wheels on the trains would grind down the rails, and at the end of their tours cops would blow out black steel dust. After a few days doing security, Wendell goes on morgue duty for two months. Some guys stay on the street, outside the morgue. They don't want to go inside. Wendell goes inside. "Being a security guard is not my thing." On the other side of the morgue doors, Wendell Stradford, who has endured an NYPD career's worth of remains of murder, is introduced to a whole new level of death.

At the same time, Detective Snead has been alternately sitting at the homes of Mitchell's wife and mother, waiting for him to appear. Wendell comes down to Baltimore three times to sit with him. They never see Mitchell. Then, in early October, Keisha calls Snead from jail. Mitchell is at her mother's house right now looking for Keisha and their baby. This is the first time anyone has seen him in about seven months. Wendell immediately leaves for Baltimore. They hit Mitchell's wife's house first. She isn't there, but someone else lets them in. They search the apartment. "It was a filthy, disgusting place, roaches everywhere," Wendell remembers. Mitchell's not there. Then the girl gets belligerent. "You can't do this." "Well, who are you?" they ask. They run her name through their databases. "She's out on parole," Snead announces. "You know you're not supposed to be here," they tell her. Robert Mitchell is on parole for another charge, and two parolees can't live together. She backs down. "I'm sorry, this is my friend's place and you guys came running in here," she said, trying to be nice now. She doesn't know where he is, she insists. But they know it's just a matter of time.

The full name of the Cold Case Squad is the Cold Case and Apprehension Squad. It's one thing to figure out who murdered someone. "Tracking people's movements, and finding people who don't want to be found is a different skill," Eddie Norris, the original Cold Case Squad commander, explains. "You can't put a picture in a cell." In the movies and on TV, the bad guy is always arrested within a day. Detectives show up at the person's place of work or home, at some nice, civilized time in the afternoon, and quietly take the guy away in cuffs. In reality, it can take months and years of painstaking searching, and the actual arrest almost always happens in the dead of night, usually around three or four in the morning, when everyone is asleep and at their most vulnerable. Norris, who came from the Warrants Division of Fugitives and Apprehension, knew the difference between detectives who could both solve cases ("homicide guys") and detectives who could actually find the perpetrators ("warrants guys"). When he and Jack Maple put together the Cold Case Squad, they recruited both.

At first, the seasoned homicide detectives, who thought they knew everything, looked at the warrants guys with the same smug attitude the Cold Case detectives had displayed during the DNA lecture. But there was a lot they routinely overlooked, steps the warrants guys would never have missed. The homicide guys knocked on doors without adequate surveillance or homework, and people were either not there or they ran. Word spread, everyone warned everyone else, and no one got caught.

The warrants guys moved slower. They watched the place for a while. They didn't just have one address, they put together lists, which included addresses of the perp's friends, girlfriends, and relatives. They made sure people were home and that they knew the identities of everyone inside. They checked the occupants of the houses and apartments across from them, and the ones next door. "They could all be associates," Wendall says, "someone they've been arrested with, or family members. If you go knocking at their next-door neighbors, and they say, 'That's my cousin,' you've just given up everything. Now they'll just yes you to death, and when you leave they'll call and say, 'The cops were just here looking for you.'"

Robert Mitchell is back in Baltimore, and Wendell and the other detectives know what to do. They decide to hit the mother's and the wife's houses that night, at the accustomed time, three in the morning. In the meantime, both residences are kept under constant surveillance. When Wendell and Steve Kaplan get there, there are uniform cops, Baltimore police, and guys from the ATF. Wendell is sitting on the wife's house, and another team is sitting on the mother's house. They watch both places for an hour or so, to see if there is any more activity before going in. "The people that we're looking for are not homebodies," Wendell explains. "They go out, they party, they drink, they get high. By four in the morning, they're usually back in their house." That's when the detectives get in close and listen at the door or peer through a window.

It's five in the morning. Wendell is sitting in a car with Steve Kaplan and Detective Bob Snead. They're dressed in civilian clothes and "raid jackets" (black jackets that say POLICE in big white letters), and the mood inside the car is anxious. They're gearing up to pounce. Wendell decides they're going to hit the wife's house first. He gets on the police radio and alerts everyone in their cars and positioned around the house. "We're going in." NOW. They swarm the house, then knock. Loudly. When the door opens, "You shine a light in their face and they're disoriented. You hit them with questions quickly, before they have a chance to realize that there are five or six cops standing at their door." All the exits and windows are covered with guns drawn in case anyone tries to run.

The wife is home. "She was screaming and yelling, calling us motherfuckers." But Mitchell isn't there. Wendell calls the other team sitting on the mother's house. "He's not here." The other team immediately hits the house. They can't wait while phone calls are made and people flee. Wendell and his team drive there as fast as they can. The house is three, maybe four, miles away and they are flying. The mother's neighborhood is as nice as the wife's is seedy. She lives across the street from the Western Cemetery.

When Stradford, Snead, and Kaplan arrive, they step inside to a wall of rage and arrogance. The mother is as belligerent as the wife was: "Why the fuck are the police at my house, scaring the children?" She's in her sixties, loud, foulmouthed, and simple. "She called everyone motherfuckers in front of the children," says Wendell. Mitchell isn't there, but his brother is, and when he sees them coming he's about to leave.

They need to quickly gain control of the situation and, if at all possible, ensure cooperation from the people in the house. Mitchell is a drug dealer and everyone in the family knows it. So the detectives say, "Listen. Your family could be in danger." Everyone stops. "Some of Mitchell's associates are after him," they tell the family, "and you could get hurt." The mood in the room changes. "Oh. Is that why people have been calling here?" the mother asks. "Somebody called and said they were going to kill everyone in the house if Robert doesn't give them the money." "No kidding," the men improvise, full of concern and sympathy. "It's probably the same people." The mother tells them about the girl Robert lives with, but she's afraid Robert will find out that she told if she takes them there. "He'll never find out from us," they assure her. Mitchell's brother encourages her. "Yeah, take them over there, Ma, show him so we don't have to worry about this." They put her in an unmarked car with tinted windows, and she takes them to an apartment complex on the other side of town. She points out the apartment. The team surrounds the building. Wendell knocks on the door. A girl's voice calls through the door, "Who is it?" and the Baltimore PD guys immediately kick down the door.

"He's not here," she yells as they come through the door. In his twenty-year career, Wendell has done a few hundred warrants. He can tell when people are lying. "When people are lying to you, telling you someone isn't there, when you know they are, you know you're going to have a problem. Either he's trying to hide, or worse, preparing to defend himself." They know Mitchell is there because his mother had called earlier that evening and spoken to him.

Detective Wendell Stradford generally carries himself with a quiet, dignified bearing. He's self-contained, professional, never says a single unnecessary word, and the few words he does utter will be spoken softly. When he's arresting a criminal who doesn't comply with his wishes, however, it's hard to imagine anyone not immediately dropping to the floor and never making another move. Gun drawn, it's like watching a horror movie transformation. "COME OUT HERE MOTHERFUCKER. I'LL PUT A HOLE RIGHT IN YOUR FUCKING HEAD." "You have to be really aggressive, really threatening," Wendell explains. "Especially if he's looking right at you and sizing up his chances. He has to believe that you're just as crazy as he is. He has to know he can't win." "Robert Mitchell!" he yells. Then every cop runs through all the rooms until they find the over-six-feet-tall and at least 250-pound Mitchell cowering under a bed in his boxer shorts. They arrest him and bring him back to the BPD headquarters.

■

On October 17, Wendell and Kaplan interview Robert Mitchell in the Fugitive Office of the Baltimore Police Department, where they're now holding him on probation violations. (Mitchell wasn't seeing his parole officer or living at his listed parole address.)

Then twenty-one, Mitchell was the youngest of the murderers that night in 1996. He cries during the interview but Wendell is not impressed. "Crocodile tears," Wendell says. Considering the magnitude of the events of the night, it's bizarre what Mitchell doesn't remember or claims never to have known. For instance, he doesn't know Denise's last name or nationality. "Indian? Light-skinned?" They were drinking a cheap brandy called E&J the whole time they were riding up there that day, he told them.

Of the four, Mitchell's interview was the shortest. "As with all drug enterprises," Wendell says, explaining how it all began, "the relationship soured." (The DEA weren't entirely wrong about a drug connection to the killings, only it came from Baltimore and not Colombia.) Esteban was living the good life, Mitchell believed, while Mitchell was struggling to sell drugs that Esteban had "stepped on" (cut with other substances).

Mitchell says he called Tony to try to talk things over. He only wanted to get his money back, but Tony wouldn't return his calls. Tony was blowing him off. So they were going to rob them, Mitchell admits, but he had no idea that they would be killed.

They get there and begin a drug deal. Robert gives Esteban money, and Esteban measures out the drugs and wraps them up. Everyone was sitting on the couch when "I goes to the bathroom, pissing," Mitchell continues. In his version, Kevin pulls the gun out of his backpack, along with the handcuffs and tape. Robert claims he was shocked. "What the fuck? Don't do this shit," he supposedly exclaims. Then Kevin taped them up. "I know them, like, personally. And their kids." He told Kevin not to do this. "He was like, twisting that shit in her ear. He was like trying to poke it through her head or something. He tried to cut her neck or some shit." Esteban's little boy remembers Mitchell's actions differently. "He covered my mommy's mouth when she was screaming." Mitchell said that Kevin called Linda a "bitch" when she cried out as he tried to cut her neck. Like it was her fault he had the wrong knife for the job.

Out of the blue, on purpose, Wendell asks, "When did you put the gloves on?" but it doesn't work. Mitchell says there were no gloves, which would have verified that there was a plan.

Mitchell continues. Kevin brought Linda into another room and came back with blood all over his shoes and pants. Mitchell says he took a bag from Kevin and was already out of the apartment when he heard the shots. He only found out later, from another guy, that Linda and Esteban were dead, and he was mad because he was the only one the children knew personally. Tío Rob.

Keisha was crying when they got out of the building, Mitchell tells them. After the murder, they sat for a while in a McDonald's. Keisha started crying again on the bus ride back. "What did you say to her?" Wendell asks. Mitchell tells him the only words of comfort he offered to his girlfriend and the mother of his child were "Fuck it."

When they got back to Baltimore, they stayed in the Baltimore Hilton, a nice hotel in downtown Baltimore, now the Radisson Plaza Lord Baltimore Inner Harbor, where doubles go for $279 a night. Mitchell says that when they split the money the first time he didn't get any. He says he was particularly upset that Keisha would be included and not him. "Why does she get money and I don't get no money?" After they redistributed the money, including him this time, Keisha and Denise went out to buy drugs and liquor. They were all talking about what they were going to buy. "Fuck it. I'm just going to buy me a car," Mitchell remembers saying, "'cause the car I had was bullshit." He traded his Maxima for an Acura Legend for four or five thousand dollars, which left him about ten or fifteen thousand. He can't remember exactly.

Wendell asks him if he worried about what would happen with the children. "Yeah. I did worry about shit. I liked them little kids." Wendell keeps going. "The Christmas tree was up when you were there. There were presents there? Decorations?" "Yeah," Mitchell answers without emotion.

Mitchell won't share any of his thoughts or feelings about the children and Christmas. He says he bought "dumb shit." Keisha got her hair and nails done. "I wish that would have never happened to them. Because they did treat me good."

■

In the crime scene photographs there are Christmas decorations and children's drawings on the front of the door of Linda and Esteban's apartment in Parkchester, a fairly nice neighborhood in the Bronx. The Christmas tree is white, and gifts in purple wrapping are piled beneath it. Esteban's blood pours out in a very large puddle on a green, marblelike floor, just a few feet from the tree. He's handcuffed. Linda, feet and hands duct taped, lies on the floor in the children's room, a poster from *101 Dalmatians* on the wall behind her. Her head is beside a child's pillow with a Casper the Friendly Ghost pillowcase.

■

Wendell has mixed feelings about Linda and Esteban. They were drug dealers. As a father himself, though, he is sure that when they realized they were really and truly going to die, their last thoughts were of the children. I will never see my kids again. Or worse, they're going to kill my babies next.

Two months after his interview, Robert Mitchell is transferred to a Maryland State Correctional Facility to begin serving seven years for probation violations. The only way they're getting him back to New York now is if New York initiates an Interstate Agreement on Detainer, which must be filed with the state attorney's office in Maryland. This would allow them to transfer Robert Mitchell back to New York for a trial. ADA Nancy Borko promises to get that paperwork started.

One cold case down, 8,893 to go.

7 Detective Steve Kaplan

The Ronald Stapleton Case

Cops are used to looking at murder this way: someone is killed, they figure out who did it, the DAs prove it to a jury, that person goes to jail. They're accustomed to working with one partner alone, someone they've gotten to know and trust, and together they focus on a murder case like detective-guided missiles. In 1967, the NYPD established a homicide desk in the Central Investigation Bureau to "collect, analyze, and evaluate all information available in connection with homicides arising from, or connected with, organized crime." Three years later Congress enacted RICO, the Racketeer Influenced and Corrupt Organizations Act. Detective Steve Kaplan had cleared a few mob-related cases, but he wasn't exactly an organized crime expert when the Ronald Stapleton case fell into his lap. Deputy Inspector Vito Spano doesn't even like these kinds of cases. Organized-crime cases are complicated.

In a RICO case, they can't just look at a murder as a murder—it's a piece of an entire operation. The suspect is not a murderer, he's a mobster, and murder is just one part of his job description. The focus is never on a single crime. A RICO investigation has many different goals: find the murderer, find the money launderer, gambler, drug seller, etc., find the bosses, shut down the operation, and it's not just you and your partner anymore. More than one law enforcement agency is involved. It's like going after someone in the mail department at Enron, but you can't pick him up and haul him in because he was just following orders and someone else needs him to testify against a guy in the sales department on the third floor, who has some information about someone in accounting, who's been saving a memo the president quietly sent to the guy running one of their largest subsidiaries.

RICO forces the NYPD, this notoriously territorial group, to look at the big picture with other notoriously territorial groups—groups they don't always get along with and can't control—and they're not too happy about it. "When I'm involving outside agencies, and I have to establish a continuing criminal enterprise and the other pieces, and maybe a piece of it is my homicide case, I'm uncomfortable," Spano explains. "There's a lot of cooks, a lot of other players involved in prosecuting a case like that. I don't get the full flavor, we're indicting a person or a group for a certain amount of homicides or whatever, and we're going to get clearances and everything, but it makes me unsettled."

"I realize RICO is a good thing. But I'm more comfortable with doing a criminal investigation, gathering actual witnesses, getting actual forensic evidence, developing witnesses and evidence, presenting it to a district attorney, getting an indictment, and going forward that way, rather than relying on their involvement in criminal enterprises and gaining cooperators."

It requires a new way of looking at crime and its investigation that took prosecutors themselves a long time to understand. "It was ten years before I found a prosecutor who was willing to try a RICO case," G. Robert Blakey, the principal author of the RICO statute, remembers. He explains how the shift in his own perspective came in the late 1960s. He had been an organized-crime prosecutor in the

Department of Justice under Robert Kennedy, and in 1967 was serving as a consultant on the President's Commission for Law Enforcement and Administration of Justice. There he met the three men he credits with expanding his criminal point of view. Ex-NYPD mob expert Ralph Salerno knew mob history better than anyone else. "I had read intelligence stuff from the FBI when I was in Justice in the sixties," Blakey says, "but Salerno made the notion of 'organized crime,' that is, the mob in NYC, vivid to me." Harvard economist Tom Schelling told Blakey "to think about crime in economics terms." Principles that are traditionally applied to upperworld markets can also be used to understand the underworld. Don Cressy, an organizational theorist at the University of California, said, "Stop focusing on the individual and single crimes. Look at the group. The criminal enterprise. Think in terms of patterns of diverse crimes."

"Don't just put crooks in jails," Blakey explains. "Put the mob out of business." Blakey was already thinking about tougher grand jury powers, immunity, witness protection, wiretapping, but now he started to think about long-term imprisonment, enhanced property sanctions, "take the profit out of crime," with civil sanctions like injunctions and treble damages. "Make them pay triple for what they did, and reform it, so they can't come back."

"RICO is a good tool," Spano concedes. "Otherwise we wouldn't be able to prosecute a lot of these cases." But not only do RICO cases force the squad to proceed differently with all these other agencies, it turns out putting mobsters in jail is not even particularly satisfying. "These people were involved in high-risk behavior, they know what they're getting themselves into," Spano explains. "They get themselves into some sort of crisis, they start killing each other, fuck 'em. I'd rather work on senior citizen murders, random murders. Some fucking predator eyeballed and attacked and murdered someone, a person working in a store, a woman who is raped and murdered during a burglary, those I want to work on. I understand we gotta work on these other cases, I know their murder is important, I gotta clear a number and the only way I'm going to clear it is this RICO thing. I've gotta kiss everybody's ass, every federal agency's ass, just to get them to give me the privilege of bringing the case folder over."

Due to their difficulty and sheer volume, a lot of the cases that go cold are organized-crime cases. And because there are a lot of organized-crime cases, clearing them produces the numbers the NYPD craves and rewards, the numbers by which the entire New York Police Department is judged. No one has ever helped their NYPD career by fighting the numbers. "Whether I like them or not, they have to get done. And if we didn't have RICO, we wouldn't have the handle on organized crime that we do," Spano finishes. "There were five thousand family members in seventeen cities in 1963," Blakey, who is now a law professor at the Notre Dame Law School, says, "and only fifteen hundred in two cities in 2004."

But it's not real detective work. "The detective's not doing anything," Spano says. "It's people giving up information to save their own ass. It's a big jerk off."

Working organized-crime cases is as much politics and people skills as investigation and forensics. A detective has to be particularly adept at getting along with everyone and making people open up. Steve Kaplan gets people to talk. He has a large, imposing presence combined with a friendly, accepting personality that just makes people want to tell him everything. People trust him. Especially wiseguys. "Actually, he's kinda the same as a wiseguy," a detective who works with him says. "He's a big guy. They like that. And he's a funny guy. He gets people to relax by joking around. Wiseguys do that." It's become a cliché, but a big guy with a sense of humor is a force in the world of crime and law enforcement, and in this investigation this is critical, because by the time the case is cleared, eleven law enforcement agencies in four states will be involved.

The Ronald Stapleton murder investigation will ultimately lead from one New York murder to another, but it all begins because of one guy who talks, Frank Gioia Jr. Gioia has been indicted and prosecuted in Boston on RICO charges. He pleads guilty and becomes a cooperating witness. A cooperating witness is different than a confidential informant, or CI. A cooperating witness has agreed to testify in court.

In the summer of 1997, Gioia tells FBI agent Steve Byrne he has information about an off-duty cop who was murdered in Brooklyn twenty years earlier while investigating a burglary. Byrne already knows Detective Steve Kaplan. So he gives him a call. Once Kaplan traces the tip to Ronald Stapleton, he needs to ask Gioia some questions. Steve Kaplan meets Frank Gioia for the first time on September 18, 1997, in the basement of the correctional facility where Gioia is being held. The FBI is there and they record the interview on a 302, their equivalent of the NYPD's DD5. They pass stacks and stacks of paperwork before they're buzzed into first one room, where all the U.S. marshals sit, and then a second room, where the actual interview takes place. The room has a small desk and a couple of chairs. "Okay," Kaplan says to Gioia. "Tell me what you know." Gioia is a good guy, a regular guy, Kaplan says. "He's not a sissy. And Gioia loves an audience." He's like a stand-up comedian, others say. At twenty-four, Gioia had become one of the youngest made men, but he never fulfilled his promise. He was never the head of a family.

If Gioia is a performer, Kaplan is his dream audience. Two imposing, charismatic guys who like to have a good time, except one is a wiseguy who wants to put on a show, and the other is a cop who is ready to listen and be entertained. They immediately hit it off. Kaplan asks Gioia about the two guys Gioia had said killed Police Officer Ronald Stapleton: Manny Gonzalez, who had since changed his name to Tony Francesehi (pronounced Fran-CHAY-zee) and Vinnie Cilone. Gioia tells Kaplan that he can't stand Francesehi. Before he went to jail, Gioia had a child with a mob daughter named Kim Smith, and they were engaged to be married. Tony Francesehi was engaged to Kim Smith's cousin (Tony later dumped the cousin and married her mother instead). He and Francesehi would see each other at family gatherings, Gioia explains, but Gioia always did his best to avoid Francesehi. Vinnie Cilone, the other murderer, was another of Kim Smith's cousins.

In 1992, Kim Smith's mobster father was working at the construction site for the new Barney's on Madison Avenue. It was supposed to be a "tit job" (no real work). But her father complained that too much was being demanded of him, and sometime after his body was found at the bottom of an elevator shaft. Kim's brother Frank Smith Jr. was in jail on a narcotics charge at the time, so Kim's family looked to Gioia to take over as the man of the house. As the future son-in-law, Gioia was expected to do what had to be done. Tony Francesehi saw an opportunity. He had always dreamed of getting in the mob, but only Italians can be made men, and even though he was trying to pass himself off as Italian, everyone knew he was Puerto Rican. Tony's only alternative would be to go on record, or be an associate, which means he is in the crew of a made man. He doesn't have the ultimate protection and prestige of a made man, but he does have the protection of the made man he works under, and some of the perks. Gioia was Tony's in. At the wake, Gioia set up his office in the bedroom. This was Tony's chance. He went in to ask Gioia about his plans to deal with the death of Kim Smith's father.

"I know what's going on," Tony said. "Let me help. I want to get even for him. Just take me with you." To prove that he was more than up to the task, Tony told Gioia that he had done "work" in the past and then he told him all about beating, torturing, and then shooting Ronald Stapleton. Gioia listened to Tony and nodded when he was finished. Tony was dismissed. "I didn't offer him to be a part of my hit team. I didn't want him to be involved with this." "Tony didn't get it," Kaplan says, amazed at Francesehi's cluelessness. "He used to brag to Gioia about hanging out with John Jr. [Gotti]. In the crazy world in his head he still thought someday he'd become a made guy."

By 1997, Gioia is estranged from Kim Smith and the rest of her family because he's in jail on a narcotics charge himself and is cooperating with the feds, and the Smiths and their cousins the Cilones know it. That summer, an AUSA (assistant United States attorney, the federal equivalent of an ADA) tells Gioia that Kim Smith has been taping her conversations with him. The family's lawyers are hoping to get some dirt on Gioia so that they can impeach his testimony in court. Up until that point, Gioia has been protecting Kim and her family for the sake of their son. He has given up a lot of people, but no one from his son's immediate family. When he learns of their deception he turns to the AUSA and says, "Okay. Take out your pad." That's when he gives them the tip about Tony Francesehi and Vinnie Cilone.

Kaplan would love to go right out and pick up Francesehi and Cilone, but although Gioia is turning out to be an articulate, forthright, and believable witness, Kaplan knows he can't go to court with one person's testimony alone. He needs someone besides Gioia to talk to him. He has to build a case. "You want someone who will roll," Gioia tells them. "Try Mike and Pixie." Pixie is Vinnie Cilone's wife, Frances, Mike is Mike Cilone, Vinnie's brother. Kaplan goes to his computer and looks up Vinnie Cilone on AutoTrack. He has just missed him. Cilone had died six months before in Florida. The Broward County Sheriff's Departments Cold Case Squad help Kaplan find his widow, Pixie, and Kaplan goes down to Florida with his sergeant and sits on her house. The first time they go to her door she is dressed like a housewife in mourning who was not expecting guests. "Come back tomorrow," she tells them. The next day her hair is teased, and she is wearing a low-cut red dress. She has just lost her husband. And here is Steve Kaplan—this big, friendly former football player who reminds everyone of a wiseguy. Perhaps Pixie was attracted to the charming detective who made her laugh and seemed like he could take care of everything. Kaplan's sergeant, who was also there, says, "Maybe she was just trying to look her best for men she had never met before." Pixie invites Kaplan and his sergeant and the men from the Broward County Cold Case Squad inside.

"Tony said he was Italian but we all knew he was Puerto Rican," she tells them. Pixie remembers the Christmas of 1977, the year her husband became a murderer, because it was unusually warm that winter. She hadn't seen Vinnie for two weeks, but this was normal. He was on methadone at the time, and he frequently disappeared.

Vinnie told Pixie that he and Tony hung out in cop bars and gay bars and that they'd rob the guys from the gay bars. One day, when she was arguing with Vinnie about robbing people, he said, "You know what? Me and Tony killed a guy a couple of years ago. We tortured him, we beat the shit out of him." "It always haunted him," Pixie tells Kaplan and all the men gathered in her living room. Not the torturing and the murdering, it turns out, but rather the possibility of getting caught. "Vinnie used to tell me often, especially toward the end, he knew that this killing was going to catch up to him. Vinnie wanted to die before he got arrested." Vinnie's official cause of death was listed as cirrhosis, but there are persistent rumors that he actually died of AIDS. In 1994 he wrote the following in a small notebook. (The letter is reproduced here with grammatical and spelling errors intact.)

> *Im sitting home alone knowing Im going to die worried about my wife and kids. Knowing me and Tony did something along time ago that might come back and haunt me. And hurt my family. I dont trust Tony because she knows about the murders that me him did. I spoke w/Frankie Joya when Uncle Frankie died about my wife left me. And I was afraid than she would say something because we were fighting. But than again she knew for 20 years and never said a word. I writing this because one day I know this I going to come out in the open. When it does I know they are going to come and see my wife start asking questions I know the mother fucker is going to say it was me because I'm dieing and cannot speak for myself and writing this when and if all come about my wife Pixie Cilone have something to show the count and also my brother knows about the faget guy that me and Tony killed with duck tape. So when this all come out one day my wife and brother will be protect also Tony set it all up. Because he is an out and out fag an scum dag that I'm*

afraid. Try to hurt my wife because she knows. PS. Pixie if you would find this book keep in save place. Love Always Vinnie 11-94.

Kaplan doesn't believe the letter is authentic. "It sounded staged." He has the handwriting analyzed, and is later told only that neither Pixie nor her brother-in-law Mike wrote the letter.

The next day Kaplan and his sergeant sit and watch Pixie's house, hoping to get a look at her brother-in-law Mike Cilone. He never shows up. They go back to the Broward County Cold Case Squad to track down Cilone's photograph from the DMV.

Kaplan then calls the Latent Prints Section. He asks them to check Tony's and Vinnie's prints against the latent prints from the Stapleton case. It might take a while, he's told, because the fingerprints are in the archives, which are in a warehouse out in Brooklyn.

For the Stapleton family, the past is about to return. Kaplan goes out to Brooklyn to look for Stapleton's now grown son, Ronnie. He needs to know that his father's case is being reinvestigated. Meeting the family of the victim is always a fraught encounter and must be carefully orchestrated. You never know what reaction you're going to get or what emotional state the family will be in. Have they moved on? Or will they now wait every day for your call? "When we first started, sometimes we were asked to leave," Lieutenant Panzarella remembers. "We were shocked. 'What do we do now?' So we left. We solved the cases anyway." Panzarella explains: "Not everybody that gets killed is an altar boy." Sometimes an elderly relative is on the other side of the door, someone who hasn't received a visitor in some time and who is in no hurry for the detectives to leave. And so the men kindly accept the offer of a cup of tea and stay for a while, long after useful information, if any, has been provided.

Kaplan first meets Stapleton's son, Ronnie, when Ronnie is still a young kid in his twenties, living with his grandparents in a two-family home and looking for his place in the world.

Kaplan knocks on Ronald Stapleton's widow's door. No answer.

Neighbors who see him tell him to hang on a second, then run around the corner to get Ronnie. Stapleton's wife, who never dated and never remarried, is in the hospital with a brain aneurysm, and Ronnie's autistic sister is living in a small group home. Ronnie has assumed all the family responsibilities. On his way to meet Kaplan for the first time he tries to think of why the police department is looking for his mother. "Mom forgot to pay her bills" is all he can think of, but that doesn't make sense. They don't send detectives to have a word with widows who are behind on their bills. Ronnie never even thinks of his father. He hasn't spoken to anyone from the NYPD about his father's death since he was ten. Ronnie looks nervous when he tells Kaplan that he will be speaking for the family from now on. This can't be easy for Kaplan, either. Ronald was a cop who was murdered and here is his kid. Kaplan likes Ronnie, and he tries to be gentle when he tells him where they are with the investigation. Ronnie isn't expecting this. "It turned it all up again." After so many years, he was resigned. He had tried to move on. And now here is this detective and it's all going to begin again. He isn't sure how to feel about that.

Ronald Stapleton's in-laws, on the other hand, have always hoped that his killers would someday be found. They've never given up. Ronald Stapleton's mother still calls for updates from Canada. (Stapleton was from Canada, and his father was deceased.)

Before visiting Stapleton's father-in-law, Vincent Cestare, Kaplan goes back to Knapp Street and the Trade Winds Bar (also nicknamed the No Name Bar), where Ronald Stapleton was meat hooked and shot. Cold Case Squad detectives love going back to the crime scene, even when there's nothing left. ADAs are baffled by the practice, and there hasn't been a time in anyone's memory where detectives have recovered any valuable evidence, but this is one of the ways they psych themselves up to begin. They are mustering with the past before resuming the battle. The Stapleton crime scene is no less unyielding. The bar where Ronald was attacked is abandoned, and a For Sale sign is nailed up nearby. The parking lot where he was found is fenced in and empty. Kaplan takes it all in, the barrenness, the lack of life or activity, and goes to see Cestare.

A weathered 1977 wanted poster for his son-in-law's murderer still hangs in the front window of Cestare's store, where Kaplan goes to visit him. "He loved Stapleton," Kaplan says. He describes Cestare as the salt of the earth. "A typical old Italian grandfather. 'Come in, have some coffee, how about a piece of cake?' He made us feel very comfortable," Kaplan remembers. "He was grateful we were there." "I haven't heard from the police department in a quite a few years," Cestare tells him. But Cestare is not a waiting-by-the-phone kind of man. He wrote the mayor (Ed Koch) in late 1981. He hired a private investigator. But Cestare couldn't tell Kaplan anything he didn't already know.

Kaplan tracks down Tony Francesehi in Jackson, New Jersey, and he contacts the New Jersey State Police. Together, they sit on the houses of Tony's wife and daughter. Tony doesn't appear. Over the next month, as he tries to build his case, Kaplan runs into one dead lead after another. He can't find Stapleton's gun, and latent print checks come back negative. By the end of the month, however, Kaplan convinces Vinnie Cilone's widow, Pixie, to become an official CI. She wants to be called the Meat Queen (she works in the meat department in a grocery store). The murderer's widow is enjoying herself apparently, but Kaplan feels pity for her. "She's a lost soul," he says. Cases like these ride on the detective's ability to get people to cooperate, and criminals and their associates no doubt talk to Kaplan in part because of his seeming inability to hate or pass judgment on them.

Over the next couple of days they sit on a few Brooklyn addresses they get for Tony Francesehi from AutoTrack. Nothing. Much of a Cold Case detective's time is spent sitting around, and this makes Kaplan miserable. He's acutely aware of his size and is concerned about the near total lack of movement. "I'm basically a spectator," he complains. "Before I came to Cold Case I was in shape. I used to lift weights. I used to run. But we're just a bunch of old guys now," he says. Kaplan recently developed a painful skin condition. The doctor told him it was from stress.

The following week Kaplan talks to Stapleton's brother-in-law, who had been a police officer in the 71 at the time of the murder. Even though he was a cop, Stapleton's brother-in-law was given the same story as everyone else. Stapleton was killed while trying to stop a burglary. He didn't have any inside information.

There is a long-standing history of animosity between the NYPD and the FBI. Cops tend to think the FBI guys are arrogant. "Prissy college guys." FBI agents find cops uneducated and uncouth. But Kaplan and Special Agent Byrne get along. "He's a regular guy," Kaplan says about Byrne. "He should have been a cop." Of Kaplan, Byrne says, "He's kind of a bull in a china shop, but he tracked down a lot of people, and these were twenty-year-old cases and a lot of people were dead. He doesn't stop until the case is resolved."

Kaplan and Byrne decide it's time to contact the Brooklyn DA. A couple of days later, they bring the case to Kenneth Taub, deputy district attorney and chief of the Homicide Bureau in the office of the Brooklyn District Attorney. Taub isn't interested. "You've got nothing here." Go away. "Detectives have trouble separating what they think to be true and what is admissible in court," Taub says. "They don't understand why prosecutions aren't going ahead." Paul DeMartini, the former bureau chief of the Trial Division in the Rackets Bureau in the Brooklyn DA's office, agrees. "The detectives don't understand reasonable doubt." Vito Spano immediately snaps back, "Beyond a reasonable doubt does not mean beyond *any* doubt."

Kaplan and Byrne take their case to Jay Shapiro, the head of the Rackets Division, and Chris Blank, the executive district attorney. They jump on it. Shapiro thinks it's a good murder case. "I'll never forget the look on their faces when I said I'd take the case," Shapiro remembers. "They were thrilled." Shapiro adds, "When you have senior, seasoned detectives who want to do an investigation, you don't want to discourage them." Anticipating trouble between Homicide and Rackets, Shapiro goes to Charles Hynes, the Brooklyn DA, and they talk about the potential problems. Hynes lets him have it. Shapiro assigns the case to an ADA.

Three days later Kaplan and his sergeant go back down to Florida to talk to Mike Cilone. Mike Cilone lives in a modest ranch house. He answers the door in his T-shirt and shorts, smoking a cigarette. He is very nervous. Kaplan asks if they can come in and Mike says no, but he steps outside and talks to them. "He was a slimeball," Kaplan says. But as Kaplan gets to know him his opinion changes. "It's like baseball, when you're on the opposing team. You hate the guys on the other team. Until you get traded. Then they're okay guys." Mike Cilone must have sensed Kaplan's change of heart. He tells Kaplan he was introduced to Tony Francesehi when Tony was dating Mike's cousin. He didn't like Tony. Not many people did, it would turn out.

Cilone doesn't offer much else that first meeting. He's done time for his crimes, he says, and he's trying to stay out of trouble now, and that's pretty much it. After Mike they meet with a friend of the Cilones'. "We try to talk to everybody in the beginning," Kaplan explains. "You never know who is going to give you a key piece of information." But Kaplan hasn't given up on Mike. He needs him to testify, and this is just his first pass.

Kaplan goes back to talk to the Meat Queen. She's had time to think since they last met, she tells him. Now she remembers that Tony wore a gun on his ankle at Vinnie's funeral. What kind of gun? She doesn't know. Kaplan pulls out his 9mm. "No." It wasn't like that. He had an "old-fashioned gun like the cops used to have on TV." A week later she calls to tell him to be very careful when he talks to Tony. She's seen him carrying a gun many times. Pixie is looking out for Kaplan.

There's something ultimately tragic about the relationship between a CI and a detective. Someone is opening up and making themselves vulnerable to someone else, but the growing trust will inevitably be betrayed. Because how do you get an informant to open up? "You lie to them," Kaplan says. Kaplan knows that Pixie's husband was terrified of being arrested, so he comes up with the perfect lie to gain her trust. He tells her that he found out that Vinnie was a murderer while Vinnie was still dying. "Then I said I waited for him to die before going forward to spare him going through arrest, a trial, and jail." Pixie has likely never experienced such tender concern from a member of law enforcement. Later, when she learns the truth, Pixie will grow to hate Detective Steve Kaplan.

On November 26, Kaplan and Special Agent Steve Byrne and others meet with Mark Feldman, the section chief of Organized Crime in the United States Attorney's Office, Eastern District, to talk about the Stapleton case.

Gioia is the crux of the case, but U.S. attorneys don't give over witnesses easily. Jay Shapiro, the head of the Rackets Division of the Brooklyn DA at the time, sums up the attitude: "Our witness, our guy." To him, it's only fair. They found and cultivated the witness. But on this case Feldman is being unusually accommodating, for two reasons. When Stapleton was killed, Feldman had just started out in the Brooklyn DA's office. He's never forgotten him, and he wants to see this case get done. The whole thing was a mystery, where and how it happened—he is sure there is a link to organized crime, but he can't prove it. Also, Feldman likes cops. Not all attorneys do. An ADA once did a parody of Kaplan. "Must solve case," he said in a low, gravelly voice, imitating a caveman and summing up the attitude some attorneys have toward a lot of cops: they're Neanderthals. But Mark Feldman not only likes Kaplan, he has Kaplan's respect. "Feldman deserves a lot of credit for dismantling organized crime in the Eastern District," Kaplan says. (The Eastern District had the heaviest mob concentration in New York.) Giuliani is the name everyone knows, but according to Kaplan, Feldman has been a key player too. Feldman wanted to see Kaplan solve this case.

Feldman tells Kaplan and the other men assembled in his office that he will assign an AUSA to act as a liaison, and call Ken Taub at the Brooklyn DA's office to let him know they are to be involved. Again, it's a matter of politics. Rackets has the case, but Taub is still chief of Homicide. Also, even though Feldman is helping out, if the case goes to court it will be tried in the state. Even though Feldman and others have always believed there was an organized-crime connection, in reality the connection is to an organized-crime wannabe, Tony Francesehi. Tony was never and could never become a made man. Therefore the Stapleton murder is technically not a mob hit. There is no RICO case here. Yet.

Kaplan and others continue to do everything they can to strengthen their case. Kaplan gets Pixie Cilone, the Meat Queen, to agree to testify in court. He now has two witnesses, Frank Gioia and Pixie Cilone, and while that gives him the corroborating testimony he needs, Pixie isn't a strong witness. He still needs Mike Cilone.

A month later, in January 1998, Pixie calls Kaplan in a complete panic. A friend of the Cilone family has been calling around, telling everyone in the family that Pixie is starting trouble. "Protect me," she pleads to Kaplan. "Do something, anything." She calls Ken Taub. Taub calls Kaplan. Kaplan asks him what he is going to do about it. "What am I going to do about it?" Taub answers. "What are you going to do about it?" Kaplan is on his own.

Kaplan goes to Brooklyn and brings Pixie's in-laws back to the Cold Case Squad headquarters. They tell him that Tony gave them the story about being half Italian, too, but they didn't believe him any more than anyone else had. After Tony married the cousin's mother instead of the cousin, they said, he was never welcomed in any of the family's homes again. By the end of the interview, the in-laws agree to have their phones tapped.

On January 12, Tony Francesehi tells Pixie's father-in-law that he is going to kill Pixie.

Two days later Mike Cilone calls Kaplan. He knows it's just a matter of time before Tony turns his attention to him. Mike tells Kaplan he has information about the Stapleton homicide and other crimes and he is ready to talk. "Come to New York if you want to talk," Kaplan responds. "If I had immediately run down to Florida, Mike would have thought he was the boss." Kaplan doesn't want him thinking he's in charge. It wasn't too much of a gamble, Kaplan explains. "He was in hot water. He had no choice. He had to come up and talk to us." Mike says he'll come to New York as soon as possible.

On January 18, they pick up Pixie Cilone at the airport and take her to her in-laws' house. Mike Cilone is already there. Kaplan has his three witnesses. He tells Mike that he'll have to talk to the FBI, and that "under no circumstances were we going to offer him any type of immunity for past criminal activities." Kaplan doesn't have the authority to make deals, and he doesn't try to pretend that he does. Unlike Pixie, "these guys know when you're lying to them," Kaplan explains. "That's why wiseguys respect him," a detective agrees. "Kaplan doesn't bullshit them."

Tony Francesehi's lawyer calls the Cold Case Squad headquarters the following week to see if they're investigating Tony in relation to an old homicide. Lieutenant Bob McHugh picks up the phone. "What homicide?" he asks. "Jan Schenley." Jan Schenley? Who is Jan Schenley? The lawyer says they'd like to come in and "take care of it." This is the first they hear of any connection between the Ronald Stapleton case and the murder of a man named Jan Schenley. What does Tony Francesehi have to do with it? McHugh walks over to Kaplan's desk and tells him about the call. Kaplan is a 1st-grade detective with fifteen years under his belt. One murder leading to another is nothing new. These guys frequently know each other, or know who's been whacking whom. Kaplan appears to take the news casually. "But he was interested," McHugh remembers. Kaplan immediately starts looking for the Schenley case files.

■

Not all detectives are aware that the NYPD's Central Records Division has a warehouse in Brooklyn. The case records for unsolved homicides are supposed to stay in the precinct where the homicides occurred, but anything older than the 1980s is often missing. They were lost in a move, the people at the precinct usually explain, or destroyed in a flooded basement. But 187 boxes of homicide records both solved and unsolved, and spanning the years 1921 to 1973, sit largely forgotten in an aisle at the very back of the Central Records warehouse. Some boxes have a few cases, some have thirty or more. They may be falling apart from age, but there are probably four thousand to seven thousand case files there. The box marked "1921" has several cases from the early twenties, including the following four cold cases: Cecil E. Landon, a nineteen-year-old from Portland, Oregon, who was murdered just after returning from military service in France; twelve-year-old Virginia Walker, who was murdered on her way to buy cream; seventeen-year-old Ream Constance Hoxsie, who was hit in the head with a hammer eight times, then posed on a bed; and the severed head of an unknown Italian man that was found in Bronx Zoological Park by two boys looking for freshwater crabs. Several days later, two women searching the same area for mushrooms found the torso.

Central Records stores other records, including crime scene photographs going back to 1948. (In the basement of 1PP, glass-plate negatives from the early 1900s sit in piles in a small caged room, cracking anytime someone steps too hard.) Also at the Central Records warehouse—a few random stacks of old logbooks and decades' worth of fingerprint cards.

Few detectives know about these records because few go back to find cases this old. But Kaplan doesn't have a date or a place yet. So he starts with the Homicide Analysis Unit at 1PP and goes through the homicide logbooks, where in the eighties every murder in New York was entered in by hand. He finds Jan Schenley. Soon after, he finds the case records. Jan Schenley was the gay pharmacist who was murdered in 1982 during a burglary in his home. An unknown man had sex with Jan, then wrapped his face in duct tape, and while Jan suffocated and died, this man took everything of value and packed it up in Jan's own car and drove away. How was Tony Francesehi involved?

On February 12, 1998, Mike Cilone proffers. He has no choice. Gioia has given him up, and Francesehi is calling around, trying to find out who has spoken to whom. Mike's best option is to roll and pray that the feds will protect him. Mike confirms everything Frank Gioia Jr. had said. Mike's brother Vinnie had told him that he and Tony Francesehi had killed Ronald Stapleton. Kaplan now officially has a third person to testify in court, for Stapleton and, unbelievably, for Schenley. Vinnie had talked to Mike about that one, too. Francesehi had also killed the pharmacist.

Mike doesn't stop there. He tells them about the 1987 murder of mob guys Carmine Variale and Frank Santora by Kim Smith's brother Frank. Mike had driven the get-away car. Gioia, the federal witness, is able to corroborate this story.

This changes everything. The nature of the investigation has just expanded. Stapleton and Schenley were killed by someone who only aspired to be in the mob. But the murders of Variale and Santora were unequivocally organized-crime hits. It's a whole new ballgame. Not only is he up to four murder victims (Stapleton, Schenley, Variale, and Santora) and three murderers plus an accomplice (Tony Francesehi, Vinnie Cilone, Frank Smith, and Mike Cilone), but Kaplan now has to confront the time and complications that come with every organized-crime case, the kind of case that Deputy Inspector Vito Spano would sometimes understandably prefer to avoid.

■

In early March 1998, Kaplan writes "Things to Do" at the top of a piece of paper and divides it into three sections representing the three cases he is now juggling: Stapleton, Schenley, and the Variale-Santora double homicide. In each section he lists the people he needs to find and talk to.

At the top of the Stapleton section he writes, "Locate and re-interview Frank Teta, the ambulance driver from Coney Island Hospital. He spoke with Stapleton at the scene." Kaplan tracks Teta, but unfortunately, he has passed. Someone else he hopes to find, one of the owners of the Trade Winds Bar, has also been dead for eight months. The Stapleton case is now twenty-one years old and counting. Helen, the wife and co-owner of the Trade Winds who first found the beaten and bleeding Stapleton in the parking lot, is still alive. Helen looks at a picture of Tony and says that a man that young would never have been allowed into her bar. But she also said that Stapleton was not in her bar the evening that he was shot, and Kaplan later learns that before he died, Stapleton admitted that he was. She's either mistaken or she's lying.

Next on Kaplan's list of people to speak to is Dennis Graf, Stapleton's old partner from the 77 Precinct. Graf says Stapleton was a tough guy and would never have been beaten up the way he was by a single guy. "Couldn't happen."

After Graf, Kaplan talks to Ron Cadieux, the original lead detective on the Ronald Stapleton case. Cadieux is a private investigator now, with an office near the Brooklyn Courts. Like Feldman, Cadieux is sure there was an organized-crime connection to the Stapleton case, and for the rest of his NYPD career, every time he interviewed an organized-crime guy he would ask them about Stapleton. No one was ever able to tell him anything. Cadieux had interviewed Stapleton in the hospital, but it was mostly Stapleton's attorney, Robert Race, talking for Stapleton, who had tubes down his throat and was now nearing death, and only able to nod or write yes or no. Cadieux has no new information to add.

Kaplan looks everywhere he can for leads; he tries to find old witnesses, old hospital records, ME's records, Stapleton's personnel files. He tries to recover the round that was pulled from Stapleton's body. He regularly meets with the ADA who gets him the subpoenas he needs. He speaks to the original cops on the scene who are now in their sixties. No help. But Kaplan keeps going.

In August, Kaplan meets with Paul DeMartini, the head of the Trial Division in the Rackets Bureau in the Brooklyn DA, who has just been assigned the case after the original ADA had to leave the office for health reasons. DeMartini is the opposite of Kaplan. Where Kaplan is a regular, unsophisticated, joking-around guy, DeMartini is businesslike, educated, and serious.

On September 4, 1998, Kaplan and DeMartini go out to the

Ballistics Unit in Queens to look for the round recovered from Stapleton's body. They find it in an envelope in a file cabinet. They also find more rounds from an earlier incident involving Stapleton's gun. A few months before he died, Stapleton had been mugged outside Nathan's in Coney Island. His gun was taken then, too, but they got it back. When guns are returned they automatically go to Ballistics to see if they're still operable. Ballistics had fired a few shells from Stapleton's gun, and those rounds were saved. Kaplan has the shells compared, and he's able to prove that the bullets fired into Stapleton on December 18 did indeed come from his own gun. No one before Kaplan had bothered to find the two bullets and check.

Next, Kaplan gets a subpoena and goes through Stapleton's personnel files. "He was a cop's cop. He was aggressive" is all Kaplan will say about what he found. Stapleton's old partner, Dennis Graf, offers a little more. "Whatever he did," Graf says, "it was always to the max. He was out there. Alive and vibrant. He was always the first on the scene." On more than one occasion they beat the FDNY to a fire. Graf remembers one particular fire in Brooklyn. He and Stapleton climbed the fire escape and a woman handed them an infant and a two-year-old. By that time, the fire had grown beneath them, and they had to take the children to the roof and hope the FDNY got a ladder to them in time. (They did.)

Another night, Stapleton and Graf got a call about a disturbance. Stapleton was a night person, and they frequently worked the midnight to 8:00 a.m. shift. As they pulled up, Stapleton checked out a guy who was leaving the building. There was something off about him, Stapleton thought. "Where are you coming from?" he asked. "The third floor." It was a two-story building. Seconds later, Stapleton was rolling in the snow with a guy who, it turned out, had just burglarized, beaten, and raped an eighty-year-old woman inside.

Graf told one last story about one of their exploits. In the summer of 1977, during the famous New York blackout, and months before he himself was mortally shot, Ronald Stapleton saved the life of a shooting victim whom he and Graf came across while patrolling during the blackout. Stapleton threw him in the backseat and held his chest while Graf drove a hundred miles an hour to the hospital. The man lived. Six months later Stapleton was dead. After Stapleton died, Dennis Graf left the police department and joined the FDNY. Says Graf, "When you lose someone like that you lose a little bit of the reason why you were there in the first place. I didn't want to be a cop anymore."

▪

One piece from the original investigation doesn't fit. As many times as they comb the DD5s, they cannot make sense of the testimony of Robert Race, Stapleton's attorney. According to Race, Ronald Stapleton said he was attacked by two men when he stopped to investigate a possible burglary, and that one of his attackers was black. Stapleton never saw the other guy. Kaplan is building a case against Tony Francesehi. Tony Francesehi is not black.

Kaplan's commanding officer at this time wants their witness Mike Cilone to say that Tony could be mistaken for a black man. It's not completely off the wall. Francesehi is Puerto Rican and was wearing his hair in an Afro-like style in 1977. It wasn't inconceivable that someone who had just been shot and had his eye gouged out, was a little confused. Kaplan disagrees. "You don't make things fit." Kaplan keeps writing DD5s without this explanation, and his commanding officer keeps ripping them up.

DeMartini agrees with Kaplan. "Oh, it's okay," another ADA says. "We can argue around that." "How are we going to argue around the fact that the only eyewitness, the deceased, allegedly has told someone immediately after the event that it was a black man?" DeMartini responds. "It's reasonable doubt as big as a Mack truck."

Everyone knows there is something off about Stapleton's attorney's story. Robert Race wasn't telling them something.

Kaplan calls Race and meets him outside court in Manhattan. He drives him out to court in Brooklyn, and by the time they arrive Kaplan has worked his magic: Robert Race finally tells the truth.

Over the next couple of weeks, from Race and later others, Kaplan will piece together what happened. Everyone knows the first part of the story, and the facts are undisputed: Stapleton's father-in-law called Race the night Stapleton was shot, and Race was one of the first to get to Coney Island Hospital.

The emergency room was in chaos. Stapleton had been shot twice in the abdomen and was suffering from wounds to his pancreas, liver, stomach, large and small intestines, right kidney, and elsewhere, and what was left of his right eye was about to be removed by the surgeons. He was bleeding through all the bandages the ambulance attendants had managed to wrap around him, and he was in agony. Lying on the gurney and looking up at everyone with one eye, Stapleton told Race and anyone who came near him, "I'm going to die, I'm going to die." "I'd never seen him scared before," his partner later said. "No you're not. You're going to make it," the medical staff and everyone else assured Stapleton.

Race immediately took charge. "He's my client now, and no one is to question him unless I'm there." Stapleton and Race knew each other from the NYPD hockey team, where Stapleton was a player and, for a while, Race was their manager. Stapleton trusted Race. The place was swarming with the top brass, but Race wouldn't let them near Stapleton. He wanted to hear Stapleton's story first. The doctors were about to take Stapleton into surgery, but Race and Stapleton asked for one minute to talk. The doctors stepped away and stood a few feet apart, anxiously waiting to begin. Before he was taken into surgery, Stapleton told Race what happened.

"I went bouncing from bar to bar," Stapleton said. He was ready to call it a night when he turned into Knapp Street. At this point he was ten minutes from home. He decided to go into the Trade Winds bar for one more drink, and he got into trouble almost immediately. "I got into an argument with some guy at the bar," Stapleton later admitted. Stapleton couldn't afford to get into any kind of trouble there. It was a mob-related bar and had been declared off-limits to all NYPD personnel. If the department ever found out Stapleton had been drinking there, he would have been brought up on charges of "conduct unbecoming an officer." So Police Officer Stapleton walked out of one fight and into the last fight of his life. He was attacked before he reached his car. One guy came up from behind him and grabbed him in a bear hug. Stapleton never got a good look at that guy, but he told Race, "It was two white guys. One guy was built like a gorilla." No one was black. The one like a gorilla whaled on Stapleton with all he had. The other guy slammed a meat hook into Stapleton's eye and pulled. Stapleton's gun fell. While Stapleton struggled against the first guy and the meat hook, the second guy bent down and retrieved the fallen gun, aimed, and fired twice. Stapleton wasn't going to die because he tried to stop a burglary, as everyone had been told. He wasn't shot in the line of duty. It was a stickup. Tony and Vinnie probably didn't know the drunk they were rolling was a cop until it was too late.

The doctors were waiting. Stapleton and Race had only seconds before they're going to be told that's it, we have to get this guy into surgery. Stapleton was having trouble talking now. "Just take care of my wife and kids," he pleads. "Oh, shut up, will you," Race said. "You're going to be fine." "I thought he was going to die that night," Race admitted later. They decided to come up with a cover story that would help Stapleton's family get a good pension. Stapleton knew he was dying. He also trusted that Race would know what to do.

Race tells Kaplan that he and Stapleton wanted to make sure the family received line-of-duty death benefits. If it's a line-of-duty death, the family continues to receive an officer's full salary, tax free. Otherwise, in Stapleton's case, his family would receive a single payment of one year's salary. They had to make it look like he died in the line of duty. The doctors wheeled Stapleton away and Race turned to face the crowd in the emergency room. Every man in the room was quiet now. They were afraid. They were afraid for their friend, their brother, and because this was the life they had chosen, and in addition to moments of glory and brotherhood there was this other side that you didn't think about it, because what good would it do? You might retire into a quiet security job. Or you might face meat hooks, pain, wounds everywhere that will not stop bleeding, and a terrible choking panic that's so bad you can't cry, you can't even scream, all you can do is throw up. He looked so scared. They were all standing right there but no one could reach out and save him. They didn't know what to say to each other. Race scanned the room and found Stapleton's father-in-law and brother-in-law. The three men knew what to do.

Three days after they came up with their story, Ronald Stapleton lost consciousness, and after that he only came to for brief periods of time. Two weeks later he was dead.

■

"The initial statement wasn't correct." Race begins his account once again, only this time to DeMartini. "That's the statement that went on the pension papers." Race is confident. "The false filing of those papers with the city, that statute of limitations has run out. Any larceny connected with collecting a bigger pension, that has run out," he repeats.

DeMartini doesn't say anything. He needs Race to testify to the grand jury in order to get an indictment for Tony Francesehi. A case can be brought before a grand jury before or after an arrest. Since they're dealing with old cases, there's usually no need for the Cold Case Squad to run out and arrest someone without an indictment, so they'll almost always go to the grand jury prior to an arrest. Race doesn't believe there will be any repercussions from his original lie, so he agrees to appear before the grand jury. With their biggest obstacle eliminated, the case against Tony Francesehi is getting stronger.

The police department is contacted about the Stapleton family's pension. A long time has passed, the wife had an aneurysm and is confined to a wheelchair, their autistic daughter is now in a home—the police department isn't going to take the pension away now.

Over the next month Kaplan and others call and meet with Mike Cilone to discuss Mike's role in the case. Mike tells them that his brother Vinnie used to carry a meat hook with him when he and Tony did "scores." Pixie remembers the meat hook, too. "He carried it for years," she tells them. Stapleton had told Race he knew one of the guys had gotten him with a meat hook. It was another bit of information that would help tie the crime to Tony Francesehi and Vinnie Cilone.

Kaplan, Cilone, the FBI, and all the ADAs and AUSAs meet with Gioia in November. Once again, everyone discusses what they have found out and run it by their key witness, Frank Gioia Jr. They are ready to move.

Gioia is brought before the grand jury on November 24, 1998. Mike Cilone testifies on December 4, and Robert Race takes his turn on December 11. DeMartini meets Race at lunchtime in front of the courthouse and the Tombs (named for the holding cells there) to go over his testimony. Race is hesitant. He is starting to think of the implications. The two of them go over which judges got the homicide cases, and Race decides he is safe with the five or six judges that might try the case. "They won't go after me." And DeMartini is thinking, "The judges aren't your problem. The problem is looking at you." It's like Race has forgotten who he's been talking to. The DA's office has an ethical obligation, and as soon as they get their indictment, they are going to write in about him. "He just assumed that we wanted this conviction so we weren't going to report him." (Later, the attorney for the Brooklyn DA will write the Department Disciplinary Committee about Race. The committee takes into account Race's inexperience at the time, his mental state, the fact that he was a former police officer, his father and brother were police officers, and now his police officer friend was dying horribly. He had no selfish motive. Still, Race will be suspended for three months.)

■

The composition of the grand jury is half black and they have some pointed questions for Bob Race. "They just didn't like him,"says DeMartini. To them, his behavior recalls the Charles Stuart case from Boston ten years before. Stuart shot his pregnant wife, then called the police claiming she was shot by a black man who had kidnapped and robbed them first. No one was happy about how the police had seemingly accepted Stuart's story without question, and the jury doesn't like how Robert Race had exploited the same prejudices.

Race tells the grand jury what Stapleton really said. While he was lying on the gurney, before being brought into the operating room, Stapleton had told Race that he only saw one guy. "A big guy with an olive complexion and frizzy Afro-type hair." A description that exactly fit Tony Francesehi. "Stapleton wasn't investigating a burglary, he was going into the bar." Race had met with Stapleton's wife and other family members over the next couple of days to discuss how the circumstances of the assault and his presence at an off-limits bar might affect his pension. The practical matter of raising a young family overshadowed any need for vengeance. They decided to say that the killers were black in order to make them appear more out of place in the neighborhood. That would have given Stapleton more of a reason to stop and get out of his car to check. In half an hour, the grand jury indicts Tony Francesehi. A warrant is issued for his arrest on December 11, 1998.

Their corroborating witness, Michael Cilone, is arrested the next day for the murders of Carmine Variale and Frank Santora, which had come up in his proffer session. This is all part of the cooperation agreement worked out during his proffer. Kaplan will get back to Mike Cilone and the murders of Variale and Santora, but for now, he is focused on the arrest of Tony Francesehi.

Now that they have an indictment the case gets hot. Kaplan, with help from countless others, has pulled it off. The brass over at 1PP are making plans to hold a press conference once an arrest has been made, and people in the Brooklyn DA are starting to talk. Charles (Joe) Hynes, the DA, asks, "Why does Rackets have this case?" and gives it to Ken Taub, the chief of the Homicide Bureau, who had wanted nothing to do with it initially. It's office politics, as usual. That's where the case should have been in the first place, even though there were some peripheral organized-crime issues. After all the work Paul DeMartini has done, they can't just pull him off, so he is made co-counsel, but Taub will be the lead attorney. "DeMartini doesn't have a big ego," his old boss Jay Shapiro said. "He was okay with it." Nonetheless, it must have been somewhat galling that Taub was handed the case after he had turned it down. But Taub has an impressive record of winning cases and everyone wanted to win.

Kaplan puts together a Tac Plan (tactical plan) for the arrest of Tony Francesehi. This includes a staging area for everyone involved, and it lists the names, pagers, and cell phones of all the teams from the New Jersey State Police, the Cold Case Squad, and the FBI, seventeen people in all. It also has a description and photographs of Tony Francesehi, his address, a list of cars in his name, and the addresses for the Cold Case Squad, the New Jersey State Police, and the nearest hospital.

On December 15, Kaplan goes to MapQuest and prints out all the directions they need.

The next day, at four in the morning, Kaplan, the FBI, and the New Jersey State Police drive to Tony's house. Other members of the New Jersey State Police are already there with Wendell Stradford and Paddy Lanigan, another Cold Case detective. They sit and wait. Former football player Steve Kaplan isn't nervous. "He knows how to take the field," Wendell Stradford describes. Everyone there is a professional, and everyone is perfectly calm while they wait. Let's get this done, is the attitude. The lights start going on in the house. People are probably taking showers, they think. Everyone watches quietly as Tony gets into his car and starts to drive away. Before Tony gets too far, they simply stop him, put him under arrest, and considerately return his SUV to his wife—a smooth and efficient hitch-free arrest operation. Sometimes arrests are made without a hint of drama.

▪

As a rule, cops aren't interested in contemplating how murderers feel or even why they did what they did. In fact, some cops get mad when you ask. They think you're criticizing them, and they immediately start defending themselves. They're just doing their job, they say, and who gives a shit how the murderer is feeling, they ask with all the disgust they can muster. Kaplan is a little different. For all his bulk—and it's true, you definitely wouldn't want to mess with him—Kaplan is gentle with murderers. "They made a mistake," he usually says. In the course of his investigation, Kaplan learns that Tony's mother has died and that Tony doesn't know. As he leads him away, Kaplan quietly tells Tony that his mother had passed on. "Thank you very much," Tony responds respectfully.

Tony is taken to the New Jersey State Police Headquarters, where he will have to be processed, since the arrest took place in their state. "I asked him about his health due to his associate being a potential AIDS victim (Vincent Cilone)," a New Jersey officer wrote in his arrest report. "He wondered why I asked and I explained he was thought to have other homosexual partners. This was the only time he became angry and enraged, denying the allegations of homosexuality until photographs linking him with a homicide victim in New York were produced." Nude pictures of Tony and other men were found among the possessions of Jan Schenley, the pharmacist who was murdered in 1982. "He explained that the activity and people in the photos occurred 'back then. That's not me, that's when I was young.'"

After he's processed, Tony is brought before a judge, where he waives his extradition rights and is turned over to Detective Steve Kaplan. Kaplan takes him to the Brooklyn House of Detention at the corner of Flatbush and Atlantic. Some jails are worse than others. "This was a bad jail," Kaplan admits. It's one of the city's holding facilities, where people wait before they are sent to Rikers or elsewhere. It's overcrowded and hostile, a place where petty thieves are put in with murderers like Tony. "Tony may be a big guy and a murderer, but he's got no heart," Kaplan explains. "He's a murderer, but he's a punk murderer. When guys step up to him he backs right down." He will not have an easy time of it.

After Kaplan vouchers Tony's possessions and deposits them

with the property clerk, Kaplan completes the arrest package, which includes a total of seven forms and reports. When Kaplan writes up what they call a "blue 5," so named for the color of the last part of the three-part DD5 form, that means the case has been cleared. "We're going to get a blue on this," detectives say when they know they've turned the corner. Twenty-two years later, they finally got a blue on Stapleton.

▪

Kaplan is now able to turn his attention to the second item on his to-do list and another of Tony Francesehi's murder victims: Jan Schenley. He begins by talking to the original lead detective, Roy Creighton, and some of Schenley's friends. People cry when Kaplan calls them. It's been decades and they still miss Jan. "They loved the guy. You should have heard them." Schenley wasn't completely out of the closet when he died, and a lot of people didn't know that he was gay, not that any of them would have cared. Like Steve Kaplan, Jan Schenley's popularity transcended barriers of culture and class, and in this case, sexual orientation. Friends from his Brooklyn neighborhood who lacked Schenley's sophistication talked about how he taught them about art and music and introduced them to a world they never would have known existed. Kaplan's not someone who spends his spare time checking out the recent acquisitions at the Metropolitan Museum of Art, and he admits that he started to like the man who had been gone for so many years now. Perhaps Kaplan wouldn't have minded someone introducing him to art and culture. "I probably would have been friends with Schenley," Kaplan says. "He was from a different world, all that opera and stuff. What's the word for when they dance around? Ballet. But the way people talked about him when I called, everyone crying. It's not my world, but I think we could have been friends."

Jan Schenley surrounded himself with art and antiques that in the end were taken out of his house one by one and piled in his car while he slowly suffocated from the duct tape that completely covered his face. Jan may have even shown these objects to his murderer, once, and had him hold them and turn them over in his hands while Jan explained their history and what made them worth cherishing. Jan could not have known that there was no chance that the craftsmanship of an exquisitely made clock could ever mean anything to the kind of man who could listen to someone struggle for air until he died, however long that took, and not think it was worth stopping for a second while he was robbing him to loosen the tape and save his life.

Normally Kaplan calls a victim's family member to let them know he has just picked up a case. When Kaplan calls Jan Schenley's sister Laureen, her brother's murderer, Tony Francesehi, is already in custody. It's rough. She hasn't heard from the police for fifteen years. "From 1983 to Kaplan's call, nothing," Laureen remembers. She's mad. She has never forgiven the police department for not moving heaven and earth to catch her brother's killer, and her first reaction is rage. But, Kaplan says, "Laureen is tough," speaking with frank admiration. "You can't bullshit her," he adds. These are very important qualities to a cop, and Kaplan, whose feelings may have been helped along by the fact that he had come to like her long-dead brother, decides he likes his sister, too. Years later, Kaplan and Laureen still have lunch together from time to time.

Laureen Schenley is living fifteen, twenty minutes away from Tony Francesehi, it turns out. She has met him before, astoundingly. "I knew him as Manny," Laureen explains, before he changed his name from Manny Gonzalez. Her brother Jan introduced them at a party in the late seventies. "Kaplan always talked about Tony, Tony, Tony. One day he said Manny, and I said, 'That one I know!' No one liked Manny," she continues. "He was arrogant, full of himself. He was just the kind of guy you instantly didn't like." When Laureen is told that Manny killed her brother she says, "I knew it was him."

Everyone knew it was him. In the original DD5s everyone said it was Manny Gonzalez. "His name was all over that case," Kaplan remembers. In addition to finding the nude pictures of Tony in

Schenley's possession, the precinct detectives were told by at least four people that Jan and Manny, who had a violent, ugly personality, were lovers. All of Jan's closest friends said Manny did it. When the detectives questioned Tony on November 21, 1982, and he said he thought of Schenley as a brother or father figure, they knew by then that he was lying. And if that wasn't enough to throw suspicion on him, the day after Jan was murdered, detectives learned that Tony Francesehi had already been arrested once for burglarizing Schenley's apartment. Semen was recovered from the scene, but there is no indication that any tests were ever performed. And while the kinds of tests they could have conducted in 1982 were not nearly as exacting as DNA testing is now, there were tests available at the time that could have been used to either eliminate suspects or keep them in the running. What the hell happened?

Jan Schenley was murdered in 1982. Thirteen years had passed since the famous Stonewall Riots, when the police raided a gay bar in the West Village called the Stonewall Inn, and for the first time, the patrons fought back. But this is the NYPD—traditions die a prolonged and agonizing death. Perhaps in 1982 gay killings were not investigated as aggressively. Things were very different back then. Detectives wrote things on DD5s they'd be disciplined for now. At the time of the murder, Laureen was told, "This is the lifestyle that your brother led and you have to expect this sort of thing." Now the detectives say they didn't mean the gay lifestyle, they meant sleeping around with strangers. One of their theories was that Jan Schenley, who they believe went cruising once a week, had picked up the wrong guy.

It wasn't just the police who passed these kinds of judgments; 1982 was the year the CDC gave the name AIDS to what until then had been called the "gay cancer," and there were still nurses at St. Vincent's Hospital who refused to touch people with AIDS. People in New York were nervous about eating in restaurants in the West Village, the neighborhood in Manhattan with the largest gay population. What if the cooks or waiters were gay? Even though it had already been reported that AIDS was not transmitted this way, the information had not been immediately accepted.

Jan Schenley himself was still in the closet when he was murdered. He was not out and about, living the life he'd surely be living now if only Tony had let him.

Vito Spano thinks the idea that the detectives wouldn't have put everything they had into investigating Schenley's murder is bullshit. But Spano never attended a meeting of the Gay and Lesbian Community Council, established in 1984 by NYPD Chief of Operations Robert Johnston. "You could see the look of disdain on his subordinates' faces as members of the gay community filed into Johnston's conference room," David Wertheimer, a consultant in the field of mental health and criminal justice, remembers. "Johnston, however, always had a warm smile underneath his gruff exterior," Wertheimer admits. But Spano is insistent. "If somebody can clear a murder they're going to clear a murder." Kaplan makes a face. His expression says Vito is saying what he has to, to defend the department. Other detectives describe the attitude in 1982 with a few words: "Who's this fag?" There were 1,668 murders in 1982, they were never going to get to all of them, and 524 remain unsolved today. It's not unreasonable to imagine that the detectives went after the most sympathetic victims first, and that to a 1982-era cop, a gay guy who was likely murdered by his gay lover (who also had a police record) was not the most sympathetic victim.

Again, Spano strongly disagrees. "I have never seen anything like that in twenty-five years of experience. When a detective makes a mistake it's usually a mistake of the head and not of the heart. Also, they've got a lot of people watching, so even if he feels that way, there's still a lot of people watching and hovering over everything he does, they'd pick up on it at the case review." Panzarella agrees with Spano. Neither commanding officer is defensive; they merely seem vaguely insulted by the suggestion and passionately believe that it is wrong.

Retired detective Glen Whelpley, who picked up the case in 1984, also agrees with Spano. They were under enormous pressure to clear a huge number of cases, and Schenley's case wasn't the only one going cold. One of the original detectives was very old school though, Whelpley admits. He was conservative. "Half Republican." He didn't think women should be on patrol, for instance. "He was part of a different time," Whelpley remembers. And the precinct where Schenley was murdered, the 70 (Midwood), would have been a completely unsympathetic precinct at the time, David Wertheimer points out. "The backwater of the NYPD with respect to gay/lesbian issues."

When Whelpley came on the case in 1984, he reached out to the gay community for help. He called the New York City Gay and Lesbian Anti-Violence Project, the National Gay Task Force, and a newspaper called *The Native.* According to David Wertheimer, who was with the Anti-Violence Project in the eighties, that still would have been a highly unusual thing for a detective to do in 1984. "But the gay community was the greatest source of information you could get," Whelpley explains. The social network that had evolved in New York was tight and well organized. Information both true and false traveled fast. Like most small, close-knit groups, it was also a gossipy community. "They love to talk. They love to tell a story." Maybe they had some information about this crime.

"The Anti-Violence Project had a hot line," Whelpley continues. It was a twenty-four-hour hot line for crime victims that had been established in 1980. They also had a decent working relationship with the police, depending on the precinct and the commanding officer. "I was looking for someone who was notorious." But they didn't have anyone that fit this particular crime. The problem was, Schenley was not completely out of the closet, and mob wannabe Manny Gonzalez would never admit that he was gay. They were not part of the gay community in New York, and therefore didn't figure in any gay-gossip loop. "They were part of it," Kaplan says. "But the underground part of it."

On February 9, 1999, Ray Ferrari, the commanding officer of the Cold Case Squad at the time, sends a memo to the chief of Detectives requesting publicity for the Schenley case. A reporter from *LGNY* (now called *Gay City News*) wants to publish photographs of some of the antiques that were stolen from Jan Schenley's home and to ask their readers to come forward if they have information. Permission is granted.

Laureen Schenley, meanwhile, puts pressure on the police department through state senator Thomas K. Duane, who writes Howard Safir. She also contacts the Lambda Independent Democrats, the New York City Gay and Lesbian Anti-Violence Project, and *LGNY*. "I felt they weren't doing what they needed to be doing for my brother," Laureen says. Tony Francesehi is in custody. What are they waiting for? *LGNY* starts publishing a series of articles about the long-unsolved crime. Kaplan, however, has only one witness who can testify, Mike Cilone, and he needs another before the case can go forward.

■

Kaplan continues to talk to every person he could find who knows Tony Francesehi. He's hoping to find someone else Tony had spoken to about the murders, particularly the murder of Jan Schenley.

On June 28, 1999, three months before Tony Francesehi goes to trial for the murder of Ronald Stapleton, Stapleton's father-in-law, Vincent Cestare, who had never given up hope, dies.

September 15, 1999. Stapleton's mother-in-law, who took care of his children when his wife no longer could, dies. Ronnie Stapleton is the only member of his family left to attend the trial the following Monday, September 20.

Ronnie goes to the trial every day. In the beginning, Tony smiles, smirks, and winks at Stapleton's son. Ronnie refuses to look away; he just stares back. Tony complains to his lawyer, who in turn complains to Ken Taub, the prosecutor, who tells Stapleton to stop staring. He is making Tony uncomfortable.

When Pixie Cilone walks in, the other family members yell at her. They do the same when Mike Cilone appears. They are both traitors.

Few who take the stand get a warm reception. Robert Race testifies on September 24. This jury isn't happy about his testimony, either. They, too, resent his fabrication of a black suspect as a scapegoat. With the recent Charles Stuart case from Boston on their minds, they believe Race.

Kaplan can't attend the trial because he keeps expecting and hoping for his chance to testify. As long as the possibility remains, he has to stay out of the courtroom. But he is never called. It must kill him to sit and wait out in the hallway every day, watching others go inside, one by one. Detectives want to testify. They're the ones who figured out who did it, who hunted the murderer down and pulled him out of the life he didn't deserve to be enjoying. Standing up in court at the penultimate moment in a sometimes years-long process to explain exactly what they did in front of colleagues and friends, and the victim's family and friends, is their one moment to fulfill the very human need to let it be known that they, too, were a part of a job well done.

■

"He blew it." Kaplan says. Ken Taub makes Tony an offer, but he doesn't take it. He thought he could win. His arrogance costs him twenty-five years.

When the trial is over, Ronnie Stapleton is glad, but he doesn't feel an overwhelming satisfaction. "What difference did it make?" he asks. "My grandparents are dead, my mother is sick, and my sister doesn't understand." Jan Schenley's sister Laureen remembers Ronnie looked "pretty burnt out. He looked like his life was destroyed." It's part of the process, hoping for something more than what you ultimately get. More relief, more retribution, more closure, and certainly not still more disappointment.

On October 20, 1999, Tony is sentenced to twenty-five years to life for the murder of Ronald Stapleton. The DA already has Tony in for life, so rather than go to trial for Jan Schenley, they are willing to negotiate a plea. "Tony was more afraid of the Schenley case," everyone connected with the investigation says, so he is equally willing to negotiate. In reality, the DA's case against Tony for the murder of Jan Schenley is not as strong. They have one witness. Francesehi never talked about Schenley to Frank Gioia, their most believable and articulate witness, and crucial evidence from the Schenley case was lost in a 1990 fire at the Property Clerk warehouse where it was stored. But Francesehi knows there are a lot of people who will remember that he was intimate with Jan Schenley. Tony thinks he's going to get off on appeal for Stapleton, however, and part of the plea agreement is, if he wins his appeal for Stapleton, he can withdraw his plea for Schenley, take his chances, and go to trial.

Tony has one more demand. He wants everyone's assurance that they will remain silent on the matter of his homosexuality. Tony Francesehi would rather be known as a murderer than a homosexual. The detectives and the prosecutors say, "Sure." Nothing is written down, it is a verbal agreement only, but it's an arrangement they all feel they can live with.

And so Tony Francesehi pleads guilty to the murder of Jan Schenley on October 11, 2000. When Tony talked to the original detective on the Schenley case in 1982, he said that he'd like to see Schenley's killer get the chair. New York didn't have a death penalty in 1982, and no one had been electrocuted since 1963 (or executed at all since 1976). In the end, for taping Jan Schenley's face from his chin to his forehead, causing his slow death, Tony gets five to fifteen, to be served concurrently with his earlier sentence.

New York has what are called indeterminate sentences; they have a bottom and a top. In this case, that would be five and fifteen years. After five years, Tony is eligible for parole. In addition, for every year of good behavior an inmate gets three months of "good time" off the back end of their sentence. That means even if the parole board continually puts a check in the DENIED field of his Parole Board Release Decision Notice, as long as he doesn't get into trouble,

Francesehi could still get out in twelve years on a conditional discharge. He would be under the parole board's supervision for what would have been the remainder of his sentence, but he'd be out.

But good time doesn't come off the back end of a life sentence. Francesehi has to serve twenty-five years for murdering Ronald Stapleton. Tony probably thought, "I'll win my appeal for Stapleton and maybe they won't prosecute me for Schenley, or, at worst, I'll still get the five to fifteen, and I'll be out in five years." "He was rolling the dice," Kaplan says.

Tony loses all his direct appeals. Schenley's sister Laureen immediately outs Tony when the family is given an opportunity to speak in court. Laureen gets up, and in addition to talking about how the murder affected her family, she talks about how Tony was one of her brother's lovers. "Ken Taub turned green," Laureen remembers, "but I felt good. I felt like I was giving Manny his going away present. I wanted the people in prison, where he was going, to know. Also, I thought, he murdered my brother, who the fuck is he to make the rules?" "I was cringing," Kaplan remembers. "I thought, 'Oh no, here we go.'" But Kaplan laughs as he tells the story. "Yeah, it was great," he admits, his affection and admiration for Laureen apparent. "She was sitting next to me. She kept asking me, should I do it, should I do it? She was so nervous. I told her, 'You do what you gotta do.' You could tell she felt good when she was done."

■

Finally, Kaplan turns his attention to the final item on his to-do list, the Carmine Variale and Frank Santora murders, and their murderer, Frank Smith Jr. Frank Smith had been given up for the murders of Variale and Santora by his cousin, Kaplan's CI Mike Cilone, and Frank Gioia Jr., the federal witness who was once engaged to Frank Smith's sister.

Smith is indicted on September 5, 2000. Ken Taub goes to the grand jury as a favor to the feds. He doesn't have a terribly strong case, but Kaplan and the feds are sure Smith will roll if indicted, and they wanted him to give up an even bigger mobster. Warrant in hand, Kaplan goes back to the prison where Smith is being held, arrests him for the murders of Variale and Santora, then brings him to the Cold Case headquarters for processing and fingerprints. Then he fills out an On Line Booking System Arrest Worksheet, and takes him right back to jail.

Kaplan and the feds are right. The next summer, on June 4, 2001, Mike Cilone calls Kaplan to tell him that Frank Smith Jr. is ready to talk. Smith has been in prison since 1988 on a narcotics conviction that he is actually innocent of, and now he has Variale and Santora hanging over his head. He's ready to cooperate. This is what they are waiting for. As bad as they are, Tony Francesehi and Mike Cilone are at the bottom of a hierarchy of badness. They're the mailroom guys of this particular organized-crime outfit. Tony, technically, isn't even on the mob organizational charts. Frank Smith Jr. is much higher up, but even he's not the guy they really want. Smith is taking direction from someone else, the acting head of operations for the Colombo family, and it's outside this guy's house they hope to sit and wait early some morning with flashlights, cuffs, vests, and warrants. If they can get this guy, then they'll be talking the kind of serious numbers (murder clearances) the department is forever after them to deliver. Kaplan and Margie Yee go out to Rikers to talk to Smith.

That meeting leads to two proffer sessions with Smith, one on June 22, 2001, and the other on August 3, 2001. Jack Maple, the deputy commissioner who insisted that New York needed a Cold Case Squad, always said that the guys who were killing back then were the same guys killing now, or they knew the guys who were. Kaplan's aggressive investigation of a twenty-year-old cold case allowed him to dig up killers from the eighties, conduct still more investigations, and to resolve more killings that took place in the nineties. Three decades of death. Jack Maple was right.

8 Detective Tommy Wray

The Christine Diefenbach Case

The current file of DD5s for Christine Diefenbach is so thick the fasteners at the top won't hold it together anymore. Every time you pick up the case folder, the top twenty DD5s fall out. It's the fall of 2003. In the past ten months, however, only four DD5s have been typed up and added to the file. DD5s may have piled up quickly in 1988, when there were ten detectives working on the case, but their number grows much more slowly now. The truth is, pretty much everything that can be done has been done. Detective Wray is waiting for test results from the evidence now. He will wait a long time.

■

Two years after fourteen-year-old Christine was murdered, a 49 was sent to the Property Clerk Division asking them not to destroy any evidence connected with the Christine Diefenbach case. The "49" comes from a now defunct form called a UF49, and it simply refers to interdepartmental memos on police letterhead. Evidence stored at the Property Clerk is destroyed after two years, except for evidence marked "homicide" on the fourth line down on the Property

Clerk voucher. That's what's supposed to happen. The commanding officer at the 102 knew how things really worked, so he sent the 49 to make sure everything was saved. It didn't help. In spite of his request, some of the evidence was destroyed. "They're dicks and they needed the room," one detective explained. A 1963 report found that the police personnel in the Property Clerk were not particularly qualified—untrained—and didn't consistently follow the few written procedures that existed. The cops who were there were there because they were on restricted or modified duty. Restricted means they're sick or have been injured; modified means they're disciplinary problems and they're being punished. No guns, no shields, no patrol or enforcement. The rubber-gun squad, they're called. A former Property Clerk employee from the seventies called it a "no-show job." People were on the payroll but they didn't show up. "Those guys don't care," another detective said. "They couldn't care less."

Not so anymore. After a long history of bad management, they managed to completely turn the place around in the nineties. Once the de facto resting place for malcontents, people at the division admit, there's only one person on restricted duty there today. Still, the earlier practices had consequences. Property Clerk officers were not able to hand over all the evidence originally stored in 1988 for the Christine Diefenbach case.

The people at the Property Clerk may have figured, what's the point? The chances of solving a cold case even as little as a few years after it happened are slim. Before DNA became a serious factor in clearing cases, they must have really believed there was no point in holding onto evidence. Few detectives came back for anything from these older cases. Plus, there are storage issues. There have been over seventy thousand murders in the past hundred years (not to mention all the other crimes). Where can they possibly keep all that evidence?

▪

When someone is murdered in New York, the first thing a detective does with the evidence is go to the precinct to see the property officer, who will give the detective vouchers with serial numbers for each piece or group of evidence. The voucher lists each object and describes it as either investigatory (needs tests), property (needs to be stored), or arrest (will be needed for court). Belongings of the victim that do not require testing are left with the property officer. From there it will either go to the property clerk's office in that borough, or to one of four large Property Clerk warehouses located around the city. Evidence for testing goes into envelopes (once it was discovered that bacteria grew inside plastic envelopes and caused DNA to degrade, the department switched to paper). Then it's taken to either the Office of the Chief Medical Examiner (OCME) or to the NYPD's Forensic Investigations Division, more commonly referred to as the Police Lab, in Queens.

Once the tests at the OCME are complete, a report is sent to the detective and the evidence is put into what are alternately referred to as DNA, DOA (Dead on Arrival), or blood barrels. Every month, ten to fifteen DOA barrels are delivered directly to the Property Clerk warehouse in Queens. The people at the warehouse make sure that what the OCME says is in there is really in there, then they issue a transfer receipt for the OCME, give the barrel a number, log it, and store it.

There is no statute of limitations on murder. Technically, any evidence from an unsolved murder should still be sitting in warehouses around the city. Given the approximately twenty-three thousand plus unsolved homicides in New York, there should be more than a century's worth of evidence disintegrating, unremembered, in a storeroom somewhere.

The first reference in the New York Police Department annual reports to storing actual biological evidence from murders appears in 1924. It mentions the "bloody and unsanitary clothing," which until that year was held at the Homicide Bureau of the district attorney's office. "The property is unsanitary," the report states, "and should be kept in a separate room away from other property, for the health and safety of the men attached to this office, and the general public." They complain about the lack of space and the fact that they have to hold onto evidence for unsolved cases indefinitely, and they cite three cases going back to 1909 as examples.

Before 1924, the Property Clerk Office was responsible for "all lost, stolen, abandoned and other property which comes into possession of the police department, and criminal courts of the city, and all property taken from persons dying intestate." The same is true today, but the description on the police department Web site is carefully worded in order to make the following point very clear: "All property coming into and leaving the Property Clerk Division is subject to strict legal constraints." The Property Clerk Division is responsible for a lot. In addition to crime scene evidence, they collect and hold for a prescribed period jewelry, cash, liquor, narcotics, automobiles, weapons, furniture, and pretty much any other object imaginable. Citizens who find money or jewelry and other items generally get to keep them if no one comes forward to claim them after six months if the object is valued under $500, after a year for objects under $5,000, and after three years for anything worth more than that.

Unclaimed property is assigned a value and sold on-line on an eBay-like company called Property Bureau. Cars are the exception—they are still auctioned off from the warehouse in Queens. Before Property Bureau, all auctions were held at the Queens warehouse. A collection of false teeth was sold for twenty-two dollars at a 1932 auction. No one made a bid for a bag of broken seashells. At a 1935 auction one man purchased a bag of horsehair for four dollars. A 1954 sale included a lot of "Carbon Rubber Doll Bodies (no heads)." Another year they sold two electrocardiograph machines. For the most part, the police department sells things like cars, bikes, TVs, cameras, and computers. In 1857, the first auction under newly assigned property clerk Charles J. Warren grossed just under six hundred dollars. By 1862 the total gross sales from unclaimed property was up to $2,404.17. In 2002, it was $2,128,000. In the past, net receipts from the auctions and any unclaimed cash they collected originally went to the Widows and Orphans Fund, then to the Police Pension Fund. Today it goes into New York City's General Fund. Occasionally, clothing from the Property Clerk is donated to charity.

Liquor, weapons, narcotics, and gambling devices are destroyed. For most of the past hundred years, weapons were taken out to sea and sunk. In 1933, 3,816 guns, knives, and swords were dumped into the sea at the Scotland Lightship station off the New Jersey coast. A couple of years later 1,575 phony token slugs were dumped into the Long Island Sound at Eaton's Neck in Huntington Bay, along with 500 slot machines and 4,000 weapons. Two years after that the Property Clerk poured 10,000 gallons of wine, whiskey, and beer into the Lower Bay. As of the seventies they were still throwing what they could into the various bodies of water in New York, but in the '80s they began melting handguns down in a foundry in Pennsylvania. Rifles and knives were put in a metal shredder.

Narcotics are burned. The police department burned millions of dollars' worth of drugs at their headquarters at 240 Centre Street in the twenties. In the thirties, marijuana was burned inside the Property Clerk Office at the bottom of Thirty-sixth Street in Brooklyn. In the fifties they used a furnace in the subbasement of the Fire Department Annex at 400 Broome Street, where the police department also had an annex. They started using a sanitation department incinerator at Twelfth Avenue and Fifty-sixth Street in the sixties. Today it's burned by a private contractor in Garden City, Long Island, but not all of it. Now they store some narcotics as evidence. Or, they try to.

Drugs, along with money being held as evidence, have been disappearing from Property Clerk offices since the beginning. A 1952 report by the Institute of Public Administration is just one of many calling for the "installation of controls and audits on the office of the Property Clerk." Their own annual reports indicated that they understood the need for a better system of record keeping and security. The biggest heist of all, and the one that led to the greatest reforms, was the theft of ten million dollars worth of heroin from the second floor at the 400 Broome Street annex. The heroin came from the famous 1962 French Connection case. Although the drugs were discovered missing in 1970, the police department suspected they were taken earlier. They hadn't kept tabs on what they had in a while, and what started out as 24 pounds unaccounted for climbed to 398 pounds following a crash inventory.

This led to enormous changes within the Property Clerk Division. However, the new controls that were effectively applied to drugs and money were not applied to evidence from homicides until the 1990s. No one was trying to walk off with old bloodstained shirts. They weren't particularly interested in saving them either. If Tommy Wray needs old evidence for further examination or testing or for an appearance in court, he has to get the storage numbers from the Property Clerk or the Police Lab, then go down to the warehouses himself to get it. That's when his problems begin.

First, was the evidence ever really stored there in the first place? A retired detective described what it was like at the Property Clerk's in a 1972 *New York Times* article: "You can walk into that office and you have to wait with maybe fifty or sixty other guys in order to get to a little window and take out evidence or return it." It wasn't worth the trouble. If the evidence was important, they held on to it, he said. I stood with Steve Kaplan at the Property Clerk window in Manhattan and waited. Some things hadn't changed. We stood for two hours, unacknowledged. When I argued that we should complain, Kaplan said, "Then we would wait forever."

Next, even if the evidence was stored there, did the property clerk save it or throw it out? "I saw a guy in there with a pitchfork, throwing old evidence out into a Dumpster," one Cold Case detective remembers. It's difficult to find evidence from cases earlier than 1990. The people at the Property Clerk sometimes attribute the missing evidence to a fire at a large warehouse that used to be located under the Brooklyn-Queens Expressway. A search of FDNY records turned up one minor fire, on November 2, 1990, which did ignite some boxes and clothing, and while some evidence was certainly lost, it wasn't big enough to explain why there is almost no evidence prior to the 1980s in the Property Clerk's possession. Jean Sanseverino's ring, her mother's wedding ring, which her father picked up while stationed in Germany during World War I, and which was likely deposited with the Brooklyn Property Clerk in 1951, was either sold or thrown out long ago. There's nothing from the fifties left there today. One vouchered handgun from a 1949 unsolved homicide case has survived, along with a few boxes containing a small number of homicide cases from the 1970s.

Evidence from more recent big cases, newsworthy cases, and any murder involving a member of the police department are more carefully stored. They still have the door from the Happyland Social Club fire in the Bronx in 1990, where eighty-seven people died. "We'll save that forever," a Property Clerk official declared. The police department as a whole, however, has shown an inconsistent interest in history. A 1924 *New York Times* article talks about five hundred bundles of clothes that were burned. The police were careful to note that "only clothing that had been used as evidence, or worn by the victims in crimes of violence that already have been disposed of, was sent to the incinerator," but in that bundle, now long gone, was the clothing worn by prominent New York architect Stanford White the night he was shot to death by Harry Thaw.

Sometimes, though, they paused before they destroyed. In 1982, Property Clerk personnel took a second look at two guns that were seized in a raid in the South Bronx in 1971. The weapons weren't like anything they'd recovered before, so they took them to the Metropolitan Museum of Art to see what they could find out about them. The museum had seen the pistols before, in 1933, when they were loaned to the museum by their then owner, Gustave Diderrich, and displayed that summer. They turned out to be handmade flintlock hunting pistols that once belonged to Empress Catherine the Great and were designed by master armorer Johan Adolph Grecke in St. Petersburg in 1786.

The police department didn't smelt them, they didn't throw

them into the Hudson River, and they didn't sell them at a police auction. They loaned them to the Metropolitan Museum of Art who put them on display for the second time in fifty years. The *New York Times* ran a piece about the pistols, which were then recognized by the family of John M. Schiff, which was able to document their purchase in 1939 and their theft in 1970. In 1986, John Schiff donated the pistols to the museum in memory of his wife, Edith Baker Schiff. After strongly expressing the difficulty in placing a value on items of such artistic and historic importance, Peter Finer, an English arms and armor dealer, estimated that the ivory, gold, steel, and brass pistols were worth a million dollars.

The oldest DOA barrels remaining in the Property Clerk's possession are from 1986, and they're stored in the Erie Basin warehouse, which is primarily used to store cars. No one knows what's in all of the older barrels. They were filled before anyone knew how to properly store these kinds of items and they're not going to open them without guys in hazmat suits. "We opened a barrel one time and it was filled with maggots," someone who worked there remembered. One detective said he'd find envelopes eaten through by rats. Another detective described the warehouses as "the bowels of hell. It was disgusting."

The area around the warehouses is generally filled with light industry, auto body shops, scrap-metal yards, recycling plants, transportation hubs. Inside, it's damp, dank, like an unfinished basement, with concrete and dirt floors. Evidence used to be piled up around poles that were numbered, and spray-painted in red, readable today. Now it's stored on metal shelves. People who work there use hand cream a lot because the powder and the latex from the gloves they use while working dries their skin. It rained and there were puddles and mud in the ground at one warehouse. "We're dirty but we're happy," one person who worked there said. The warehouses look like that final shot of *Raiders of the Lost Ark,* when they are putting away the Ark of the Covenant among endless stacks of wooden crates. Here, there are fifty-foot-tall towers of cardboard DOA barrels, with some showing signs of fluid damage. Each barrel holds twenty to twenty-five envelopes of evidence. There are roughly five or six thousand barrels. At twenty-five envelopes per barrel, that could represent up to 150,000 crimes.

The inventory and storage operations at the warehouses are crude. They don't use computers. They've got pens and logbooks and file cabinets. If there's anything on a computer, it's because an individual who knows the software program Excel took it upon himself to put it there for his use alone. There's no climate control at the warehouses. No air filtering. A few half-open barrels and boxes with torn paper envelopes exposing knives that presumably still might hold biological evidence sit on the shelves. Contamination seems like it would be an issue, but Dr. Robert Shaler from the OCME argues, "You can't deny the results. These are storehouses. You go into this old evidence, and even though it wasn't handled in the best mechanism, you still get results which are valid. You have a blood stain, and it's a big, huge juicy blood stain. Even though somebody may have handled that with their fingers forty years ago, there's going to be so much less DNA from the person who handled it than there is of the evidence. The evidence DNA is going to swamp out whatever contamination is there.

"If the suspect's DNA is there you still have to explain it. There has to be a reason for what you are seeing."

Money is a big part of the storage problem. Computerization is not in the budget. There's no more space to be had even though forty to fifty barrels come in every single month. The Property Clerk processed 29,000 vouchers in 1943. They've got 1.2 million now. Still, despite a lack of funds and decades of bad habits, in the nineties, around the same time the police department got serious about DNA, the Property Clerk Division got their act together with respect to homicide evidence. The problems at the Property Clerk have been pronounced under control many times over the years, but DNA finally did it. Rape kits are refrigerated. Homicide evidence, particularly any serological evidence, is no longer thrown out. The newer barrels are inventoried, sealed, and marked. Armed personnel and motion detectors are on every Property Clerk floor. Nothing leaves without a 49 from a commanding officer or a letter from an ADA or a subpoena. Different controls exist at each local borough office, but at the Brooklyn office, for instance, only so many people can stand at the Property Clerk window at any one time. The rest must wait outside a locked door until they're buzzed in and photographed. Before anything leaves any borough storeroom, the officer taking away the evidence will be fingerprinted, and those fingerprints are attached to the Property Clerk invoice.

Inspector Jack Trabitz, the commanding officer of the Property Clerk Division, claims they now have a 100 percent inventory, and they conduct unannounced spot checks to prove it. When I visited the warehouse, even though their inventory methods were not state of the art, they were still able to quickly say where everything was.

The people at the Property Clerk today are thorough and intent about their work, but many of the murders being investigated by the Cold Case detectives happened before these diligent officers got there. This might explain the attitude Cold Case detectives sometimes encounter when they show up looking for decades-old evidence. When they request evidence from the 1960s, '70s, and '80s, the people at the Property Clerk point out that those items were stored before their time, before they got things right. They don't want to be held responsible, and, anticipating the traditionally low opinion many within the NYPD have of people in the Property Clerk, they sometimes go on the offensive. "Find it yourself," the officer at the Property Clerk's warehouse told Wendell Stradford and his partner, Carl Harrison (aka Chuck), when they came looking for evidence from a 1988 case in which a nine-year-old girl and her mother were raped and murdered. Harrison had just picked up the case and was trying to track down about a dozen Property Clerk vouchers. He called the Property Clerk two or three times a day for a month asking about them. They finally gave him some storage numbers and told him he'd have to find the rest himself. Chuck was most interested in a vaginal swab that had been taken from the little girl. According to a piece of paper in the case folder, there was a possibility that the vaginal swab was at a private DNA lab in Maryland called Cellmark Diagnostics. The people at Cellmark told Chuck that they had extracted DNA from the swab and sent it back to the Police Lab in small tubes. The Police Lab said they sent them back to Property Clerk. Chuck and Wendell went back to the Property Clerk and looked themselves. No tubes. They went through the Police Lab logbooks for that week looking for a clue. Then they found the answer. The lab was supposed to send the evidence back to the Bronx Property Clerk, but they gave the package a Manhattan storage number. It never got to the Bronx. Chuck and Wendell found the tubes sitting in a box at the Manhattan Property Clerk. They took them to the OCME and got a hit. They now have a new suspect.

Clearly, there are people in the Property Clerk who hate their job and are miserable, but they no longer define the division. The best detectives find out who the best PAAs are (police administrative assistant, the people who actually look for evidence), the ones who know where everything is and won't give up until they find it.

∎

While much of the evidence from the Christine Diefenbach case has been destroyed or lost, Tommy Wray and a PAA in the Property Clerk named Cathy Farrell still manage to find all of the most important items, the ones from which they might be able to recover the killer's DNA. Before Wray can start testing for DNA, however, he needs DNA samples for comparison. He needs a suspect. Wray's search begins on June 12, 2001, with someone the original detectives had always intended to get back to—the man with the nickname Trucker.

Wray first calls the former owner of Finnegan's Bar, the place where ten years earlier a distressed, anonymous drunk picked up the phone to tell the officers at the 102 about a guy named Trucker who had actually bragged to him about beating a young girl to death on the Long Island Rail Road tracks. I remember Trucker, the owner says. He and his friend Russell Burns were in his bar until 2:00 a.m. the night before Christine was murdered.

But Burns had told detectives in 1997 that while he had heard of Trucker, they never hung out together. Wray now knows that Russell lied. Why? Before talking to Russell himself, he wants another person to confirm that Russell and Trucker were friends. Russell's wife, Angela, might know. What else does she know? Tommy goes to see her and finds her mother instead. "I told her not to marry him," Angela's mother tells Wray. Then three months after her mother's warning Angela had called to say that it was done, they were wed. But Angela is living with a girlfriend now, her mother says. Tommy goes to the hair salon where Angela works, only to find she hasn't shown up or answered the phone for a week.

Tommy starts looking for others mentioned in the DD5s. He finds a friend of Trucker's who won't say much but confirms that Trucker knew Burns. A former girlfriend says she was terrified of him. She wants to help, though, and she gives Wray the names of six more friends.

Tommy is working his way through the list of friends when he decides that enough people have already verified that Trucker and Russell were friends. On July 26, Wray drives out to confront Burns, who is in prison on a burglary charge.

Russell Burns and Christine Diefenbach were both fourteen years old when she was murdered. Burns is short, thin, pale, and tattooed. In a mug shot he looks innocently, almost dumbly, into the camera. He has the beginnings of a smile but it's a smug smile, which only makes him look naive, like a kid with something to prove. Tommy Wray describes him as a wannabe tough guy.

Burns throws up his hands when he sees Tommy Wray. Yeah, he and Trucker were in the bar together every night in those days. So what? "Why did you lie?" Tommy asked him. "I was in that bar every night with him, how am I supposed to know what night you're talking about?" What can he tell them about Trucker? "I don't know anything, I'm no rat. I would never say anything bad about him. He took me in when I was down and out. As far as I know he's an okay guy." Russell Burns is not going to cooperate.

When Tommy and his partner get back to New York, Tommy has a message from a lieutenant at the prison where Russell is incarcerated. Burns was so shaken by Wray's visit, the lieutenant is sure something has to be up. "I think he knows all about the homicide." Tommy is thinking, *Not only does he know all about it, he was there.*

Tommy continues to track down Burns's friends. While he looks for people to talk to about Burns, he follows up on another tip from an anonymous caller about a guy who had a rape conviction and was known to beat his mother and sisters. A surveillance tape during a robbery shows him dancing around and smiling while he wraps a man in duct tape and pronounces himself "the duct tape king." The guy was an early riser in prison, Tommy is told. Christine was murdered very early on a Sunday morning. There's a chance. Wray checks his prison records. This guy was in jail when Christine died.

The same lieutenant from Burns's prison calls back. All of the inmates' phone calls are monitored, and Burns has just phoned a friend and told him he lied to Tommy Wray. He did know something about the murder. He also said, "Angela opened her big mouth."

Tommy Wray and his partner, Mike Solomeno, immediately drive back to Angela's. Angela is thirty years old. In photographs, she's a big girl who looks vulnerable. Her face has that simultaneous hard-soft look of a girl whose life hasn't gone as she dreamed it would and who has since gotten into some trouble. Angela's had a few arrests, but she's in a drug rehab program now and is working as a hairdresser, trying to get her life together. Yes, she was married to Russell, she says, but she's trying to end it, and it's proving difficult. She sent him divorce papers and he sent back an envelope full of ashes.

Trucker and Russell were once very close, she begins. Trucker took Russell in when Russell's mobster father threw him out. Still, it was possible that Russell was afraid of Trucker, she says. Trucker got into a lot of bar fights. And he wouldn't back down. Ever. Even if Russell knew anything he might be afraid to talk. "What kind of shoes does Trucker wear?" Tommy asks her. He's curious because the blunt object that was used to kill Christine was never found. Trucker wore steel-tipped boots, Tommy is told. What if the weapon was never found, Tommy wonders, thinking of Christine's wounds, because the killer walked away wearing it? "He wore those construction boots," Angela answers.

Angela hasn't seen Trucker for eleven years, but she is willing to visit him to try to get him to talk about the investigation. Killers always tell someone, the detectives say. "Some people brag about it," Lieutenant Panzarella explains. "Some people can't live with it and they have to tell somebody. Other people, they're drinking, they lose their composure, they'll go into detail about it, and then a day later they'll go, 'You know I was drunk and I was only making shit up,' and they really weren't. They really are the killer."

■

Tommy keeps talking to everyone he can find. Detectives can never proceed in an orderly, linear fashion. They can't wait until they find one guy before moving on to the next. It's not practical. Even if they'd like to have information from one before approaching another, they might find one guy in a day, another in a few months, and another in a few years. People and test results come back chaotically. A detective has to be all over the place all the time, making phone calls, dropping off evidence, faxing and e-mailing and catching people and information as it randomly comes in, working in a semicontrolled free-for-all.

Tommy contacts some of Russell's prison buddies to see if Russell ever told them anything about Christine. Then he and Solomeno go out to see a man living in a sad, dilapidated neighborhood in Queens. They pull out a picture of Trucker. Yeah, he's a friend, the man tells them. They used to hang out at Finnegan's Bar and another bar called Joe's. "What kind of shoes did Trucker wear?" Tommy asks. Construction-type boots.

They drive 250 miles to see a bartender named John Sanderson. A friend of a friend of a friend of Sanderson's said Sanderson had over-heard Russell talk about the murder in the bar where Sanderson worked. Sanderson is large, gruff, and physically menacing. He doesn't know anything, he insists.

The next friend of Russell Burns's that they visit has been expect-ing them. Russell has told him all about Detective Tommy Wray. He told this friend he lied to the first detective he spoke to, but he didn't say why.

Also that summer, Wray introduces himself to Christine's father. He wants him to know he's working on the case now that Annunziata has retired and that Christine will not be forgotten. John Diefenbach is a small, gentle, and soft-spoken man. Wray never meets Christine's mother, who to this day has trouble talking about her daughter. That is not an unusual response for the parent of a murdered child. Christine's father is glad to know that her case will not be dropped. He doesn't want another child to die. "I don't want to see someone else go through what me and my wife went through." But the idea of Tommy actually succeeding brings up complicated feelings.

"The thing I dread, if they catch him, is now I have to live this again," Diefenbach admits quietly. "He's going to sit up there and tell what it was like, her last few minutes. I dread that. I always think about what she must have felt those last few minutes. Did she know she was going to die? When they first grabbed her, whatever they did to her. I really don't know what they did. That's what I think about. The terror." Diefenbach feels what any father would have felt. He was supposed to protect her and he wasn't there when she needed him. Did she suffer? It's unthinkable. But when it's your child who is murdered, it's hard to stop thinking about it.

Dr. Sherwin B. Nuland offers some reassurance in his book *How We Die.* There's a lot of evidence, Nuland found, to indicate that there's an absence of pain and fear in the face of even the most hor-rifying deaths. In his chapter about murder, Nuland recounts the story of a nine-year-old girl named Katie who was stabbed to death across the street while her mother watched. What haunts John

Diefenbach is echoed in the words of that mother. "Later, I went through months and months of asking myself, How much pain did she feel? I needed to know that . . . I had to know what she went through, what she felt. . . ."

Nuland cites example after example of "serenity and languorous comfort in the face of what would seem to be frightful and agonizing wounds." He includes accounts from people who survived terrifying accidents only to say that at the worst possible moment there was no pain, no fear. Nuland writes, "It is not farfetched to believe that the human body itself knows how to make these morphinelike substances [endorphins] and knows how to time their release to correspond with the instant of need . . . I am convinced that nature stepped in, as it so often does, and provided exactly the right spoonful of medicine to give a measure of tranquility to a dying child.

"Whatever the source, humankind and many animals often seem to be protected at the instant when sudden death approaches—protected not only from the horror of death itself but from certain counterproductive actions that might ensure it or extend its anguish."

"I wish I was there," Diefenbach repeats. "Maybe something would have changed."

▪

September 11, 2001. Over the next year, for two days a week, all the Cold Case detectives work one 9/11-related assignment or another. Like Stradford and Kaplan, Tommy Wray has his 9/11 assignment. He works at the Family Bereavement Center, talking to the families, taking DNA samples, and filling out missing-persons reports. And, like NYPD cops everywhere, many Cold Case detectives start packing it in and retiring. The Cold Case arrest logs start filling up more slowly now.

In late September, Sanderson the bartender calls back. He's had some time to think about it and wants to speak to them. He asked for a safe phone number to call and they give him the "Hello" number. This is the telephone number they give out to informants; there's one in each Cold Case office. When the Hello phone rings they answer, "Hello" instead of "Cold Case Squad, may I help you?" or something else official-sounding. That way, if Russell ever finds the number in Sanderson's pocket and dials it, he won't find out that Sanderson is working with the police.

Sanderson calls the Hello number on September 28. The information he gives is so good, Wray gets back in his car and drives 250 miles to pick up Sanderson and take him to the office of the Queens District Attorney to repeat everything he just said.

Like so many others Wray and his partner talked to, Sanderson doesn't like Russell Burns. "He's got a big mouth." Still, Russell listened when Sanderson complained about his problems, so Sanderson returned the favor and listened to Russell when he complained about his problems, which was fine until Russell started talking about some detectives who were trying to connect him to a homicide investigation. Russell "was worried about an ex-friend by the name of Trucker who was with him when he 'stomped' a girl to death." Russell said they killed Christine because she fought when Trucker tried to rape her. It all took place near Finnegan's Bar and a diner, Russell said. He and Trucker were living in a trailer, and they were both high on crack and beer at the time.

But he and Trucker parted on bad terms, Russell said, and he was afraid if detectives got to Trucker, "Trucker would roll on him." So Russell was making phone calls and raising money in order to put a contract on Trucker. Wray and the Queens ADA want more. Building convincing cases years after the crime is difficult.

Sanderson goes on. Russell showed him how he used an object to push down on Christine's throat, he said. Christine's autopsy report does indicate oral trauma and deep bruising in the back of the throat, neither of which Sanderson could have known. Russell wouldn't say what the object was, but he left it at the crime scene. He also told Sanderson he may have lost a belt buckle there, and he was worried that the detectives might have it.

By the time cases reach the Cold Case Squad, crime scenes are usually long gone, but if there's even the remotest possibility that something remains, the detectives have to try. If it's still there, with the right tools they can recover it and use it as one piece of physical, irrefutable evidence, bringing at least some measure of peace to a family that has been waiting so long for resolution.

When they're looking for a body they'll bring a cadaver dog. In one cold case investigation a cadaver dog found a body that was wrapped in plastic and buried under concrete four years earlier. To train a dog to find dead bodies, they construct something called a scent tube. It's made from PVC and is sealed at both ends after the insertion of a piece of gauze that's been doused with one of the following perfumes: Pseudo Corpse I or II (II is a corpse further along in the decomposition process), Pseudo Drowned Victim, or Cadaverine. They get the stuff from the Sigma Chemical Company in St. Louis and it's expensive. To make a comparison, 1.5 ounces of the famously expensive perfume Joy by Jean Patou, which requires the blossoms of 10,600 jasmine flowers and 336 May roses, retails for $100. The same amount of Pseudo Corpse II would run you $276.75.

Depending on what the detectives are trying to find, they might bring teams of personnel and equipment, like a device called a surface penetrating radar. "We're looking for shadows," one guy said, describing how it works. Detective Wray is searching for one belt buckle. He goes back to the tracks where Christine was murdered with three ESU (Emergency Services Unit) guys and a metal detector called a wand. They try even though they know they're divining for miracles. On railroad tracks there are countless small metal objects in every square inch. They never find the buckle.

After this, Tommy turns his attention back to his first suspect. "Let's find Trucker," he says. He and Solomeno park outside Trucker's last known address in a small, off-the-beaten-track neighborhood in Queens. Back in the eighties, the area's town bar was in someone's home. On some corners, instead of standard, city-issued signs, there are hand-painted street signs nailed to telephone poles.

Wray and Solomeno arrive and wait. When Trucker pulls up in a blue 1983 Chevy at 4:40 in the afternoon on November 27, Tommy and his partner go home. For now, they just want to confirm that Trucker lives there.

Over the next month, Tommy makes more phone calls. More friends talk. When they learn all they're going to learn from every source at their disposal, Tommy decides it's time to bring Trucker in for questioning. On January 3, 2002, they drive out and sit on Trucker's house until he pulls into the driveway at the end of the afternoon. Trucker comes back with them voluntarily. In snapshots taken at the precinct, he has an unexpected expression. The camera must have disarmed him. The look on his face is hopeful, embarrassed, self-conscious, and exposed. In one picture, Trucker tries to put his arm around Tommy Wray. It's like he's striving for a "we're all just a bunch of guys here" feel, but Tommy leans away, clearly uncomfortable. Wray says he wanted to appear friendly in the pictures. They plan to take those pictures to Russell, to make him think Trucker was cooperating with them.

Yeah, I'm called Trucker, he admits when he sits down. His friends told him detectives were asking about him, but he had nothing to do with the death of Christine Diefenbach. It's true that he and Russell were living in a trailer at the time. A lot of people were coming in and out of his house in those days. It was "party central." But Trucker kicked Russell out in 1988 or '89, he says, when he found out Russell was doing angel dust. He hasn't seen him since.

He also admits that hitting a woman isn't totally out of character for him. He's had problems in the past, beating up women, but that was when he was drinking heavily. He has cirrhosis now and doesn't drink anymore. He broke up with his girlfriend Carolyn in 1986 or '87, specifically because they both liked to drink too much and they got into fistfights when they did. And yes, he did hit that girl in Joe's bar, but she broke a bottle over his head first. The charges were dropped when she didn't show up in court. Then Trucker starts talking to Wray about a girlfriend named Doris who was a psycho. "Did you talk to Doris? Don't believe a thing she says," he tells them. Tommy notices Trucker's construction boots. "I've been wearing construction boots ever since a car accident in the late eighties," Trucker says. "I wear them for ankle support."

Trucker also confirms that he and Russell were hanging out in bars in the area in 1988. But his liver was starting to go, and he sometimes blacked out when drinking. A crime could have happened, he concedes, but he doesn't have any memory of it.

Over and over, he asks for a polygraph test or to be hypnotized and says he wants to provide DNA. Anything to prove that he didn't do it. They take him to the Queens DA's office for a polygraph test. He passes. The sergeant who administered the test says that if the crime really was performed during a blackout, however, this test gets them nowhere. Trucker would have no memory of the event, and his answers would appear truthful.

Wray and Solomeno spend the next few days unsuccessfully tracking down more friends of Russell's and chasing down dead-end leads. Such is the unglamorous work of a Cold Case detective. But you never know what the original detectives may have missed, and you don't want to be yet another detective who overlooks something crucial.

Still, for all his effort, after all the phone calls and hours of driving, Tommy has only uncovered one person whom one of his suspects talked to about the murder. Once more, he turns back to the physical evidence, wondering: what did we miss? He pulls out all the original Property Clerk vouchers. One voucher lists seven plastic envelopes containing hair and fibers that were removed from the deceased during the autopsy. They were never tested. Tommy goes to the Police Lab in Queens, where the envelopes were taken at the time. They check their logbooks. The items were sent to the OCME at Bellevue. The OCME says they sent everything to the Manhattan Property Office at 1PP. Tommy calls the Manhattan Property Office. They have them.

Wray picks up the seven envelopes and drives them over to the Office of the Chief Medical Examiner on February 15, 2002. For the second time in fourteen years, the evidence is in the hands of the OCME. Let's see what we can get this time, Wray thinks.

Lieutenant Panzarella sends a 49 to the Property Clerk, explaining that Tommy has the hair and fiber evidence from the Diefenbach case and that he's taken it to the OCME for DNA testing. Panzarella is just following standard operating procedure. The Property Clerk expects evidence back the next day, and if it's not coming back immediately you have to explain why. We've got a suspect, Panzarella writes.

Meanwhile, Tommy is still trying to find someone else Trucker has talked to about the murder. He goes back to the former owner of Finnegan's Bar and takes one more shot at learning the identity of the anonymous caller who supplied their first tip about Trucker. "I think I know who the caller was," he tells Wray this time, and he gives him a name. Tommy tracks the possible caller to a small town in Pennsylvania. He and Solomeno drive two and a half hours but he isn't home. Tommy writes "Please contact me" on one of his business cards and sticks it in the front door. It's not unusual for detectives to leave their cards when they're someplace they can't get back to easily. People almost always call back, too. It's irresistible. They have to know why a cop left them a note.

A couple of days later, in the Queens Cold Case kitchen, Trucker lets them take his DNA. Tommy Wray wraps a cotton swab around a wood pencil and puts it in Trucker's mouth. "Nothing better was available and I didn't want to wait and give him a chance to change his mind." It's a strangely intimate and vulnerable act, taking someone's DNA, but Detective Wray doesn't stop to contemplate what to him is merely evidence collection. He drops the pencil off at the OCME the next day.

Now he needs Burns's DNA. In order to compel Burns to cooperate he has to get a warrant. Two weeks later Tommy brings John Sanderson before a judge and directs him to "just tell him what you told us." Wray knows the judge will be satisfied with what Sanderson has to say.

March 20. Warrant in hand, Wray and Solomeno go back to confront Burns. They try one more time to get a confession. "We know you lied to the police," they begin. Burns hunkers down. "I don't know what you're talking about and if you have evidence then charge me, and I'll see you at the trial." He's calling their bluff. They try for an hour and a half to get him to tell them something, but Burns insists, "I don't know nothing." Tommy gives up and places a Q-tip in Burns's mouth. They bring the sample to the 105, pick up a Property Clerk voucher, then deliver the sample to the OCME. Now the OCME has both Trucker's and Burns's DNA. Tommy asks them to compare the DNA against the hair and fibers he delivered the month before.

The next day they hear from the possible anonymous caller in Pennsylvania. He knows Russell Burns. They used to hang out at Finnegan's Bar. Burns was just a kid when he met him for the first time, and not a bad one, but he got into drugs and in with the wrong people and he changed for the worse. He doesn't know about the murder, but Trucker was a violent person, he says. Particularly when drinking. He got into fights all the time. Wray asks, "Is there a way to get to the railroad tracks from Finnegan's Bar?" "Sure, right in the back of Finnegan's, we used to go up there all the time to smoke pot and get blow jobs." Tommy asks him point-blank, "Were you the anonymous caller?" "No." Tommy believes him. Before they hang up, the man gives him some names of a few more people from Finnegan's.

Tommy runs the names through their in-house databases: BADS (Booking Arraignment and Disposition Inquiry System), CARS (Computer Assisted Robbery System), and NITRO (Narcotics Investigative Tracking of Recidivist Offenders). He is looking for arrests and finds that two of the men on his list have a history.

Wray and Solomeno go looking for one of them in another remote town in Queens called Broad Channel. Broad Channel has a shabby, wrong-side-of-the-tracks feel. Culturally, it dug in its heels sometime in the sixties. This is the place where a police officer and two firefighters lost their jobs after appearing on a 1998 Labor Day Parade float in blackface with watermelons and fried chicken buckets while mimicking the murder of James Byrd, who had been dragged to his death in Texas three months earlier. (In 2003, a judge ruled that the city had violated their right to free speech when Mayor Rudolph Giuliani fired them. In 2004, the judge ordered the city to reinstate them and pay them for lost wages, pending the result of the appeal. The current mayor, Michael Bloomberg, plans to appeal.)

They check three places, but no one is home. They leave cards with notes to please contact them, then head back to the office. Each person they talk to gives them more names to call, and for a while their list grows and they pick up a useful fact here and there— "Yes, the stairs to the railroad tracks were only a few feet from Finnegan's" and "I always expected Russell would end up in jail"— but as they work their way down the list of names, they don't come up with a single person who can tell them anything about Christine's murder.

"I hit a wall," Wray says. "Yeah, it's frustrating, but it was just another wall. I just have to figure out how I can walk around it and attack this case another way." At times Detective Tommy Wray seems to run on faith alone, for him a seemingly inexhaustible energy source. His determination is never grim, but unfailingly, almost perversely, upbeat.

Once again Wray thinks, I've got to find at least one concrete piece of physical evidence. He goes back one more time to physically check every piece of evidence that remains in their possession. The ADA writes the Property Clerk to request that the property listed in thirty-one vouchers from the Diefenbach case be released to Wray for the purpose of DNA analysis. But thirty-one is a lot of envelopes, and these were stored back in the days before the Property Clerk kept a careful watch. They will have to search by hand. Finding them is going to take some time.

For a month, nothing happens. Burns is up for parole, but Tommy hasn't finished building his case. He writes Burns's parole officer, arguing for a denial of Burns's parole, and faxes a copy to the ADA. Russell has a sixty-forty chance of making his parole, Wray is told, but in the end his letter helps. Russell's parole is denied.

On September 26, 2002, Cathy Farrell from the Property Clerk calls to say that they checked their logbooks and some of the vouchers are in storage, some were destroyed, and they don't have any record of the rest. She gives Wray storage numbers for the ones she believes they have, and he goes to Queens to find them. Half of what he is looking for is there. Three vouchers are found, and two are confirmed destroyed.

Cathy Farrell calls again on October 18. She hasn't given up. Another voucher turned out to be lost, but she's found five more. In the end, Cathy Farrell manages to recover most of the vouchered items that came directly from the crime scene. Tommy has what he needs. On October 28, Wray drops everything off with Mark Desire at the OCME for DNA analysis.

The Office of the Chief Medical Examiner in New York is the largest forensic lab in the United States, according to Dr. Robert Shaler, and they have the best turnaround time in the country for a large lab.

Tommy does not have the personality to do nothing while waiting for test results—he goes back to the Tips Log. Perhaps he can find something useful that everyone else missed. Two tips naming one guy Tommy hasn't looked into before had come within days of the murder. There wasn't anything about him in the original DD5s. Wray gets his rap sheet. (Rap sheets list someone's arrest and prison history, their Social Security, NYSID, and FBI numbers, a physical description, their place and date of birth, and their address.) The rap sheet lists six out-of-state arrests and thirty in New York. One arrest was for sex with a minor and another was for attempted rape. Tommy calls a detective in the New York Department of Correction's Investigations Division. Was this guy incarcerated on February 8,

1988? Yes. He was in Rikers. "Is it possible that he was on work release on that day, or in a mental health facility with the ability to come and go?" "The way the records read," the detective says, "I seriously doubt if any of the programs would have been granted to him." The detective can't say, with 100 percent certainty, however, that he was incarcerated that day. Only that he should have been.

December 18, bad news. Cathy Farrell verifies that two more vouchers were destroyed in 1996.

Then the OCME calls with more bad news. They weren't able to recover any nuclear DNA from a hair from Christine's vaginal area that he'd delivered ten months earlier. Does he ever feel defeated? "Never," Tommy answers without hesitation or doubt. "This is what it's about. You gotta keep plugging away." Besides, he has another idea. Wray calls Mark Desire at the OCME on December 19 and asks for mitochondrial DNA analysis of the hair. There are thousands of mitochondrial DNA molecules per cell. as opposed to just two of nuclear DNA. When they can't recover nuclear DNA, sometimes they'll shoot for mitochondrial. "Also," Dr. Robert Shaler explains further, "with degraded samples, we might use mitochondrial DNA if the STRs don't give good or 'strange' results, and if the sample was important enough." (STR stands for short tandem repeat, a method of analyzing/mapping DNA.)

The problem is, mitochondrial DNA is inherited from the mother only and doesn't identify the person exactly; it only establishes a maternal connection between DNA samples. If there's a match, it could mean that both DNA samples came from the same person, but it could also mean that it came from two different people who had the same mother. If the mitochondrial DNA from the scene matched Trucker's DNA, for example, his lawyer could argue that the DNA could have just as easily come from Trucker's brother. It may be a long shot, but it's all Tommy has. "Christine's case is one of the things that's keeping me on the job. I want to bring an answer to this family." Mitochondrial analysis is just one more investigative tool, and he is going to use every tool he has to find Christine's killers. "No one had done mitochondrial tests on that hair. It was worth that shot."

The OCME is not currently set up for mitochondrial (mtDNA) testing. If they need mtDNA analysis, the police department has to send their samples out to private labs, which are expensive. The FBI will conduct the tests for free, but results from the FBI can take a year or more to come back. The Cold Case Squad favors an outfit called Mitotyping Technologies, LLC, in Pennsylvania. Mitotyping Technologies charges four thousand dollars to test one sample and a known source (i.e., a suspect), compare the results, and send back a report in a week to ten days. If the testing is done before an indictment comes down, it usually comes out of the NYPD's budget. After that, the money may come out of the DA's or the U.S. attorney's office, depending on who is trying the case. Wray doesn't want to postpone possibly bringing an answer to the Diefenbach family for yet another year. As the commanding officer, Vito Spano will have to write to get approval to send the samples to Mitotyping.

"The sole purpose of mitochondrial analysis is for comparison to a separate source," Mark Desire reminds Tommy. "If you are going to perform mitochondrial analysis on a sample left at a crime scene, you need a suspect's DNA to compare it to." If you don't have a suspect yet, the OCME believes that time and money is better spent elsewhere. "That's fine," Tommy responds. They had taken Trucker's and Burns's DNA. "We have something to compare it to." Tommy will have to gather up all the samples again and arrange for testing elsewhere.

At around this time a different criminalist at the OCME, Lisa Dzegliewski, takes over the Diefenbach case. Lisa goes back and re-examines the evidence and performs additional tests. Trucker's and Russell's DNA have now been analyzed, but at this point Wray doesn't have any nuclear DNA evidence from the crime scene to compare their DNA to. Trucker's and Russell's profiles are checked against Linkage, the local DNA database, but they don't get a hit. This doesn't really tell the detectives much either way. New York's local DNA database has two DNA collections. One contains the DNA from suspects and the other stores DNA from crime scenes. The fact that they don't get a hit only means that no one else had entered Trucker's and Russell's DNA in the system and that their DNA had not been recovered from a crime scene in New York. They can't check the profiles against the state or national databases. State policy prohibits it at the local level and federal law prevents it at the national level. In any case, what Wray really needs is something from the Diefenbach crime scene to compare their profiles to.

Everything is taking months. Because of 9/11, the OCME is in turmoil, and Dzegliewski has a lot of evidence from the Diefenbach case to go over. And everything she does has to be reviewed by two levels of supervisors. Dzegliewski is finally able to recover nuclear DNA, but everything she finds came from Christine. There isn't anything else Lisa can do.

On July 24, 2003, Wray goes back to the OCME to go over his options with Lisa. The original hairs have already been consumed by testing, she tells him, but he might be able to recover mitochondrial DNA from a hair recovered from Christine's vaginal area that they have in storage at the OCME, and possibly from two metal bars with hair that Wray had dropped off on October 28, 2002, and are now back at the Property Clerk. These hairs have not been tested.

Tommy wanted to get mitochondrial analysis back in December, but mtDNA testing is still relatively new in law enforcement circles. It was only admitted into a U.S. court for the first time in 1996. The Police Lab has sent only five hairs out for mtDNA tests, ever. Not everyone was exactly clear on the procedure. Once again, Tommy goes back to the Property Clerk with the storage numbers for the bars. They say they'll look for them. Wray will end up waiting three months.

It's a familiar story. If it's a big case that's getting a lot of attention, or the evidence is needed for a court date, there's no wait. If it's a twenty-year-old case and the only person showing any interest is one detective from the Cold Case Squad, it takes a while. "Are they less important because they're old?" Tommy Wray asks. He doesn't think so. "They're more important because they've been waiting longer." The Property Clerk can't win. Like the Cold Case Squad, they have to put down what they're doing sometimes to work a special detail or a parade. Vito Spano says the reality is "if you're not on top of them, and I don't care if you're talking about the DA, the OCME, or the Property Clerk, it's not going to happen." You've got to be a pain in the ass. Tommy Wray manages to be a pain in the ass and cheerful at the same time.

On October 2 Tommy hears Russell Burns made parole. There was nothing left for him to do to prevent it. He already stopped Burns's parole once and he couldn't postpone his release indefinitely. Burns is free. Tommy is resigned. "It doesn't matter. In or out, I still had to finish building a case. I did the best I could." Wray is accustomed to near-constant frustration.

Tommy continues to chase down leads. At the end of October, the OCME finds the hair they had in storage and the Property Clerk finds the two metal bars. The procedure for getting mitochondrial DNA analysis has been set. Wray has to first take everything over to criminalist Lisa Faber at the Police Laboratory. She will determine if the hairs are animal, human, or fibers and if they belong to the victim. If she finds they are human hairs of unknown origin, she'll get them ready to be sent to a lab for testing. Meanwhile, Vito Spano has to send a 49 to the Central Investigation and Resource Division in the Detective Bureau to get approval to spend the money. Tommy has to go back to the OCME and retrieve the Trucker and Burns swabs that he had dropped off in early 2002. When everything is ready, Lisa will call Tommy. Then, in order to maintain a strict chain of custody while tests are being conducted, Tommy will drive the package down to Pennsylvania himself.

In November 2002, a local television news station airs a piece about the Christine Diefenbach case. CBS has a new fictional show called *Cold Case,* which is doing well, and cold cases are hot. Tommy Wray doesn't have an enormous ego, he's more of a blend-into-the-background kind of guy unless a different approach is called for, but he is more than willing to get on TV to help his case. "People need to be reminded," he says. In the final piece they show the place where Christine was killed, an agonizing interview with Christine's father, and a clip of Tommy making a plea for anyone with information to contact them. "Maybe the anonymous caller will finally come forward," Tommy says hopefully, before the piece airs. No one does.

■

According to the U.S. Department of Justice, homicides of children are the most likely to be cleared.

As the sixteenth anniversary of Christine Diefenbach's murder approaches, the former principal at Christine's junior high school, Jules Weisler, talks about Christine's murder. "The kids were destroyed, crying in the halls, kids who knew her and kids who didn't." A memorial wall was set up in the auditorium in Christine's honor, and a number of student paintings and drawings were hung there, along with a plaque that reads, "The Christine Diefenbach Gallery." There's a drawing of Christine's in the middle, a black-and-white landscape. It's haunting, lonely, no people or animals, and it's very well done. Today, the gallery is a sad, ignored thing. The students' work hangs way over everyone's heads, and it's hard to read the signatures. Three paintings have been removed and empty slots with only nails remain. "I've been here thirteen years and I didn't know it was here," a woman who works in the principal's office said. The wall was supposed to give the children something to focus on, Weisler explained, and to help them find closure.

Lieutenant Panzarella hates the word *closure*. "You always hear some idiot prosecutor or cop say, 'Well, we got them closure.' Everyone wants the killer captured and convicted, but what is closure? It's an invented word. It means nothing to no one. If you're born on October 21, October 21 comes every year. It's your birthday. Do you think because we captured somebody and convicted them that no one's ever going to think about their murdered daughter on her birthday? And then comes Christmas, and then comes New Year's, anniversaries. What closure is there? It's a silly word."

"Christine would have turned thirty this year," her father re-members.

On November 24, 2003, Tommy Wray takes the last package of evidence to Mitotyping Technologies for mitochondrial analysis. They say they need a month. Wray has exhausted all his investigative angles. Everything is riding on the results of these tests.

9 Detectives Walter Duffy, William Kelly, et al.

The Jean Sanseverino Case

"You want to know how I heard about Bessie Jean's death?" Joann asks. "I had just been married a month, and we were living with his mother right down from my sister Blanche. A photographer from Birmingham, Alabama, knocked on the door. He wanted to know if I had a picture of my older sister from New York. I was young. I said, what has she done, is she getting in the movies or a model or getting something exciting? And he looked so sad, his face drained of color, and he said, 'No, hon, it's to go in the paper. Your sister's dead.' I ran a half a mile up the dirt path to where my mother was keeping my sister Blanche's children while she worked in Gadsden at Elmore's five and ten." She stops to think. "That was really something, for Gadsden, Alabama. For a young woman to go off and get murdered in New York. It was really something."

A little over a year after she left, Bessie Jean's body came home, by train, in a plain wood box. She was clothed in a terry cloth robe, and her hand was puffy. "Of course it would be, she was out so long." Ray took his time releasing her body. It wasn't until Bessie's uncle

173

Charlie got on the phone that Ray agreed to allow her body to come home to Alabama. Bessie's parents didn't have any money. Uncle Charlie paid for her body to be returned to Webster's Chapel. Bessie's mother's wedding ring wasn't on her finger when her body was returned. Lillie wrote her roommate Sylvia several times, asking about the ring and other things, but never received a response.

Bessie was buried in a pink chiffon dress at Oak Grove Baptist Church Cemetery in Glencoe, where her family went occasionally for services and revivals. It was a white wooden church then; it's brick now. The ground was frozen on March 14, the day of the funeral, and there were snow flurries. Bessie's Gadsden friends and former bosses, F. C. Elrod, Claude Smart, and Guy Alford, were among the pallbearers. Lillie and Lawrence East never really got over Bessie Jean's death. Like the parents of Christine Diefenbach, they endured this loss every day of their lives until their own deaths.

■

Bessie Jean's body was found by her roommate, Sylvia Krumholz, at 11:35 in the morning on Thursday, March 8, 1951. Detective Duffy of the 82 Squad caught the case that would defeat him and every other detective that looked at it. They didn't have a lot to go on. There wasn't much in the way of crime scene analysis in those days. James D. Watson and Francis Crick were still two years away from discovering the double-helix structure of DNA. Still, detectives began their cases the same way. They started by talking to people. But everyone has their own version of the truth, and all of their stories have to be questioned. "You have to ask yourself, what do they need to be true," Wendell Stradford explains. When Bessie Jean wrote her mother to say, "We're doing fine, know it's going to remain that way," when things couldn't possibly have been less fine, perhaps that's what Bessie needed her mother to hear to protect her from worry.

Later, detectives have to consider how time has altered people's memories. It's been fifty-two years since Joann saw her big sister off at the Gadsden bus station. When we first spoke, Ray Sanseverino's oldest son knew less about his father's history than I did. The people in Alabama who knew Bessie Jean or who were living in the area at the time told me two things: that Bessie Jean was strangled with a black bra, and that after he killed her, the murderer cut her mother's wedding ring off her finger. Neither turned out to be true. It had been up to Detective Duffy to figure out what happened at the time, and we already know he failed. All we know is that after Jean got on that bus with curlers in her hair everything went horribly wrong.

After all this time, and with a killer who is probably long dead, does it even matter that over half a century ago someone either didn't care or couldn't stop themselves from holding a girl down and doing the worst possible thing one person can do to another? Sixty-four of the sixty-five murders in Brooklyn that year were cleared, every one but Bessie Jean's. What is one unsolved murder?

■

Detectives keep their case files in brown accordion-style folders that look like something schoolchildren might carry. The older files are tied shut with string; the newer ones are sealed with Velcro. If it's a complex case, and the folders start piling up, they're moved into cardboard cartons. As the case grows, the detectives start stacking cartons. The cartons for Etan Patz, the six-year-old boy who disappeared from SoHo in 1979, fill an entire wall. Christine Diefenbach's take up a shelf. Jean Sanseverino has one collapsing brown folder. The manila card stock has lost its snap and it's beginning to feel more like cloth.

Inside Jean's folder are the remains of what all her New York friends, boyfriends, neighbors, acquaintances, and suspects had to say for themselves. After 1951, few of them appear again in any public record. People who lived in the same neighborhood can't recall them. Except for the few fragments inside the folder, the people around Jean at the time of her death came and went without leaving a single mark. In a tiny rural community in Alabama with no name, no electricity, and no plumbing, people remember you. In a large metropolitan city like New York, where countless people have since slept quietly in the room where you endured the ultimate annihilation, you're less than the air you were denied.

When Jean rejoined Ray in March 1950, they lived for a time with Ray's sister and her husband, Eleanor and John Kraus, in the Bedford-Stuyvesant section of Brooklyn. They weren't entirely happy there, and Jean was glad when they moved into their own apartment at 372 State Street, in an area in south Brooklyn then called North Gowanus and now called Boerum Hill. "Boy I'm thrilled to death," she wrote her mother. "While we were at Eleanor & Johnny's we had to pay $10.00 a week & everything was so damm dirty. The damm mean kids drove me crazy. That Jeannie is the meanest brat I've ever seen. At least we have a clean place & a good bed that's not pissy ha ha."

State Street was already well into a period of decline. After World War II, the charming brownstones changed from one-family homes to rooming houses and places that rented by the hour. The Brooklyn Navy Yard was nearby, and when the ships came in, the girls came out. Prostitutes walked around making no effort to hide what they were up to. "We weren't allowed to walk down State Street," a woman who grew up nearby remembered. The older neighbors occasionally complained and patrolmen were assigned to see what they could do, but times being what they were, the women had few options, and a couple of men in blue were not going to keep them away for long. In those days girls would go to a man's room and have sex for five dollars.

Jean and Ray got a great deal on State Street, though. They lived rent free in exchange for light housekeeping duties. "It's a good break Mom," Jean wrote. "It's nothing at all to do. Oh yes besides we get $20 extra every month. Ray is very good to me. We have lots of fun now that we're all alone."

The next nine months of their life is one big blank. Then, a twenty-two-year-old waitress named Sylvia Krumholz moved into 372 State Street. If things had been genuinely fine, which doesn't seem likely, they were about to change. Sylvia and Jean "were always running parties," the landlady, Barbara Curtis, complained to the police after the murder.

By the end of January, whatever was left of Jean and Ray's relationship was over. Inside the case folder is an old bank deposit slip with a note penciled on the back.

To Whom it May Concern:

I, Raymond P. Sanseverino, consent to give my wife Bessie Jean (East) Sanseverino, full rights to proceed divorce action against me as of January 27, 1951. I agree not to interfere in any way with proceedings filed against me, so long as fair play is insued [sic]. I will not consent to divorce if unfair action is used against me.

Soon after writing this declaration, he moved into the Brooklyn Navy YMCA at 167 Sands Street and slept on a couch in the lobby. After five days they gave him a room and a locker and a job as a short-order cook. Ray wanted Jean to go back home to her family on Webster's Chapel Road, but Jean had other ideas. "I'm going to stay in New York and have fun," she told him and anyone who would listen. She would be dead in a month.

Two weeks after settling in at the Y, Ray met Marie Rizzo. Detectives used to be infuriatingly casual about spelling names and other facts, such as house numbers, which change from DD5 to DD5. Marie's last name appears sometimes as Rizzo and sometimes as Russo. Marie Rizzo/Russo was the ward of Carrie Boyd, who owned a building at 180 St. John's Place.

This may not have been the first time Ray and Marie lived in the same place. Twenty years earlier, Raymond's mother put all her children in orphanages. According to the 1930 Federal Census, Raymond and his sister Eleanor were living in the New York Foundling Hospital on East 68th Street at the same time as a two-year-old foundling named Marie Rizzo, possibly the same Marie Rizzo. The age fits. Perhaps they discovered their common roots, and it became a bond between them.

On February 7, Ray cleaned out his locker at the Y, collected his final paycheck, and moved into the basement at 180 St. John's Place.

Jean stayed closer to the home she and Ray briefly shared. She and Sylvia found a room a block away, at 366 State Street. They needed a little money to move in, so Jean wrote her mother and Mrs. East sold her sewing machine for fifty dollars to Mary Johnson, their neighbor across the street. The money order arrived on February 3.

"Received money will write you tonight," Jean telegrammed her mother right away. "Don't worry everything going good Love Jean." There were some problems with the new room. The heat didn't always come up and sometimes Jean and Sylvia had to light the oven to keep warm. They didn't have a private bath. But there were pretty tin ceilings, and wallpaper with flowers. And the windows looked out on trees and a church across the street with an open lot next door, which combined to give the place a light, restful feel.

The next few weeks are another blank. We don't really know what happened. Then, between Saturday, March 3, and the early morning hours of Thursday, March 8, the last days of Jean's life, one troubled swirl of activity after another kicked up around Jean. She had bounced from man to man and had set so many erotic disturbances into motion that decades later Detective Wendell Stradford has the same problem the original detectives had, picking the most likely suspect from such a crowded field.

The aging DD5s in Jean's folder detail her final week. First, Ray Sanseverino had a fistfight with Bill Miller, a thirty-six-year-old sheet-metal worker who worked in Queens and who, up until two days before, had lived at 372 State Street, where Jean and Ray used to live. Miller's landlady asked for his back rent and he left without paying instead. Like Jean, Bill Miller didn't move far. He found another room two blocks east, at 490 State Street. There's no record of what the fight was about. Roomers at 372 State Street said that Jean didn't like Miller, and she complained about the smell in Miller's room whenever she had to clean it.

The night after the scuffle between Ray and Miller, March 4, Jean went to the Sheridan Bar & Grill, a favorite hangout on Atlantic and Hoyt, a block and a half from where she lived. When she left for the ladies' room, a man known only as Red tried to follow her, but the night cook, Vassillios Evangelinos, a thirty-three-year-old sailor whom everyone called Bill the Greek, stopped him.

Bill the Greek was very close to Jean, and they frequently spent the night together. According to her roommate, Sylvia, he and Jean would often stay in bed all day until Bill had to work at night. But sometimes Jean would tell him to go home. She'd say she was afraid Ray might find them together, which may indicate that Jean and Ray still had some semblance of a relationship even though they were living apart. But maybe that's just what Jean said when she wanted Bill to leave.

Jean had lots of boyfriends. Bill the Greek was not the only one. There was a guy named Al. He dressed neat, had beauty marks on his face, and according to one detective's notes, "Jean really liked him." She bragged about the time Al and his brother gave Bill Miller "a licking." And, when she and Ray split, Jean told friends that she wasn't going back to Alabama because she knew "a fellow with a six room apartment and he would take care of her." However, Bill the Greek was her most constant companion. More than one person said they saw Bill either coming or going from 366 State Street during the weeks before she was killed.

Three nights later. Wednesday, March 7, the last night of Jean's life, was also the night of the big heavyweight match in Detroit between Ezzard Charles, aka the Cincinnati Flash, who was defending his title, and Jersey Joe Walcott. Everyone in Jean's circle of friends was sitting in one bar or another, watching the fight on TV. The fight began after 10:00 p.m. Charles and Walcott went fifteen rounds, but Walcott lost and Charles got to keep his heavyweight title, briefly. He lost it to Walcott four months later in Pittsburgh. Ray Sanseverino watched the fight with Carrie Boyd and Marie Rizzo/ Russo over at 180 St. John's Place, then went to bed.

At eleven o'clock that night, Jean was back at the Sheridan Bar &
Grill. A lot of people she knew were there. Sylvia Krumholz was
there. Another good friend, Margaret Hunter, who went by the
nickname Frankie, was there. Frankie was a nineteen-year-old unemployed salesgirl who had just gotten out of the Villa Loretta
Home for Wayward Girls in Peekskill, New York, where she'd been
committed when she was sixteen, four months after her mother
died. Run by the Sisters of the Good Shepherd, Villa Loretta was
where you went if you were young and in trouble, but not yet
prison material, and they wanted to get you on the right path.

A number of people at the Sheridan that night lived on State
Street, it turned out, including Joe Moore, aka Big Joe, a forty-five-
year-old sailor who lived at number 318. Elias Fellours, a twenty-six-
year-old from number 304, made a tentative date with Jean to see
the singer Johnny Lee at the Manhattan Center on Sunday. Fellours
told police that he had known Jean for about six months, but he had
"never had her." Elias went home at 11:45.

David Poole, who lived at number 352, walked into the Sheridan
at 12:30 in the morning, after getting off work at Con Ed. He hung
out with Sylvia while Jean sat alone in a booth, not drinking. David
and Sylvia had something to eat and left at one in the morning.
They walked to 79 Bond Street, where Sylvia knocked on the window of her boyfriend Joe Bernard's room. Bernard let her in and
David continued home.

Bill Miller showed up at the Sheridan next. Although some said
Jean didn't like him, Miller, who in a description later given to detectives was said to be missing three teeth and the thumb on his
right hand, sat down with Jean, who was still alone, and they drank
a few highballs. Jean shared the steak Bill ordered for himself. Then,
sometime around 2:00 or 2:30 a.m., Bill said he wanted to go home.
Jean wasn't ready for him to leave her. "Take me where you took
Frankie last night," she suggested. Bill the Greek was not at all
happy when he saw them walk out together, and he complained repeatedly to Joseph Russo, the bartender at the Sheridan Bar & Grill.

Inexplicably, Jean and Bill took a cab to Terry's Bar & Grill, which was only four short blocks away. Neither of them had much money. Perhaps Jean was wearing heels and Bill wanted to impress her. When they got to Terry's it was closing, so they went two doors down to the 7 Corners Bar & Grill instead. Later, the bartender at Terry's hinted that they weren't actually closing when Jean and Bill arrived. He didn't want to serve them because they were drunk.

Ben Hapoienu, the owner of the 7 Corners Bar & Grill, poured Jean and Bill more highballs, and Seagram's 7 and ginger ale. Bill Miller didn't like the guy at the jukebox. "Some strange fellow kept looking at her," he said. Jean noticed him, too. She gave him a look that prompted Miller to tell her "not to pick anyone up in the joint." But Jean wandered away from Miller anyway, and over to the cigarette machine. "How do you work this thing?" she asked Bill Gerber, the man standing at the jukebox. Gerber was thirty years old and a bartender from a local bar. "Push it," he answered. Jean turned to the jukebox. "Pick a number." Gerber later told police that Jean "appeared to be on the make." She was "trying to be a bobby-soxer and he [Miller] looks like a pug," he said.

Richard Heaney, who also lived on State Street, was at the 7 Corners with his friend Johnny Neary, watching the whole thing. Both were members of the Bartender's Union, and Heaney was currently running for election, he later told detectives, although he never said for which office.

According to Heaney, Miller put a ten-dollar bill on the bar to pay for a drink. When he turned back he had four dollars in change. It should have been nine dollars. Don't ask the bartender about the short change, Jean insisted. Later, the bartender said that Jean "clipped the five dollars from the change." At some point during the evening, Jean told Miller she was meeting someone else later.

Richard Heaney left the 7 Corners at 3:00 a.m. for another bar. Bill Gerber, the jukebox man, followed him twenty minutes later. Miller was looking at him funny, he said, and he didn't want any trouble.

When the Sheridan Bar & Grill closed at 4:00 a.m., Bill the Greek and the bartender Joe Russo walked together down Hoyt Street toward the A train. Bill the Greek was nervous and upset, Russo told the detectives. "He did not like the idea of Miller taking her out." "Jean was supposed to come back," he recalled Bill saying repeatedly. "She said she'd come back." But she never did. He also told Russo that "Jean had taken Miller to her room for sex." Russo and Bill the Greek boarded the A train together and got to the 42nd Street station around 4:25 a.m.

Joe Moore went straight home when the Sheridan Bar & Grill closed.

Just after 4:00 a.m., Jean and Bill Miller left the 7 Corners Bar and started walking west on State Street. They walked only a few feet and Miller fell down in front of the old Oxford Theatre, where fifteen years before on the very same spot scared and desperate strippers stood and cried when the burlesque show that had run for so many years there finally closed and they were thrown out of work. Miller got up and they walked a few more yards. "Come up and see my lousy room I am living in now," he said. No, Jean answered. I'm meeting someone, Miller told detectives she told him. Jean then walked quickly away down State Street, toward her room farther west. Miller gave slightly different versions of this story each time he told it. In one version he said he was having trouble walking. "I told her to go ahead, and she walked in front." In another, Jean pushed him down. One piece never changed. Bill Miller said he last saw Jean when she reached Third Avenue, half a block from where he fell.

According to everyone's stories, at a little after four in the morning, Jean, Bill the Greek, Joe Moore, and Bill Miller were all within four blocks of each other, or closer. Jean was walking west on State Street. Bill Miller was limping west to 490 State Street, behind her. Joe Moore was walking west on the same street, toward his room at number 318. Bill the Greek was walking north on Hoyt, past State Street, on his way to the A train at Schermerhorn. Depending on the timing, Jean and Bill the Greek would have been within half a block of each other. By his own account and confirmed by both Carrie Boyd and Marie, Ray Sanseverino was sleeping a mile and three quarters away at 180 St. John's Place.*

The next hour is crucial but little about it is known. A cab driver named Louis Castro was dropped off at his 366 State Street room at 4:55 by his partner, Alfred Diaz. Fifteen minutes later he woke up landlady Mary Friga to complain about the noise in Jean's room. Mary and Louis climbed one flight to Jean's room on the second floor and knocked. No answer. Mary put her ear to the door. She reported hearing a loud noise that sounded like someone falling to the floor, then three or four heavy footsteps. Then she said she heard the soft sobbing of a woman and a man shushing her. Louis said he heard grunts. When they didn't hear anything else they both went back downstairs to bed. Neither Mary nor Louis nor anyone else called the police.

Three sixty-six State Street is a small four-story brownstone. If Jean had screamed even once, everyone in the building would have heard. Mrs. Urso, who had a room on the same floor as Jean, said she never heard a word. Jean didn't or couldn't yell for help when Mary knocked.

The medical examiner later estimated that Jean Sanseverino died around 5:30 in the morning. Sometime between 6:00 and 8:00 a.m., Rudolph Skeet, another roomer at 366 State Street, said he heard "a sofa" knock up against the wall in Jean's apartment.

Sylvia Krumholz came home from her boyfriend Joe Bernard's a few hours later, at 11:35. She telephoned Bernard. "Come over quick," a DD5 states that she said. "It looks like Jean is out from a beating." Jean had already been dead for four to almost six hours. Sylvia must not have looked too closely. When the police arrived, Bernard was on the stoop waiting for them.

*See map on page 200.

It's hard to say if Jean would have been safer if she had gone home to Alabama, as Ray desired, instead of staying in New York to have fun. While there were sixty-five murders in Brooklyn in 1951, and none at all in the Webster's Chapel area where Jean grew up, Alabama was actually more murderous than New York that year. New York had 1.27 murders per 100,000 people, and Alabama had 15.27.

▪

The first man on the scene was Patrolman Eugene McCarthy from the 82 Precinct. The Brooklyn West Homicide Squad was called to let them know that "a white girl was found DOA at 366 State Street." Whenever there was a murder in those days, a detective from the nearest Homicide Squad would be assigned in addition to the detective from the local precinct who caught the case. They'd help each other out and share information, but each detective would write up and maintain separate DD5s, and both would work the case from beginning to end. These days, someone from the Homicide Squad will help chase down leads the first day or two, and try to provide some expertise, but it's primarily the precinct detective's case. Unless it's something high profile, the Homicide Squad detective will be on to something else in a day or two. "They can't spend a great deal of time with the precinct squad, they have to be the cavalry and assist the other squads," Spano says.

In 1951 the lead guys on the Jean Sanseverino case were Detective Walter J. Duffy, a good-looking Irish guy with brown curly hair and glasses, from the 82, and Detective William J. Kelly from Brooklyn West Homicide Squad. Duffy was a 1st-grade detective, and there were even fewer 1st-grade detectives in those days, and the 82 was a busy precinct. Their territory covered the waterfront. Detective Kelly showed up with his captain and another patrolman. Detectives from the Brooklyn Photo Gallery and the Police Laboratory followed. The assistant medical examiner walked in, pronounced Jean dead on arrival, and ordered her body removed to the Kings County Morgue for an autopsy.

Over the next couple of days, more than a hundred different detectives, suspects, and witnesses did everything they could think of to either find, supply, or hide information. The killer faced possible death by electric chair. The other men probably preferred that no one learn what they sometimes did with Jean. And the detectives knew that if they didn't have the case nailed within a week, they probably never would. "You've got one initial shot at the crime scene, witnesses, and suspect," Vito Spano explains. "You want to get it right the first time, and quickly, so time does not slip by and you lose your opportunity to maximize your evidence and solve the case."

When the police arrived, Jean was lying on her back in a bed, dressed in white socks, a black bra, and a blue sweater, which was pushed above her breasts. A pencil was stuck in her bra, pointing to her chin. One line of blood trailed out of her mouth and down her cheek, and her black slip was lying on the floor beside the bed.

When asked about the significance of the pencil, Spano initially theorizes, "Maybe he was trying to retrieve something without leaving a print or mark or trace of something." But this was before DNA analysis was available to them, so Spano goes in a different direction. "People had a different view of sexuality in the early fifties. Women were held to a higher moral standard than men. This guy may have been upset over her behavior. Maybe it was meant to symbolize some sort of black mark on her soul." Are killers usually that poetic? "Yes," Spano answers.

Jean's family was told that Sylvia cleaned up before noticing anything was wrong, but that doesn't seem likely. Detectives described the excrement they found everywhere. Sylvia would have guessed the minute she walked in that something terrible had happened. There also isn't any evidence of housecleaning in the crime scene photographs. An ashtray full of cigarette butts sits on an ottoman in front of the bed. Clothes and papers cover every surface in the room. A box of feminine napkins is sitting out on a table in front of the fireplace that didn't work.

The detectives started bringing everyone with information back to the 82 for questioning, beginning with Rudolph Skeet, who lived in Jean's building, Sylvia Krumholz, and Bill the Greek, who spoke with a very thick accent, one detective wrote. Also questioned that day were Bill the Greek's roommates, Bill Gourgouvas and George Dougatzis; Joseph Russo, the bartender at Sheridan Bar & Grill; Rusty Ruenes, the bartender at the Alcazar Bar & Grill across the street; Eleanor Kraus, Raymond's sister; Jean's landlady, Mary Friga; Louis Castro, the cab driver who heard the noise in Jean's room; and Joe Moore, who called Jean "Bams," and passed along an intriguing piece of gossip. He told detectives that he had heard that Jean, Sylvia, and Frankie solicited. Given the girls' background and prospects, and the neighborhood where they were living, it's plausible. Maybe for Jean it wouldn't have been for much longer. Bill the Greek said he planned to marry her.

"If she is soliciting, she's not doing it like a streetwalker," Spano says. "She is doing it with men she has a relationship with." He tries to imagine her state of mind. "She wants to be happy. Her husband left her, she doesn't have family around her. She is looking for attention or love or comfort and this is a means for her to find it. The problem is, this is high risk-behavior and it would have made her highly vulnerable to violence."

In the first few hours of the investigation the detectives knew there was a husband named Raymond Sanseverino but no one knew where he lived or worked. Someone said he didn't have a job and was homeless, and a detective wrote "possibly a transient." Someone else said they heard he was staying at a Y.

Later in the afternoon, a woman living across the street from Jean told Mary Friga that she saw Jean walk in the door to 366 State Street at five in the morning with a tall man, but that was all the description she could offer.

Sometime that day, Detective Kelly called the INS about Bill the Greek. Bill had jumped ship in Baltimore in 1949, they told him, and had come to New York to stay with his sister and her husband in Brooklyn. In photographs, Vassilios Evangelinos always appears well dressed and groomed. He doesn't have the tough beaten-down-but-just-try-messing-with-me look of longshoremen and sailors. Perhaps he didn't start out on the sea. Greece lost a lot of young men in World War II, and a number of factories there stopped operating. Getting a job on a ship became the thing to do. The INS told Kelly that Bill was ordered deported on November 29, 1949, but was granted a new hearing on March 13, 1950. They released him on a thousand-dollar bond, and he was currently "still at liberty under the thousand-dollar bond."

A couple of detectives went back to Bill the Greek's apartment on Forty-fifth Street in Manhattan at the end of the afternoon to question his roommates about the morning Jean died, but neither of them had seen him come in that night or leave the next morning. Before they left, the detectives took all of Bill's clothes and brought them back to the 82.

Early that evening, four unidentified middle-aged men discussed Jean's murder at a bar on the northwest corner of Pacific and Hoyt streets. "The night cook at the Sheridan Bar & Grill did the job," they were overheard saying. The detectives had their own opinion by that time, too. Even in 1951 they knew how quickly a case can go cold, and they were already beginning to focus on four main suspects: Raymond Sanseverino, Bill the Greek (Vassillios Evangelinos), Bill Miller, and Joe Moore. "Four good suspects," Spano clarifies. "They had motive, means, and opportunity."

Later that night, Detective Kelly sat down and called every YMCA in Brooklyn looking for Raymond Sanseverino, without success. "They didn't want to just speak to him," Spano points out. "They wanted to actually see him. By now they knew what her behavior was like, and he might have strangled her out of a jealous rage. Maybe he has scratch marks. He was their best suspect," Spano says. "They would have been thinking what I would have been thinking, almost a full day has passed since the start of the case and they haven't located him. A prime suspect. The detectives were probably wired to find him."

At 1:15 in the morning, twenty hours after Jean was murdered, Bill Miller showed up at the 7 Corners Bar to meet her. They'd made plans to meet the night before, and he hadn't heard. "Do you remember me," he asked Ben Hapoienu, the owner and the bartender from the night before. "I was with a nice-looking girl?" Ben showed Miller the newspaper and the article about Jean's murder. Miller's reaction, according to Ben, was to say that he recognized the man in the picture as Ray, but that the woman couldn't be Jean. (It was.) Miller didn't appear nervous or strained, Hapoienu said. He mentioned falling down in front of the Oxford the night before and bruising his right knee.

Bill Gerber walked into the 7 Corners Bar at 2:00 a.m. He hadn't heard about Jean, either. When Hapoienu told him she had been murdered his only recorded reaction was, "It was a good thing I went home early." Miller left the bar an hour later. The next morning, the foreman at Bill Miller's job told him the police were looking for him. When the detectives talked to him shortly after, Miller told them about his evening with Jean. He also told them he was divorced and hadn't visited his two children for seven months.

Dr. George W. Ruger's autopsy report showed up that afternoon. Jean died of manual strangulation at approximately 5:30, he declared, and she had had sex just before death. "You see that a lot," Dr. Robert Shaler, the head of Forensic Biology at the OCME, explains. "There's a problem to begin with. Maybe he wants sex, she doesn't, but she gives in, maybe because he's angry and if she gives in this will put him off, and 'I can get rid of him.' And then it continues afterwards and she dies."

Jean's eyes were red and congested and had tiny red dots— petechiae—a common side effect of strangulation. The left side of Jean's face was swollen. Her upper and lower lip were split, probably from a punch or a slap, and there were two areas of bruising on her chin. Her chin was also scratched, another common effect of strangulation. The victim lowers their chin to protect their neck. There were more bruises and scratches on her neck and upper chest, a group of three bruises on her right breast, possibly from fingers holding her down, and a bruise on the back of her right hand. Looking over Jean's autopsy report fifty years later, a senior medical examiner said brightly and without humor, "That's love."

In 1951, they couldn't measure alcohol levels as exactly as they can now. They used a scale of 1 to 4. Jean measured at 3+. She must have been plastered, but she probably sobered up quickly. "Being strangled—having your neck grasped and crushed until the blood stops flowing, and the air gets trapped in your throat and the small blood vessels in your face and eyes start to pop—hurts," Dr. Jonathan Hayes, a senior medical examiner at the OCME, explains. "Eventually, the victim will lose consciousness, but her struggling can prolong her own suffering, as she repeatedly pushes away the killer's hands, briefly letting the breath flow and the blood circulate again, before they are abruptly cut off as the hands go back around her neck and the choking continues." Richard Speck, who murdered eight student nurses in 1966, said it took up to five minutes to strangle someone.

The detectives were at this point beginning the process of confirming everyone's stories, and seeing what else they could pick up about their suspects. After reading the autopsy report, Detective Kelly went to Holy Family Hospital to check Bill the Greek's claim that he had been treated for a cut on his nose on January 8. Kelly learned that Bill did in fact receive four stitches for a cut on the left side of his nose, a little after midnight. He told the doctor the cut had been made by glass.

Detectives then searched Joseph Moore's furnished room on the second floor of 318 State Street. They found nothing of value. His landlady, Mrs. Clarice Austin, said she's never had a single complaint about Moore, who'd been living there for two years. As far as she knew, he never brought a woman to his room or acted disorderly. "He spends most of his time away at sea," she told them.

They interviewed Moore's neighbors next. One woman said Frankie Hunter rang her bell at nine o'clock the week before, asking for Moore. She came back again at ten, saying she wanted to get some money from him. This was the first time the neighbor ever saw a white girl asking for Moore, who was black. She'd seen colored girls leaving Moore's room, but never white girls, and never Jean.

Once again, detectives picked up Bill the Greek, who was at his sister and brother-in-law's, and took him into custody for further questioning at the 82.

They also went back to George Tsaprones, the owner of the Sheridan Bar & Grill. On the night of the murder, Bill the Greek took off his cook's jacket, put on a "civilian coat," and left for half an hour. When he got back he told Tsaprones that he'd gone across the street to the Alcazar Bar and Grill for a couple of beers. They talked to Rusty Ruenes, the owner of the Alcazar. Bill looked nervous, Tsaprones told the detectives.

At some point during the day on March 9, Jean's husband, Ray Sanseverino, showed up at the 82 Precinct on Butler Street with his sister, Eleanor. They had been looking all over for him, still working their way through every YMCA in town. And here he was, walking in on his own. "The uniform cops downstairs would not have gotten excited by this," Spano says. "They don't have the same interest in the case as the detectives sitting upstairs in the squad room. But if I was upstairs and received the call that he was there, I would have been telling the desk sergeant to make sure he doesn't leave, we will be right down. I would not have just casually said send him up." The detectives questioned him for an entire afternoon, but there is no DD5 describing the interrogation, only some handwritten notes.

"I suspect it was the preliminary interview," Vito Spano says. "And the investigators felt that his statement was inconsistent or not forthcoming, and they wanted another crack at him. Or, they wanted to corroborate or disprove his statement before going forward and memorializing it on a DD5."

Detectives have to be very careful about what they write on a DD5. "It could come back to bite you on the ass," Spano explains.

"Everything you memorialize on a DD5 is given to the defense when they file a pretrial discovery motion."

"Criminal investigations go in many different directions in the beginning," Spano continues. For instance, when detectives arrived at 366 State Street, they didn't know what had happened. Jean had been with a number of men that last night, and there were a lot of leads to follow. "As the investigation progresses, issues become clearer. We're not all over the road looking at different suspects, motives, and time lines, trying to determine what events transpired.

"But anything you wrote on those 5s may be used by the defense as ammunition to attack your case." If they wrote in a DD5 that they suspected Raymond Sanseverino, for example, but all later evidence suggested that it was Bill Miller, Miller's attorney could use that early DD5 to defend his client. "You were so sure it was the husband," the attorney could say, to introduce reasonable doubt. "Now the prosecution has to explain away the inconsistencies in the case," Vito concludes.

Detectives never forget that their DD5s are going to be pored over by the defense. The very absence of a DD5 on Raymond Sanseverino could indicate that he was their number one suspect. They were just waiting until they had his story straight.

Raymond said he was living at 180 St. John's Place with Carrie Boyd and Marie Rizzo/Russo. It is not known how formal the relationship was between Carrie Boyd and Marie Rizzo/Russo. Was Carrie her legal guardian? Or did Carrie simply take in a young girl without family, perhaps also in exchange for some help around the house? Carrie operated what detectives described as a "sort of nursing home" for the elderly at 180 St. John's Place, and probably could have used the help.

The last time Raymond had been inside Jean's room was three weeks before, to get his watch and ring, which he immediately pawned on Atlantic Avenue. After questioning him for hours, Captain Peter Terranova of the 17th Detective District announced to the press that "he is not a suspect and at the present time, we believe he has no connection with the murder." This had nothing whatsoever to do with what they truly believed. If they weren't going to write it up on a DD5, they damn well weren't going to tell the press.

There's a picture of the lock to Jean's room among the crime scene photographs. According to Wendell Stradford, the lock does not look tampered with. Either Jean let her killer in or he let himself in, and by the end of the day detectives knew that both Ray Sanseverino and Bill the Greek had keys to Jean's apartment.

The next day, detectives talked to Mr. Banat, Bill Miller's landlord, who saw Miller hours after Jean's murder. "They're trying to find a witness to corroborate Miller's story," Spano explains. "They want to either eliminate or implicate him, and they want to do it quickly, so they can focus their energy on the other suspects."

Banat was in the building at 7:30 that morning, cleaning the rooms and changing the sheets. He got to Miller's room at 8:30 and changed his sheets, but he didn't see Miller until he came back later to mop the floors. That was around 12:30. Miller was home by then, and lying in bed fully dressed.

"Why aren't you at work?" he asked Miller. Miller told him that he got paid the day before, and that he went out and got drunk with some friends he used to work with. He didn't mention Jean. He tells Banat that he fell asleep on the bus to work and rode past his stop. "And being that he didn't feel too good, he came back home to sleep." Banat said there was a stain on Miller's right sleeve, "which to me looked like blood." Miller paid him $7.50, the rent for the coming week, and that was the sum total of conversation that day. While Banat was on the top floor of Miller's building cleaning, someone came in around 9:00 a.m. and went into the bathroom next to Miller's room. The person stayed there until Banat left to take care of another building. Banat thought that whoever it was, he was avoiding him. Normally, he says, his tenants would come out to say hello.

Detectives went to Jean's room to search in vain for the five-dollar bill that Jean had taken from the bar the night she died. "A waste of time," Wendell says. "What does it prove? They want to confirm Miller's story, but even if they found it, how are they going to prove that the five-dollar bill they found is the one she took from Miller? Any decent defense attorney would have that thrown out in seconds." Then they canvassed four buildings on State Street and interviewed thirty-seven people to see if anyone had seen or heard anyone go into Jean's building the morning of the murder. "Doing a thorough neighborhood canvass in the vicinity of a homicide scene is basic fundamental detective work till this day," Spano says. "Always will be." No one in Jean's neighborhood had seen anything.

Detective Kelly continued to talk to people well past midnight. Then, at three in the morning, a woman who lived next door to Jean on the second floor told him that she had woken up at 3:30 a.m. the night of the murder. She'd gone in to pull a blanket over her sleeping daughter, and when she looked out the window to see if her car was all right, she saw a man and woman go into 366 State Street. Maybe it wasn't a complete and total waste of time knocking on every God damn door, Kelly might have thought, before the woman said she couldn't tell him who they were.

"Canvassing is tedious, repetitive work," Wendell explains. "And you have to keep going back. You look at who lived in which apartments, and who actually had a view of your scene. Maybe you get lucky, but usually on the first night people tell you they didn't see anything. Or you knock and no one's home. You have to go back a second and a third time. It was five years before a neighbor of Esteban and Linda's admitted to me that she saw the killers leaving the apartment."

Sylvia Krumholz came by the 82 later with a letter that had arrived the day before for Jean. The note began, "Dear Jean, I just can't go through with it . . . I know my wife is having me watched day and night . . . ," and was signed simply, "Johnny." The post office stamps indicate that the letter had been mailed either Thursday or Friday, picked up by a postman in Maspeth, Queens, on Friday, and distributed from the larger post office branch in Flushing that morning. Would the detectives have thought they finally caught a break? "Maybe," Spano answers. "But I don't think so. They already know Jean is popular and has a lot of male friends. If anything they're feeling frustration because now they have yet another lead to follow, another element to corroborate."

Detectives had so far come across two men named John in the investigation—Jean's brother-in-law, John Kraus, and John Johansson. Witnesses placed Johansson at the Sheridan that night but the detectives hadn't gotten to him yet. There would be a third Johnny— bartender Johnny Neary—but his name would only come up after they interviewed fellow bartender Richard Heaney, who was with him that night at the 7 Corners. Johansson wasn't home when they tried to pick him up, so they brought his wife, Rita, back for questioning instead. She said that on the night of Jean's murder they left the Sheridan at nine o'clock and went home. When she woke up the next morning, her husband was gone, and she found ten dollars and a note explaining that he was shipping out that day.

Detectives checked with the Gulf Oil Corporation, where Johansson worked as a deckhand. The gangway log showed that Johansson boarded his ship the SS *Gulfcrest* in Staten Island at 3:45 a.m., two hours before Jean was strangled. The ship sailed from there to Texas at 1:15 that afternoon. He can't be the Johnny in the letter, they decided. If Johansson had a friend standing watch that night, however, that friend could have signed him in on the log any time he wanted. Given the hour, there'd be few witnesses to either confirm or deny Johansson's presence on the ship at the time Jean died. Even Rita had her suspicions. "I don't know whether he sailed or not," she admitted.

Why didn't the detective pursue Johansson more aggressively? "Just because Jean was sleeping with him doesn't mean he killed her. Jean was sleeping with a lot of guys," Wendell points out. "This guy gave them an alibi they couldn't disprove. They had nothing they could bring to court. They had a lot of suspects. They moved on."

The detectives never talked to John Kraus. And, according to what's in the file, they never looked for any other man named John.

The detectives were continuing to zero in on Raymond Sanseverino, Vassillios Evangelinos (Bill the Greek), Bill Miller, and Joseph Moore, and they were back-burnering "Johnny" the same way the detectives back-burnered Trucker in the Christine Diefenbach case and Robert Mitchell in the Linda Leon–Esteban Martinez double homicide.

That night, everyone at the Sheridan was talking about the letter that had arrived for Jean from "Johnny." They all agreed it was Johnny Johansson. They knew he was seeing Jean. His wife didn't know, but Jean and Johnny had had several dates and Johnny wanted more, they said. Not one person there believed that Johnny actually had gotten on that ship on March 8.

On Monday, March 12, Detective Ira Schwartz from the 82 retraced Bill the Greek's trip home the night of the murder. Schwartz started out from the Sheridan Bar & Grill and took the A train to the Forty-second Street station in Manhattan. Then he crossed the platform, and took the downtown train back to Brooklyn. He wanted to see how long it would have taken Bill the Greek to go home, then turn around and come right back and knock on Jean's door. "Total elapsed time for trip was fifty-one minutes." That would have put Bill the Greek on State Street around 5:00 a.m. Louis Castro was woken up by noise in Jean's room at 5:10 a.m.

While Schwartz was checking Bill the Greek's trip on the subway, Detective Kelly was talking to a dispatcher about Bill Miller's ride on the bus. Then he went to see Benjamin Morgan Vance, the deputy chief medical examiner. Vance was an old-timer. He'd been working at the OCME since 1918, shortly after it was established. He had coauthored a book called *Legal Medicine and Toxicology* in 1937 and was known in law-enforcement circles for the watercolors and pastel sketches he liked to make of crime scenes and autopsies. Kelly gave Vance a man's undershirt (unidentified), and asked him to check it for possible semen stains. He also gave him three envelopes containing scrapings from the fingernails of Bill the Greek, Joe Moore, and Bill Miller. He was hoping to find a piece of physical evidence.

Meanwhile, new information about Joseph Moore came in from Coast Guard Intelligence. Moore had signed off a ship the year before and failed to return because he was in jail. The ship sailed without him, and Moore was currently suing the owners for lost wages and gear, claiming he'd been fired from the ship.

Just before one o'clock that day, Duffy and Kelly went to the Seaman's Institute to wait for Moore, who was due to return that afternoon. They waited until 4:45, but Moore never showed.

Also that day, a laundry ticket was found in the pocket of one of the articles of clothing that had been taken from Bill Miller's room. Desperate to recover a possible key piece of evidence before any trace of the crime was washed away, detectives checked every laundry in the area. They went to the Police Laboratory at 400 Broome Street for help, and a detective took Duffy and Kelly over to a printer on Bayard Street who produced the laundry tickets that were used by all the Chinese laundries in New York. The owner said the ticket was one of his, but they were sold in bulk and they didn't keep records of the purchasers. He couldn't tell them which laundry the ticket came from.

Later in the day, detectives interviewed Carrie Boyd, Raymond's landlady. Even though in truth he'd been living there roughly three or four weeks, Carrie told them that Raymond had been living there for the past three months. She said that Ray had just started working as an elevator operator at Rockefeller Center the week before, which was true, and that he performed odd jobs around the house. He came and went at various hours, she said. On the night of the murder, Ray was home from work at 7:30, and they all had cheese sandwiches and coffee cake for supper. He was in a "jovial mood." They watched TV together until one in the morning, then Raymond went to bed. Carrie woke him up the next morning at 7:30 for breakfast and work. At 8:45, while they were reading the newspapers, Raymond showed her the article about his wife. He put his head on her shoulder and cried. Carrie said that he never left the house that night, and even though the basement has a separate entrance he couldn't leave the basement apartment without her knowledge. When the detectives checked, the front iron gate leading to the basement was locked, and the door to the basement itself was locked from the inside. Yet, in the DD5 they described the thick layer of dust and dirt on the doorsill as having been disturbed.

Marie Rizzo/Russo was questioned next. In her account, Raymond returned home the night after the murder around 8:00 p.m., and asked her to open the basement door. She watched him remove the bar from the basement door, carry in a bundle of clothes, then place the bar back on the door and lock it. The detectives checked Ray's room. They found Jean's clothes, which Raymond had taken from the scene of the homicide. Raymond, who had finally arranged to have Jean's body sent back to her family, may have taken the clothes to select something for her to wear home. Still, it's odd that the DD5s do not describe in any detail the clothes they found. Spano disagrees. "It's not an issue. If he removed the clothing after they released the crime scene—so what?" The detectives took one pair of Raymond's green army fatigue pants, brought them back to Detective Kelly, and never mentioned Jean's clothes again.

In his last interview of the day, Detective Kelly went to see cab driver Joseph Carey, who lived at 435 State Street. Carey told Kelly that he had picked up Jean and a guy from the corner of Atlantic and Hoyt and took them to Terry's Bar & Grill. Kelly checked the time card. Carey punched out that night at 2:30 a.m. The timing matched Bill Miller's story.

■

The next day, Tuesday, March 13, Jean was buried at Oak Grove Church in Glencoe, Alabama. Almost a week had passed and the detectives still didn't have a case. Things moved slower in 1951. "They didn't have databases in the fifties," Spano points out. "They had card files, long drawers full of index cards that took weeks to go through instead of the seconds it takes to search a database today." The detectives were probably starting to feel the pressure to find just one lead that caught fire. With the limited forensics available to them, "they have to rely on witnesses or an admission from the killer, and they had no witness, and so far they hadn't caught any of their suspects in a lie," Spano says.

The detectives started double-checking every story and talking to everyone they could think of. They called the garage where the cab driver Louis Castro worked. They spoke to four roomers who lived on the same floor as Bill Miller, who told detectives they never saw Bill Miller come or go from 10:00 p.m. on the seventh to 9:00 a.m. on the eighth. They interviewed twenty-two employees at the G. M. Ketcham Company in Glendale, Long Island, where Miller worked, trying to find someone who could identify the Venus H pencil they found in Jean's bra. They visited ten bars in Jean's immediate neighborhood. While Jean was known by the owners of eight of them, they were of no help either. One detective rode a neighborhood bus until the end of the line to check if there were any Chinese laundries that might be able to identify the laundry ticket they took from Bill Miller, but he didn't see a single one.

Patrolman Eugene McCarthy, the first cop on the scene, went to the Brooklyn Property Clerk's office on Bergen Street to drop off one white sock, one black brassiere, and one blue knit sweater—the clothing taken from Jean's body. He also dropped off four dollars, some change, one red woman's wallet, and four yellow metal rings. Perhaps one of those rings was the wedding ring the family longed to recover.

For a couple of days, not much of anything happened. Then, Captain Pete Terranova received an anonymous note, written in pencil and postmarked March 12, 1951, 10:30 a.m. *Trail Heaney 46 Hoyt Street He knows Sylvia. Friends got Jean 366 State St go slow, cozy. Investigate. This is hot.* Heaney is Richard Heaney, the bartender who lives at 410 State Street and who was in the 7 Corners Bar with Johnny Neary the night Jean died. They brought him in for questioning.

Heaney admitted to seeing Jean that night, but he didn't know who she was until he read about her murder in the paper the next day. He knew Miller, who came into the bar where Heaney worked. More than once he'd refused to serve him. On the night Jean died, Heaney said Johnny Neary dropped him off at his home on 410 State Street in a cab at 4:15. While Jean was walking west on State Street, Richard Heaney was in a cab with Johnny Neary, heading toward her, stopping one block away from where she lived. That makes five men who were within a block of Jean sometime after 4:00 a.m.: Bill Miller, Bill the Greek, Joseph Moore, and Richard Heaney and his friend Johnny Neary.

So they had a love letter from Johnny. And they had just received another letter that said Heaney's friends "got Jean." They knew that Heaney and his friend Johnny were in the 7 Corners Bar with Jean the night she died and that they were on State Street at around the same time Jean was walking home. Still, there's no record of a conversation between the detectives and Johnny Neary.

Instead, Detective Duffy went back to talk to Ben Hapoienu, the owner of 7 Corners Bar & Grill, perhaps hoping Hapoienu noticed something between Jean and Neary. But Hapoienu only verified that Jean and Bill came in around 2:30 a.m., that they had about five drinks each, and that Jean had taken the five dollars. Miller confronted her about the five dollars, but Jean denied taking it. She said if he kept arguing about it she'd leave. Ben let Jean and Bill out at around 4:10 a.m., and he last saw them heading west on State Street.

At the end of the day, Duffy took two packages to the ME's for analysis. In the first was a "container with human stool found at the scene and to be analyzed for type of food, drugs, etc.," and a pair of women's panties, also covered with excrement. Inside the second was Bill the Greek's tie, fingernail scrapings, and another white cotton undershirt, which Duffy wanted examined for semen stains.

Two days later, on March 17, the Police Laboratory sent Duffy a report dated March 14. They traced a dry-cleaning tag found at the scene back to the YMCA at 167 Sands. The clothing belonged to Ray

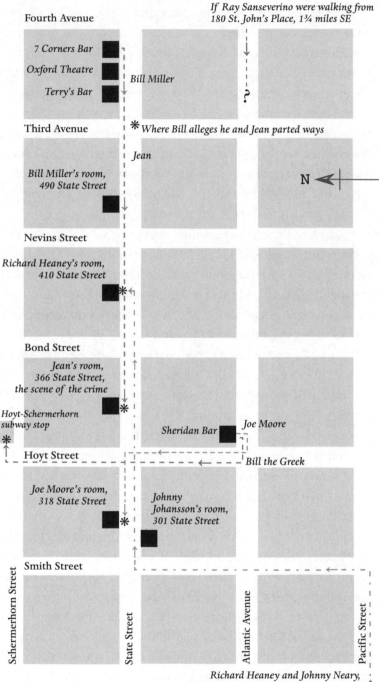

Fourth Avenue

7 Corners Bar

Oxford Theatre

Terry's Bar

Bill Miller

If Ray Sanseverino were walking from 180 St. John's Place, 1¾ miles SE

?

Third Avenue

✱ *Where Bill alleges he and Jean parted ways*

Jean

Bill Miller's room, 490 State Street

N ←

Nevins Street

Richard Heaney's room, 410 State Street

✱

Bond Street

Jean's room, 366 State Street, the scene of the crime

✱

Hoyt-Schermerhorn subway stop

Sheridan Bar

Joe Moore

✱

Hoyt Street

Bill the Greek

Joe Moore's room, 318 State Street

Johnny Johansson's room, 301 State Street

✱

Smith Street

Schermerhorn Street

State Street

Atlantic Avenue

Pacific Street

Richard Heaney and Johnny Neary, heading toward 410 State Street in a cab ↑

Thursday, March 8, 1951. Sometime after 4:00 A.M.

Sanseverino, but it had been picked up before the murder, on February 3. Just another of many leads that went nowhere.

The fingerprint report showed up on Duffy's desk next. They got smudges and partial prints from the scene, but "no fingerprints of value." Another dead lead.

The last report to arrive that day came from Benjamin Vance, the deputy chief medical examiner. He had examined the fingernail scrapings from Bill the Greek, Bill Miller, and Joseph Moore. He found epithelial cells, fiber, tobacco, the down hair of an animal, and, under Bill the Greek's in particular, "much dirt." "All of these findings might occur during ordinary everyday existence and standing alone are not significant," the ME's report read. No help anywhere. After these tests they were no closer to either eliminating or implicating four main suspects, Raymond Sanseverino, Bill the Greek, Bill Miller, and Joe Moore. "At this point you gotta go back and re-interview everyone yet again," Stradford says. "Not the suspects but the people around them. You need to get a better story, and more time has gone by. People are becoming less afraid. They'll tell you more."

Duffy's lieutenant paid a visit to Mrs. Barbara Curtis, Jean and Ray's landlady from 372 State Street. Mrs. Curtis said she put Jean and Ray out on January 8 because Jean never cleaned up all the rooms or put up clean curtains for the holidays like she was supposed to. Jean was always complaining about being sick, but Mrs. Curtis found out later that Jean was a heavy drinker. She wasn't sick every night; she was drunk. She spent all her time at the Sheridan Bar & Grill and left the house filthy, especially the bathroom. All the tenants complained. Once, Jean set her clothes on fire in the room. Another time, she tried to commit suicide by cutting her legs. When Ray went to call the police she said she'd kill herself if he left. She was never friendly with the tenants, Mrs. Curtis said, and she was never friendly with Bill Miller.

Duffy spoke to Miller again on Monday, March 19, but his story hadn't changed. After Miller left the 82, Duffy focused once again on Joseph Moore. He sent a message to the Philadelphia chief of police, asking for information about a February 22, 1951, arrest of Joseph Moore, aka Arnold Berry, aka John Brown, aka Joe Pigiren. He also described a brass key they had found in Jean's wallet and asked the chief if he could find out if the Seaman's Home on Walnut Street used the same key for their rooms or public lockers.

Then Duffy sat down and typed out the contents of the notes found in Jean's purse.

1. A note written in ink on the back of a menu: *Come to 318 State St 2nd floor, front, the door will be open and I'll be waiting for you. Signed, Joe Moore. P.S. The front door will be open.*
2. An address and name written on the back of a restaurant check, in pencil, *W. 45th St. between 9 and 10th, 438 Bill Gourgouvas R5.*
3. Written on the back of a restaurant check in pencil the words *I love you.*
4. A piece of white paper with lipstick imprints and the following written in ink: *W. 45th 9AB No 438 R5 Bill Gourgouvas.*

Bill Gourgouvas was Bill the Greek's roommate. Why was his name on two pieces of paper in Jean's purse? There's no DD5 showing that they ever asked. Bill the Greek was already beside himself with jealousy the night Jean died, knowing that she was out with Bill Miller. If he discovered that night that Jean was seeing his roommate in addition to everyone else, that might have sent him further into a rage.

The next day Moore came back to the 82, where Duffy questioned him once again. He hadn't worked since last September, he told Duffy. He spent his afternoons at a beauty parlor on Atlantic Avenue owned by his landlady. Jean had asked to borrow money the night she died, and that was why he wrote her that note. When Duffy asked him about the February 22 Philadelphia arrest, Moore said he got into a fight on a trolley. He was arraigned the next morning and ordered to leave the city.

Moore's answers were plausible and weren't helping Duffy build a case. Once again he tried to uncover a piece of physical evidence. Duffy went to the Property Clerk and got Jean's bra and sweater and brought it to the ME. He wanted them compared to the fingernail scrapings from Joe Moore, Bill Miller, and Bill the Greek.

A week later Benjamin Morgan Vance sent Duffy the following analysis. *The blue sweater is made up of unbleached and undyed wool fibers and a few blue stained and purple stained fibers. The colored fibers do not closely resemble the colored fibers in the nail scrapings, none of the unbleached and undyed wool fibers are in the nail scrapings. Result: NON-COMMITTAL.* Still nothing.

The Philadelphia Police sent Duffy a message saying that Joe Moore's February arrest was for a drunk and disorderly, and that the Seaman's Home didn't use keys like the one found in Jean's wallet.

It was a long shot but maybe the key would lead them somewhere useful. Detectives hit the streets to find the locker that fit the key. They checked every public building and store in south Brooklyn. Duffy and Kelly eventually traced it to a locker at the YMCA on Sands Street, where Raymond stayed after leaving Jean. They didn't know what they'd find but they were trying everything now. They open it up. The locker was empty except for a single business card. On one side was the preprinted address for a photographer. On the other was a girl's name, address, and telephone number. The card was never mentioned again. If they talked to the photographer or the girl, they didn't write it up on a DD5.

At the Y, Duffy and Kelly met Vincent Rivard, who'd been living there for twenty-six years. He'd been friends with Ray and Jean since the previous summer, and up until a few months prior they'd gone out drinking together two or three times a week. Duffy and Kelly brought him back for questioning. It was Rivard who had gotten Ray the job at the Y. Ray had told Rivard about coming home unexpectedly and finding Bill the Greek in the room with Jean. Rivard said he last saw Jean on February 24, with Sylvia, at a place called the

Victoria. Jean asked how Ray was, and he told her Ray was going into the marines. She cried. "That son-of-a-bitch wanted to send me to Alabama," she said. Then she told Rivard about the man with the six-room apartment who was going to take care of her.

Rivard described Jean as moody. "She was nice one minute, and very nasty the next, and smacked Ray in public." They asked Rivard where he was the night of the murder. Rivard watched the Charles-Walcott fight at the Cozy Spot Bar & Grill on Willoughby and Jay Street, then he left at 11:45 p.m. and went to a bar across the street from the Y, where he had a beer, and went home.

Later that day Duffy got a message from the Criminal Investigation Division of the U.S. Army about Raymond going AWOL and his Honorable Discharge.

After that, things stopped happening on a daily basis. The case was going relentlessly cold. In early April, Kelly sat down and read a letter from Jean's mother to Sylvia Krumholz.

April 6, 1951

Dear Sylvia this is Jean Sanseverino mother writing to you asking you if you can tell me enything about Jean's things I have been so bothered I thought maby you could tell me something I sure would apreshate it if you can be eny help to me I would like to get hur things you let me here from you. I loved my daughter so much and I guss you were hur friend and I sent hur the money to come home on but I no she received the money for I got a tellagram that she did if you know eny thing about hur things you write and let me here from you. I no Jean learned to love you if you can you write and tell me all about it. Just how long it was that hur and Ray was seperated are not She did not have eny of hur rings or hur watch eather did she have them the last time you sean hur they were not eny on hur fanger when she got here so if you loved Jean you write to Mrs. Lillie East Wellington Ala R1

Sylvia never answered.

On April 13, Duffy went back to Jean's apartment. All their leads were going nowhere, they were running out of options—maybe they had missed something. He found a page from an address book with a phone number and the name "Peppy." He traced the number to a candy store on Court Street in Brooklyn. The proprietor told him that a bunch of teenage boys hung out there and got phone calls at the pay phone. Peppy, they learned, was Thomas Pennino, a twenty-year-old prizefighter from the area. They also learned that four capsules of heroin had been found in his car and he was currently out on bail and due to appear in court in two days.

When Thomas Pennino showed up for his court date, Duffy and Kelly were there waiting for him. They brought him back to the 82, and took a sample of his handwriting, and asked him about his whereabouts on March 7 and 8.

Pennino lived with his parents and four brothers, he told them. He worked as a longshoreman, but he was also licensed by the New York State Athletic Commission as a prizefighter. He knew the Sheridan Bar & Grill, and a girl who hung out there named Frankie Hunter. They'd been friends for five years. "We went out on occasion," he said. "We'd spent the night in various hotels." They showed him photographs, and he didn't recognize Jean. When they showed him the slip of paper they found in her room with his name on it, he said, "I gave that to Frankie." On the night Jean was murdered, Pennino was at the movies, then he went to the Clinton Bar & Grill to watch the closing rounds of the Charles-Walcott fight. After that he went home to bed. When they asked him about his arrest he told them he wasn't a drug addict, but one of his four brothers was a user. Pennino is never mentioned again.

Later that day, Duffy and Kelly heard about two men who were seen watching 366 State Street. The two men turned out to be cops who were investigating complaints of prostitution. Duffy and Kelly talked to the patrolmen but they had nothing to offer.

On April 19, detectives got a copy of a letter from Jean's sixteen-year-old sister, Joann. It was dated April 2.

Dear Sirs,

    I am a sister to the slain Mrs. Jean Sanseverino who was found murdered in your town on March 8th, 1951 in a furnished room.

    I would like to know if you have any clues that might lead to the sorry person that did it? If not, let me tell you a few things about the husband Mr. Raymond Sanseverino.

    I lived with Ray & Jean while they were in Alabama & believe me things very seldom went smoothly.

    Ray very seldom had a job and Jean had to support him, but of course she didn't mind because she loved him so dam much.

    One night Ray & Jean & I were talking about money and its evils & Ray got very mad because Jean asked him to try to find a job that made things worse & they began to curse each other Ray jumped up and slapped Jean in the floor & told her "If you ever mention money again so help me God I'll kill you", and that's the way it always was he was forever more threatening her & me too. I really thought he was loco for a while the way he did. Why he came to me one night closed his fingers around my throat & said "Dam Jo, you have a small neck it would be so easy to break so just don't ever make me mad or I might do it". He even told me that he had taken pictures of me nude & that I had a very lovely body and for me to be careful around him he might do something he would regret.

    Please believe me those are just a few sample of what went on I could write 20 pages on times he threatened Jean's life. Now don't misunderstand me I'm not just telling you this just to make it hard on him because if he isn't guilty we can forget about this but I know you didn't know anything about their married life down here.

    I'll admit she wrote home & said he was better to her than he had been but when he left Alabama he left Jean with the intentions of never seeing her again, because he only left a note saying "I've gone to Chicago I'll see you around someday" Jean found the note when she came home from work. She almost went crazy after that, she even wrote a letter to June Pruitt the guy who left with Ray telling him that if he knew where Ray was or any thing about him to please tell him if he didn't come back to her or send for her that she was going to kill herself. Well June of course knew that Ray was staying with his sister in Brooklyn Eleanor is her name and he called Ray & told him about the letter Ray just laughed and said "Well if she doesn't kill herself before she gets here I'll do it for her God dam her". See June Pruitt told me this when we heard of Jean's death.

All Jean's friends down here thinks he did it on the account of they knew how he treated Jean.

I could say a lot more but I'm disgusted writing about him he is so darn sorry. So in closing I'll say when you're through with her clothes & belongings send them to this address C.O.D Mrs. Blanche Vice, Glencoe, Alabama.

And by the way my name is Jo just ask Mr Ray Sanseverino if he doesn't remember me.

> *Sincerely yours*
> *Mrs. Jo-Anne Jones*

Duffy asked the Correspondence Bureau to let Joann know that he had received her letter. "That was the protocol in those days," Spano explains. "The Correspondence Bureau contacted all outside agencies and parties." Duffy asked that they tell her "that every effort is being made to apprehend the perpetrators of this crime. Further, that all personal belongings of the deceased were delivered to the husband Raymond Sanseverino in accordance with the law. Any further information that may be of value in helping to solve this case will be welcomed." Which was pretty much all they wrote. All correspondence with Jean's family was cold and formal and to the point.

On August 2, Detective Kelly wrote the first filler 5. "On numerous occasions since the time of this occurrence, the undersigned has made discreet inquiries in the vicinity of this crime, in an effort to ascertain some information that would assist in bringing this case to a successful conclusion but to the present time has met without results. Every effort is being made, and diligent and constant attention is being given to this case, in order to apprehend the perpetrator of this crime." That's all there was left to do, occasionally recanvass the area, and hope you find someone who was up at the hour and saw something.

Six months passed without a break. Then, on January 28, 1952, the chief of Security at the Seaman's Institute told Detective Duffy that Joseph Moore was a known troublemaker. It doesn't explain why he's saying this just now. Two months before Jean died, the chief was told that Moore was sharing his room at the Institute with a nineteen-year-old "known homosexual." They told Moore that two men couldn't share a room, and asked him to leave, but they had to forcibly evict him from the building. Duffy asked that a message be sent to the U.S. Department of Justice, in Washington, D.C., for the complete police record of Joseph Moore.

Three months later, on April 5, 1952, Duffy heard from the FBI. A warrant for Joseph Moore had been issued in Norfolk, Virginia, on March 10, 1952, signed by U.S. Commissioner Percy S. Stephenson. Charges: theft of government property. Then they asked Duffy for help apprehending him.

After that, another lull. Then seven months later, in November 1952, Duffy sat down to read another letter from Alabama. Lieutenant Ned Simmons of the Gadsden Police had written the chief inspector of the NYPD (the same as the chief of Department now). Simmons had information that might help them with their investigation, he wrote.

June Pruitt, white, male, who lives in Gadsden left New York on the day Mrs. Sanseverino was killed and arrived in Gadsden two days later. Pruitt had been drinking and has stated he was with Mrs. Sanseverino the day she was killed, he has a police record here dating back several years. Mrs. Sanseverino and her husband had trouble with Pruitt before they left here to go to New York, although Pruitt and Sanseverino drank together and were together in New York.

If you will send me the facts as to the circumstances how she was killed I will pick Pruitt up and question him, also if you care for them I will send you his prints and picture.

While two ADAs made arrangements to go to Alabama with Detective Duffy, Kelly and Duffy went to Orangeburg, New York, to speak to Raymond Sanseverino. Ray was working at the Wright Airplane Plant in New Jersey as an electrician's apprentice now, and living with a Mrs. Long, whom he said he planned to marry. He and Jean knew Pruitt in Gadsden, he told them. Pruitt came to New York with Ray in February 1949, and they lived for a couple of months with a girl Pruitt knew before going their separate ways. The DD5 says this occurred in 1950, but given everyone's movements and countless other testimony, either Ray said the year wrong or the detective wrote it down incorrectly.

Duffy took a train down to Alabama with the ADAs and arrived on November 24. When they called Lieutenant Ned Simmons to tell him they were in town, Simmons asked them to start the investigation right away because they'd been holding Pruitt in jail since the twenty-second.

They interviewed Joann first. She ran into Pruitt in a Lanes Drug Store one afternoon, and Pruitt told her that he was in Jean's apartment on the day she was murdered. He had said the same thing in March, when he got back from New York. He also told Jean's sister Doris that he used to visit Jean and Ray at their apartment on State Street and that he had made a play for Jean.

June Pruitt made his statement next. "I'm twenty-two years old, and live with my mother and family, and am unemployed." He talked about his history of drunken and disorderly arrests and his dishonorable discharge from the U.S. Army in November 1949, following a court-martial, which is not explained in the statement. Pruitt knew

Raymond Sanseverino. Ray paid for their train trip to New York by selling the camera he got when he went to photography school under the GI Bill. Pruitt came back to Gadsden three months later. He was arrested in Gadsden the next year, on February 17, 1951, for drunkenness. When he didn't show up for court the following day, he was rearrested on March 12, at a dance. "Between February seventeenth and March twelfth I never left Gadsden." Lieutenant Ned Simmons checked. It was all true.

They brought Joann and Doris to the police headquarters to face Pruitt. "He said he was in New York," they insisted. Pruitt denied it, but admitted he might have told them that when he was drunk. Then Joann remembered seeing Pruitt on March 9, when she went to his house to tell Pruitt's mother about Jean's death. Duffy and the ADAs probably gave each other a look. She couldn't have remembered that she saw him the day after her sister was murdered *before* they came all the way down to talk to her? Duffy and the ADAs talked to Jean's friends and neighbors and family. Lieutenant Ned Simmons made a few calls. They determined that Pruitt was not in Brooklyn on the morning of March 8, 1951.

The next month Simmons sent Duffy copies of Jean's letters to her mother. In one letter Jean refers to her brother-in-law as "Johnny." Duffy had interviewed Eleanor and John Kraus at the beginning of the investigation, but there's nothing in the DD5 to indicate that he considered a possible connection between Johnny Kraus and the Johnny who wrote Jean the week she died. "Maybe he did, but he didn't learn anything worth putting down," Wendell says. "Also, they already interviewed this guy at the beginning of the investigation. He might have provided them with a solid alibi then."

Simmons also included the letter Ray's mother wrote to Mrs. East, warning her about Ray.

Dear Mrs. East:

I really don't know how to begin this letter because you don't know me or anything about me. I am Raymond Sanseverino's mother. He will be home soon on furlough & from what he tells me he intends to go out to Alabama & bring your daughter to New York.

I beg you please if you love your daughter don't let Raymond marry her. This is very hard for me to say but it has to be done. Raymond is a dear he doesn't love your daughter or anyone else he only loves himself.

When he was home in January he proposed to a girl that lives two blocks away from us & gave her a ring. At the same time that he was receiving letters from Jean that led me to believe he proposed to her. At the same time a very sweet little girl that I think a great deal of was writing to him and sending him gifts every day. She came to the house while he was home on leave and I quarreled with him because he lied to me about Rosie the girl he gave the ring. He said she was a tramp and wouldn't be seen with her & then he went to her house and asked her mother for her hand in marriage. It finally came out that he had also proposed to Bernadette the girl I liked so well and he had asked her not to say anything to me because he wanted to surprise me.

Recently I got a letter from a girl in the Bronx by the name of Florence Gramble. It was addressed to Mrs. Sanseverino and begged me to tell her if Raymond was alright. My son Pat went out to see her and she told him that Raymond had proposed to her. Then he let some of his buddies write to her and tell her that he had been killed in action. She was a nice girl who was keeping house for her brother and raising five young children for him.

Leave it to Raymond. He always picks them young and pure and innocent. Before Raymond went into the Army he drifted from one job to the other and he looked like a tramp. He got a job in coney Island as a clean up boy in one of the bath houses. He got so drunk every night that he couldn't get home. He used to lay in the gutter. I made him quit and took him to the priest to try to straighten him out. Nothing helped. I threatened to throw him out of the house but because he was going into the Army so soon I stuck to him. I figured that the Army would straighten him out. I had high hopes and was most anxious to see him when he came home in January. It wound up by him proposing to Rosie, breaking Bernadette's heart, trying to take Pat's girl away from him, and borrowing money all over the neighborhood. With the money that he borrowed he bought himself a ring and Rosie two rings. He left the house flat broke and left me in tears hoping and praying that God would take him before he did any more harm.

May I tell you what I think will happen if Raymond goes to Alabama. First he will bring Jean to New York and marry her probably leave her pregnant and go to Japan. He may never come back or if he does he may be wounded. Anyway the first pretty girl he sees that appeals to him will mean that Jean doesn't exist anymore for him anymore. She will be stranded here in New York maybe with a baby. No hom. No friends.

New York is not exciting or glamorous. It is just a struggle for existence unless you have plenty of money. ["Some things never change," Spano comments.]

I am going to give you the addresses of some of the girls of whom I have told you and please if you don't believe me write them and ask them what Raymond has done to them.

Now just a little bit about us here at home so that you will know our background and what Jean can expect if she comes to New York.

Eleanor is the oldest she is 19 years old and will be 20 in September. Raymond is next and will be 19 in August. Pat is going to be 18 in November and probably go into the service. Christina is 14 born in April, Donald will be 13 in August and Emily will be 17 on the 11th of July. Their father is dead. I had to put them all in an institution they were all there for five years or more. Then I remarried to get them home. They are all home now thank god. The marriage didn't last because my husband couldn't get used to all the children. We separated the day after Raymond's furlough ended in February. I am working every day. The oldest girl is looking for work and Pat goes to school but works during the summer.

If Raymond comes home, or when he is eventually released from the Army I will not allow him to live with us because he caused to much unhappiness in the house. Believe me Mrs. East I am sincere when I tell you these things and I hope you will give this letter serious thought. It would certainly be better for Jean to be disappointed now then to spend a life of misery with Raymond. By the way I myself am a protestant and what religion the girl is doesn't mean a thing to me.

Here are the addresses of the girls. [Addresses omitted here.] And there are many more.

> *Sincerely, Mrs. Eleanor Ames*
> *Please let me hear from you.*

Perhaps letters like this confirmed what they already believed—it must have been the husband. Ray's mother's letter would have only further entrenched them in their conviction. They could not be deterred. Ten more months went by. On October 26, 1953, two and a half years after Jean's murder, Kelly heard from a lawyer representing a woman in a separation action against her husband. She had some information regarding the death of Jean Sanseverino. Two years prior she was going through her husband's personal effects and came across a newspaper clipping about Jean's death. Her husband, a philanderer, drank all the time and got very violent when he was drunk, she claimed.

When Duffy and Kelly talked to the husband a couple of weeks later, he said he'd never heard of Jean Sanseverino. He didn't know the section of Brooklyn where she was killed. In fact, he barely knew Brooklyn at all. He had always lived in Queens. If they had information that he was mixed up in the killing, it probably came from his wife. She'd been suing him left and right, and he'd won all the suits so far. When they were married she was always cutting out articles "about wives that had either killed or attempted to kill their husbands because they refused to give them money for furs and the like." She needs help, he told them.

This time three years went by before another DD5 was added to the file. In March 1956, the commanding officer of Brooklyn East called Duffy to tell him about a tip from a North Carolina truck driver. The trucker heard that his brother Edward Silver had been arrested in Brooklyn for the rape and strangulation of a white woman. His sister, who lived in Brooklyn, sent his mother a newspaper clipping about it in 1949. Even though Silver did not have a record for rape, Duffy and another detective went down to Petersburg, Virginia, where Silver was living at the time.

Another false lead, and another useless train trip south. Yes, it was true that Silver was living in Brooklyn at the time, but he never knew Jean. And while he'd been arrested twice on drunk and disorderlies, he was never questioned or arrested on a rape charge. The next day they went to talk to Silver's sixty-year-old mother, Bessie, on a farm in North Carolina on Bear Hunter's Crossroad, also known as Drake Crossroad. Neither road appears on maps today. Bessie said her daughter didn't send her a newspaper clipping, but she remembered a radio broadcast three years before, saying that her son had been arrested in Brooklyn. "Talk to Lucille Andrews," Bessie said. She heard the same broadcast. They found Lucille at a corn mill in Whitakers. She didn't remember the broadcast. The detectives came home.

William Kelly left the Brooklyn West Homicide Squad the following summer, and the case was reassigned to Detective Charles Kaiser. Two months later, Kaiser put in a filler 5. Three years after that, Kaiser retired and the case was reassigned to Detective Charles A. Damiano. Six months went by before Damiano put in a filler 5. Half a year later, another filler 5. On May 2, 1961, Walter Duffy retired from the 82 and the case was reassigned to Detective Thomas Kelly, who never added a single thing to the file. Seven years after that, Damiano put in his last filler 5. In 1969, the case was reassigned from Damiano to Salvatore Nicolosi, who added filler 5s until 1972. Then nothing.

A handwritten sheet with information about four other Brooklyn homicides sits among the filler 5s. Some unknown detective thought there might be a connection between these murders and Jean's. The number after the date is the precinct; that's followed by the case number, then the name of the victim and how they died. In some cases the information is incomplete or unreadable.

12/23/44	71	1388	Sadie Fisher, loss of head & [illegible].
11/2/45	81	754	McCormack, street stab, negro.
45	73	531	Richardson.
3/3/46	78	142	Mary Griffin, stab & [illegible].
3/8/51	82	202	Jean Sanseverino, strang.

These case records were later found at the Central Records warehouse. No connection could be found, beyond the fact that they were all unsolved murders of women.

On January 16, 1984, Detective John F. Loy reviewed the files, and with his commanding officer's approval, marked the Jean Sanseverino case inactive. Three years later, when Vito Spano took temporary command of the 82, which is now the 76, following a precinct reorganization, he gathered all the old cases, made sure everything was in order, then he put them together in a box, marked the dates and case numbers on the outside, and stored the box in the closet. For almost twenty years they sat there untouched. Then, after answering countless questions about why a certain detective did this, that, or the other thing on the Jean Sanseverino case, an exasperated but now curious Detective Wendell Stradford said, "All right, give me the folder. I want to take a look at it."

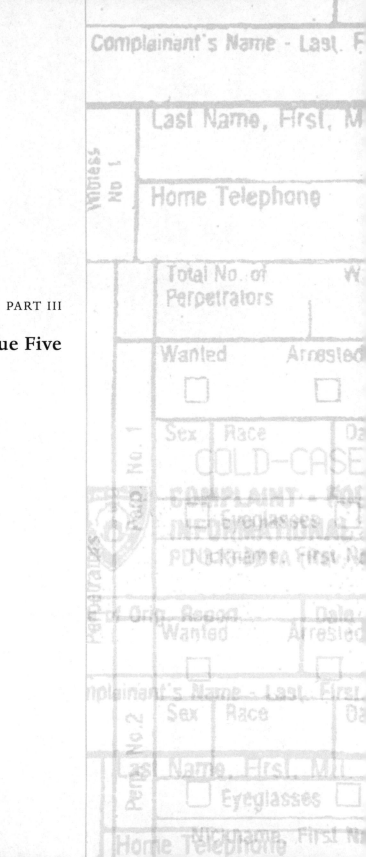

PART III

The Blue Five

10 Detective Wendell Stradford

The Leon-Martinez Double Homicide

It's hard to look a man in the eye as he's being led away in handcuffs. It's uncomfortable to see anyone so exposed and vulnerable and wholly without dignity—even if he deserves it. On TV it's always presented as a moment of triumph. In reality, it's awkward. For Wendell, this is ultimate detective-job-satisfaction. "I feel accomplished. I did my job," he says. Of the perp, he says, "All their defiance goes away. They don't give you that motherfuck-you look anymore."

Once the detectives make an arrest, they take their prisoners to the precinct or Cold Case Squad holding cell. They fill out the seven different forms and reports, then notify the ADA. Sometimes the ADA comes out and "rides the case." If they do they'll be referred to as the riding ADA, but ADAs usually ride only live homicides, and not cold cases. Unless the prisoner agrees to make a statement on camera, the ADAs wait until the prisoner is brought to Arraignment Court. Before the detective takes the prisoner to Arraignment Court they go to Central Booking.

Every borough is a little different, but from here to Arraignment Court, the Central Booking process is basically the same. The following describes what takes place in Manhattan when arrestees are brought to 100 Centre Street, aka the Tombs.

The prisoners are taken to what's called the sally port, the place for on-loading and off-loading prisoners. (*Sally port* is an archaic term that refers to the opening in a fort through which soldiers "sally" forth to attack or defend.) Inside, each prisoner gets a movement slip with a barcode, and at every step in the booking process that barcode will get scanned in and time-stamped. It's like being on a conveyor belt of corrections, it's so efficient. Everywhere you go prisoners stand in small groups connected like chain gangs, quietly waiting. While this is going on, an independent outfit called the Criminal Justice Agency gets the prisoner's rap sheet and begins to prepare a report for the judge who will be making a decision about bail. Every few feet there is some sort of security device—people, cameras, locked doors where you must be buzzed in and out. Fingerprints are electronically scanned on a red, glowing surface. You can't turn a corner without hitting a new set of holding cells. Some are for men, some are for women, and some are called special, where they put people who have medical problems, are openly gay, or in the case of informants, are in protective custody. The last thing they want to do is endanger a valuable informant. It's hard to meet the eye of anyone sitting in a holding cell, too. They're caged. Everyone looks down, except for a few people who are trying to look tough or others who appear permanently damaged. One girl looked up through the bars. Her eyes were excited; it was as if her heart was racing. An officer checked some papers. She was there for selling fake watches on Canal Street.

After the prisoner gets his movement slip he goes to Medical first, for an initial screening from an FDNY EMT. Next, he stops by the room that houses Criminal Justice Agency personnel. Then he's searched. It's a standard metal scan and pat search or frisk. Strip searches at this point are no longer conducted without probable cause. Even though the place is spotless, occasionally it smells like urine.

The next room is the one formally referred to as Central Booking. It's a large space that's completely encircled by still more holding cells. Here the prisoner will meet with his lawyer. If he doesn't have his own lawyer and is assigned a member of Legal Aid, he'll meet with them later, in one of the court holding cells upstairs. The court draws up a docket number, and the prisoner is put in a cell to wait. At this point, the arresting officer will leave. Wendell or Steve or Tommy is off to the next bad guy.

In movies, the police can be either heroes or villains. The correction guys are almost always bad guys. *Prison guards*—a term they won't even use anymore, it's always correction officer—are frequently as vilified as the prisoners they care for. But the correction officers at the Tombs are extremely polite to everyone who is brought in. Perhaps extreme politeness is how you repeatedly get through this awkward situation. A correction officer offers another explanation. "They're innocent," he says of the prisoners here. This is America. No one has been to trial and sentenced—innocent until proven guilty. Everyone in the custody of the Department of Correction at this point is innocent, so, to the best of their ability, Correction treats them as such. "If the prisoner acts up, though," Wendell says, "everything changes. I've seen corrections officers clock guys."

When all the prisoner's paperwork is together and complete, a court officer will tell a New York police officer to bring the prisoner back up two levels from his Central Booking cell to be arraigned. The prisoner is signed out and brought upstairs to another set of cells with rooms where he can talk to his lawyer. From there he goes to court.

Arraignment Court is just like the old TV show *Night Court*. It's a courtroom like any other courtroom, except not as fancy. This is the Grand Central of courtrooms; it's a bit run-down, reflecting the amount of traffic they get daily. Most of the people here look bored.

Or tired. The court personnel look professional. When their number is called, the prisoner goes up before a judge, and their lawyer and the ADA make their case about bail. It would be unusual to get bail in a homicide case today. "That's why there are all these guys running around wanted for murder, because they were given bail years ago," Wendell says. These days, in spite of any defense attorney's arguments, the DA won't offer it, and the judge won't grant it. Instead, the prisoner will be committed to the New York City Department of Correction until his trial. He will be handed over to the Department of Correction along with an accusatory instrument (anything that gives Correction the right to hold the inmate, a court order, an out-of-state warrant, or a parole violations warrant, for example). He's their responsibility now.

The whole process is conducted like a two-leg relay race. They've got twenty-four hours from the moment of arrest to get the person in front of a judge, and then the Department of Correction has twenty-four hours to process and house them either in the Tombs or at one of roughly nine facilities at Rikers Island. The moment the judge bangs his gavel, the second leg of the race begins. When the prisoner walks out of the courtroom, the accusatory instrument is stamped by the Department of Correction and the clock starts ticking. It doesn't matter if ten or ten thousand people are committed that day, they've got twenty-four hours. "My staff can handle it," says Captain Fred Sporrer. But they'd have to bring in extra medical workers, he admits. Correction has to accommodate whatever population is brought down to them, people in wheelchairs, people with contagious diseases, people detoxing. And they have to make absolutely sure that no adolescents have mistakenly come into their care.

The prisoner is taken to the New York City Department of Correction Court Division, where they're fingerprinted and given a Booking Case number. Correction starts a form called a 239, which will be used to classify the prisoner and decide where he will be housed. From here they go to Intake. A big fat packet of forms associated with each inmate is brought to Intake and administrators make sure they have everything they're supposed to have. Instead of a movement slip, they start a card to track every step and how long it took.

The prisoner is fingerprinted again, just in case a switch was made and someone thought they'd get someone else to take their place in prison. They'll get photographed once more, and Correction will issue an ID card. More paperwork is initiated that will end in visit cards, phone cards, and an inmate account. Then the prisoner will get a complete mental health screening. Is he suicidal? for instance. This is followed by a complete medical screening, including blood work. Does he have any contagious diseases or require any special medical care? Then his security risk will be assessed and he'll be classified from 1 to 57, 1 being the lowest. Anything above 17 is considered high risk. If they are a registered informant they may ask to be separated from the general population. Correction will verify if this is true and honor this request.

The security classifications are marked above the entrance to each housing unit at the Tombs (they don't say cell blocks anymore). Inside the doors are food warmers. Inmates are not taken to great big cafeterias for meals like the old days. Too much potential for trouble. Instead, they eat in their housing unit. Housing units look like every other jail you've seen on TV. An open area with a TV, surrounded by two levels of cells.

Prisoners will endure one more search before they are finally housed. Inmates who are being held on homicide charges will now be strip-searched. They'll be instructed to remove their clothes, turn around, squat, and lift their genitals. No physical contact takes place during a strip search. "But you can see if there's anything up there. Sometimes there'll be a string hanging out so they can pull the stuff out later," Captain Sporrer explains. "Sometimes it just pops out when they squat." Cops do not like conducting strip searches and some wince when describing it.

Most prisoners would prefer to remain at the Tombs. The work here is less strenuous. It's easier for friends and relatives to visit, and the inmate doesn't have to get up at 4:00 a.m. to get on a bus for their court date. It's also safer because no one stays here long, so dangerous cliques aren't really given a chance to form. Everyone is on their best behavior, hoping to stay. But space at the Tombs is tight. If the prisoner was medically cleared, then like it or not, before twenty-four hours are up, he will be getting on a bus to Rikers with anywhere from fifteen to seventy of his fellow inmates.

Within six days every inmate is brought before a grand jury, who will either decide that there is a case and indict, or they will decide that there isn't sufficient evidence and vote No True Bill (the prisoner won't be charged). From here on in there will be a series of pretrial motions, court appearances, conferences, hearings, followed by a trial. If the prisoner is convicted, he will be sentenced, generally within a month if it's state court, longer in federal court.

Once sentenced, the prisoners are put back on a bus to Rikers. At this point, the Department of Correction wants them out. The inmate is not their problem anymore, and they need the cell space. They'll be out of the city jail and into a state prison within a week. (City holding facilities are called jails, the state facilities are called prisons.)

They'll be taken to the Downstate Reception Center opposite Matewan State Hospital in Dutchess County, where they may spend up to eight weeks getting classified once again. They'll go through a whole new set of screening and testing procedures to determine their background, history of violence, health, and whether they have any program needs (an academic program, for example). They could be sent to one of seventy possible prisons, as their destination is based on what's learned during the classification process and what space is available.

■

In December 2003, after waiting more than two years for the Bronx DA's office to complete the paperwork needed to bring Robert Mitchell back to New York, Wendell loses track of him. Robert

Mitchell, the last person Wendell found and arrested for the murders of Linda Leon and Esteban Martinez, is no longer in the Baltimore facility where he was being held. "They might have put him in a halfway house," Stradford worries. "If Baltimore lets him go, we'll never find him again. He knows we're after him."

Technically, Baltimore can hold Mitchell until 2008 for probation violations, Wendell explains, "but they probably thought, 'why should we pay to keep him all that time when we can release him to New York and New York can absorb the expense of holding him?'" Senior Assistant District Attorney Nancy Borko, a competent ADA with decades of experience, may have thought, "Okay, Mitchell's locked up tight in Baltimore for a while, let me focus on some other bad guys."

That's what Wendell was thinking. "I wasn't too anxious about Robert Mitchell," he says, "because I didn't think he was going anywhere." Wendell has also been in regular contact with an attorney in the Homicide Division of the Maryland State Attorney's office. Borko, meanwhile, has been busy negotiating plea agreements with Keisha and Denise and preparing for Kevin Washington's trial. Everything has been moving forward, if a bit slowly. No one feels pressed.

Somewhere along the line, however, Mitchell vanishes. Wendell makes calls. He learns that Mitchell was moved to a prerelease facility in Hagerstown, Maryland, and is due to get out on July 7, 2004. That is just a few months away. "If you don't come to get him before then, we're going to release him," Wendell was told by the facility. They've been holding him for two years. Enough already. "If Nancy Borko doesn't complete the paperwork in time," Wendell explains, "he's out."

If she does file her paperwork, they will continue to hold him but only because of New York's detainer (this is a paper signed by a judge, informing Baltimore that New York has a warrant for Mitchell's arrest for murder and instructing them to hold him until they get down there to pick him up). Mitchell will likely ask for an extradition hearing, and he'll either waive his extradition rights, at which point Wendell has ten days to get him, or he won't. In that case Borko has ninety days to get a governor's warrant.

Shortly after Wendell learns where Mitchell is being held, Keisha Washington and Denise Henderson, the women who told three young children that everything would be okay while their parents were being murdered, take pleas. In exchange for agreeing to testify, they get six to twelve with time served, which means the soonest they can get out is the summer of 2007. Wendell doesn't think they'll be granted parole at their first hearing. "Keisha still doesn't think she did anything wrong," Wendell says. She writes a letter to the judge asking for bail, saying that she didn't belong in jail, and that her children needed her. She gets her minister to write as well. But Linda and Esteban's children needed their mother and father, too. The judge keeps her behind bars.

No friends or family fill the courtroom when Kevin Washington's trial begins in March 2004. So much time and work and money led up to this trial: investigations, jury selections, endless meetings and paperwork and research, and no one is there to witness the outcome.

ADA Nancy Borko has a complicated style that is interesting to watch. While dressed elegantly in an Upper East Side ladies-who-lunch Chanel-like suit, she still comes off as someone you don't want to mess with. Cordial and attractive, she's like a librarian, but one who might attack at any moment. She and her co-counsel use the same accordion-style case folders the detectives use; the desk is piled with them. Foam-board displays of crime scene photographs of Linda and Esteban lying in pools of blood in their Christmas-decorated home lean against the balustrade that separates the participants from the observers.

Keisha is brought into the courtroom for her brother Kevin Washington's trial. For the first time in a year, she and her twin look each other in the eye. They smile at each other self-consciously, like strangers meeting on a blind date.

There's a lot of sitting around and waiting. The attorneys move

and look at their paperwork at the same time, and all the simultaneous rustling sounds like it has just begun to rain in the courtroom.
Keisha cries to herself on the witness stand while waiting for the
jury to come in and for questioning to begin. The chains around her
ankles clank whenever she moves her legs.

When the jury is finally brought in and Borko begins drawing her
out about the night they murdered Linda and Esteban, Keisha takes
a deep breath. She looks so frightened. She calls ADA Borko "Miss
B," in what seems like a last-ditch attempt to connect with her and
somehow normalize her situation. But her casual air is both unnat-
ural and pitifully implausible. Borko is polite and businesslike in response. Keisha says she wasn't supposed to go to New York originally,
but when she found out Denise was going she didn't want to be left
out. She tries to make it sound like she went along to protect the
children. "Robert said if you go the children won't get hurt," she
claims. "Robert wanted to do the kids. Robert was going to do Tone
[their nickname for Esteban]. Kevin was going to maintain and do
the woman." The woman. "What was Tone's wife's name?" Borko
asks her. Keisha doesn't know. After all these years, and all the interrogations and preparations for the trial, Keisha never took note of
the name of the woman she helped to kill.

Robert went to the bathroom, she continues. That was their pre-
arranged signal to be ready to act. To do what? Borko asks. "To tie
them up and stuff." They didn't resist, Keisha says. "They were cooperative." Keisha talks about counting the money they found in
front of the frightened children.

What did you buy with the money? she is asked. Keisha bought
herself a car and some Christmas presents for her child. She also
used some of it to move out of her mother's house, where she was
living at the time. It appears the murders had bought her some inde-
pendence. Borko asks her if she ever thinks about what happened.
"The only time I think about it is Christmastime, because that's
when it happened." Eight Christmases to date.

Linda and Esteban's children, who have been living in the

Dominican Republic, are brought back to testify. They probably think about what happened every Christmas, too. At the time of the trial, the children are thirteen, twelve, and ten. Some of Linda's family members are now in the courtroom. Each child nervously takes the stand. They are upset but speak clearly. The two oldest boys keep glancing at Kevin Washington, while the youngest looks away. Later, everyone agrees that they've all been very brave. Neither attorney asks the children if they recognize Kevin. The prosecutor doesn't want to hear no, and the defense attorney doesn't want to hear yes. When the oldest son takes the stand, he says he was afraid that he gave the wrong address to the 911 operator. The 911 tape of his call is played in the courtroom. No one moves. The sound of paper rain is replaced by muffled crying throughout the courtroom.

During the trial, it comes out that Esteban was shot first in order to terrify Linda into telling them where the drugs and money were. When she told them, they killed her, too. Then they grabbed up the cash and drugs and left the children alone with their parents' bodies. How long was it before the children left the room where Keisha and Denise held them down, their hands over their mouths, to find the bloody, still bodies of their parents? How long did they cry and try to wake their mom and dad before the six-year-old picked up the phone, dialed 911, and with his younger brothers crying in the background, said, "I'm here on my own. My father and my mother died. Somebody killed my mother and my daddy. Please help me, okay?" And then he gave their address correctly.

Wendell also testifies. After all these years, Wendell doesn't feel a lot of emotion when he takes the stand. In his twenty years on the force he's been up there explaining what's he's done over a hundred times. Keisha sobs. The children are brave. Wendell Stradford is calm and professional. It is not at all surprising then that the defense attorney doesn't ask him much. There is no help for his client here. He isn't going to break Detective Stradford. Instead, he wants Detective Wendell Stradford off that witness stand as soon as possible. It is clear to everyone in the courtroom that Wendell has done his job.

Kevin Washington is also confident when he takes the stand. Everyone is lying, he says, it's all one big conspiracy. "A laughable defense," Stradford says with disdain. "It's a game, a complicated game, and I guess he thought saying anything is better than saying nothing at all." It is not a long, drawn-out trial. The jury doesn't take a lot of time to deliberate. On March 26, 2004, Kevin Washington is found guilty of murder in the second degree, and robbery in the first degree. His various sentences total seventy-five years. When he is given a chance to address the court at his sentencing, he doesn't show a bit of remorse. He asks God to forgive the judge and the police for sentencing the wrong man. Then he gives Wendell the eye. Wendell blows him a kiss.

The same month that Kevin Washington is convicted, the *New York Times* features the Parkchester apartment complex where Esteban and Linda were murdered. It's one of those "it's coming back" type articles that appear whenever there's a rise in real estate values. The Parkchester complex, it turns out, was built by the same company that built Stuyvesant Town and Peter Cooper Village in lower Manhattan. In the article, Parkchester residents talk about how apartments there were rented to drug dealers before renovations began and rents started climbing in 1999. Now, criminal background checks are conducted on all prospective renters. Not to protect people like Esteban and Linda, but to protect the people there from them.

During an investigation, the closer the detective gets to the family, the closer he feels to the case. "You identify more," Wendell says. As a parent himself, Wendell has been especially determined about Linda Leon and Esteban Martinez's case. He hasn't had a lot of contact with the family during the trial because he hasn't been allowed in the courtroom. He has to wait outside until he's called to testify. But when it's over, Linda's cousins come up to him and thank him through an interpreter. The relatives haven't all been there from the beginning, so they have to ask someone to point out the detective who caught the people who murdered Linda and Esteban.

Wendell can be so soft when he wants to be. He knows how to turn around, drop the sometimes frighteningly efficient 1st-grade-detective shield over his emotions, and say "You're welcome" in a way that lets people know it meant everything to him, too. He was never going to give up. "We thought it was a lost cause," the cousins tell him. The aunt who had been caring for the boys says, "They want to come back now." They left the country initially because the killers were still out there. But now they feel safe. "The boys want to come back to America." At this Wendell probably hides his embarrassment at receiving a compliment but not how glad he feels to be part of the team that is able to stand outside the courtroom and look them in the eye and smile because they did everything they could, and succeeded. He allows himself to enjoy it. Because these cases can break your heart. Detectives can try for years and never have this one, brief moment where they get to be someone's hero and make it safe for three young sons to finally come home.

According to his alleged accomplices, there is still one murderer left to deal with: Robert Mitchell, the one who had planned it all. A few weeks after Kevin's conviction, Robert Mitchell waives his extradition rights. Wendell drives back down to Maryland the day after Kevin's sentencing to get him. The drive back with Mitchell takes almost six hours, due to traffic. What's it like spending six hours in a car with someone you've arrested for murder? "He's an asshole," Wendell says. Then he adds, "He's an *asshole* asshole," because the first description doesn't feel strong enough. "We were just talking shop, about things like basketball, and I'm saying to myself, this guy is a scumbag and a murderer, and I'm sitting here, breathing the same air he's breathing, and he's acting like we're buddies and we're in this together." Playing make-believe and making small talk with the malignant is unsettling. "I had to separate myself, because how he's acting is not how it is, or who he is. He killed people. And if he could, he'd kill me, too."

Mitchell's mother calls Wendell. She talks to Wendell like she didn't know all of this was happening. "I raised him to be a good boy." She tries crying to Wendell, and then she tries berating him. Wendell quietly explains that Keisha and Denise have already taken pleas and that Kevin went to trial and was convicted. "What'd he get?" "Seventy-five years," he tells her. Robert Mitchell's mother screams.

Mitchell pleads not guilty at his arraignment. From here, Borko and Stradford will prepare for the trial, and once again, everyone will wait. Given the outcome of Kevin's trial, Mitchell might be more willing to accept a plea, but the DA doesn't need to offer him one, and while they might put something on the table to spare the time and expense of a trial, it won't be much. If it goes to trial, Linda and Esteban's sons will have to come back again to testify. The oldest boy will take the stand once more and this time he will repeat what he's said since the beginning, when he was only six years old, and what no one else really heard until Wendell picked up the case: "It was Robert."

11 Detective Steve Kaplan

The Ronald Stapleton Case

Organized crime doesn't amount to much anymore. In the most mundane ways, the business of organized crime is like any other business. Sometimes people feel trapped in dead-end jobs. Take Mike Cilone, Kaplan's witness from the Ronald Stapleton case who came to speak to Lieutenant Pollini's organized-crime class at the John Jay College for Criminal Justice in the late spring of 2002. A group of young, determined law-enforcement types sat in the classroom and listened as Mike gave a brief, very brief, outline of his life in organized crime, then invited the class to ask questions. "You can ask me anything you want," he instructed them, with his New York street accent, the same accent, by the way, of half the NYPD. "I'm not saying I'm going to answer all your questions, but you shouldn't be afraid to ask." He had a certain lack of awareness about himself and how the rest of the world worked that made him scary above and beyond the fact that he was a criminal and he had helped kill people. He began by describing a life so depressing it's surprising he wasn't in a hospital bed heavily medicated. He turned informant, so *no one* liked him, not the bad guys, not the good guys, and he couldn't have relationships with anyone or lead much of a life because anyone he associated with would have good reason to believe they were in danger. He was drafted into crime in early adolescence, he had no choice in the matter, and he'd been stuck there ever since, for very small gains. He never made a lot of money. He wasn't powerful. And then he was hunted. After clearly demonstrating the hopelessness that is his life, he looked out at the class and said "Now, I know you think my life was glamorous . . ." with an expression of pride, like he was the big man on campus, or Tony Soprano, oblivious to the fact that not one person in the room, not one person anywhere in the world, would perceive his life as glamorous. When asked, "Why are you even here?" he replied without irony, "I want to do something good." He looked so proud it was painful to watch, and a lot of the students had to cast their eyes down.

■

Once Kaplan had wiseguy Frank Smith Jr., they were able to arrest someone else they wanted even more, and with him, they had answers for years of murder.

There is quite a crowd at the Frank Smith proffer sessions. Kaplan is there with Special Agent Steve Byrne and many others, including Mark Feldman, the head of Organized Crime in the U.S. Attorney's Office, Eastern District. Even though Smith is still in state custody for the narcotics charge and has come to Detective Steve Kaplan to roll, Feldman is there because Smith was already a federal target when he contacted Kaplan. Also, the Frank Gioia Jr. proffer sessions included revelations about murders committed by Frank Smith Jr., and because Gioia was a federal witness, that gave Feldman leverage to take over. No one has a problem with it. Feldman has been generous. Between all the various law enforcement groups, they have developed their own system of working these delicate, territorial issues out, and it has been effective. They have been putting these guys in jail, and what remains of the mob in New York is left fighting over scraps.

Their new witness, Frank Smith Jr., is a nice guy, Kaplan says. "But he has a bad temper." He's a murderer. Kaplan shakes his head and repeats, "He has a bad temper. What? You don't think you're capable of murder?" Typically, Kaplan can't bring himself to hate the guy.

Frank Smith doesn't use the word *death;* he says "mayhem." "I was responsible for a lot of mayhem," he admits to all the men in the room. "Let me start off," Smith begins, "I committed a crime every day of my life." Everyone looks at each other. Their hearts beat faster. "Of course we were excited," Kaplan says. An already complicated case is about to get even more complicated, and cause the excitable deputy inspector Vito Spano to later jump up from his desk, his face red and heart pounding, barking out commands for charts and time lines. "I need a God damned time line for these murders. And give me a fucking chart of this family." "Okay, forget about the crimes," they tell Smith, to keep things as simple as possible. "Let's move on to the mayhem."

As with any proffer session, Smith has to tell them about every murder he knows about, not just his own. In the end, Smith tells them about ten murders, five of which he carried out himself, six of which were ordered by Joel Cacace, the acting boss of the Colombo family. Joel Cacace is about to become their ultimate target. (The true boss of the family was Carmine Persico, who was in prison. The boss is the boss for life, unless he abdicates or is removed by the Commission—a consortium of the heads of all the families. This is why Cacace is always referred to as the "acting boss.") As the total number of murders kept going up, every man in that room must have become positively delirious as they envisioned the clearances and reports and statistics they'd be able to deliver to their commanding officers.

Among the murdered was seventy-eight-year-old George Aronwald, the retired civil lawyer who was shot to death in a Laundromat in 1982, for reasons no one had been able to fathom. Smith tells them what happened. Cacace had told Smith and his two other favorite hit men, Vinnie and Enrico Carini, that federal prosecutors William Aronwald and future mayor and 9/11 hero Rudolph Giuliani had disrespected members of the Colombo crime family and had to die. (The order had actually come from Persico.) Aronwald would be first.

Cacace gave the Carini brothers William Aronwald's license plate. They mistakenly traced the plate back to William's father, George. They knew something was off, however. They went back to Cacace. "Are you sure you got the right guy? It's this really old guy." Cacace brushed them off. "I don't care how old he is," he answered. They went ahead with the hit. The next day, they read in the papers that they had killed the wrong guy. Then federal prosecutor Rudolph Giuliani was supposed to have been hit next, but they were forced to call it off. "Don't worry. I'll straighten it out," Cacace assured the Carini brothers. He straightened it out by having them killed. "He blamed it on them and then he whacked them," a law enforcement source explains. Organized-crime guys are not the men of the *Godfather* movies. No one resembles the brilliant and frighteningly efficient Al Pacino as Michael Corleone. "With a few exceptions, they're the losers who were beat up in grade school and had their lunch money taken, so now they're taking it back from everyone else," says Special Agent Steve Byrne. "They have gambling and substance abuse problems and sleep with each other's wives." "And that's against the rules," Kaplan adds. "That's why they're killing each other. It didn't used to be like that."

Every day, the amount of evidence indicating that things just aren't what they used to be in the organized-crime business grows. Amy Zelson, a forensic anthropologist at the OCME, called Steve Kaplan about a number of skeletons she'd been collecting. The skeletons were older and victims of homicide, and by definition cold cases. Kaplan stopped by to take a look. The clothes on some were nice, and the dental work was expensive. Kaplan read the list of locations where they were found. Then he looked at the jewelry left on the bodies. "Wiseguys," he said. There were so many skeletons, though, he had to stop her. "It was too much," Kaplan said. "Yeah, organized crime has changed." It's done, everyone says. Anyone not in prison at this point was never the cream of the organized-crime crop. The mobsters who are left are generally venal and stupid, and they don't exercise judgment or restraint. And the more they break the rules, the greater the call for retaliation, and the more often they end up in Zelson's growing stack. (Organized Crime Investigation Division detective Lynn McCarthy disagrees. "It's never done. They're still out there making money, getting married, and having kids." Future made members. While the NYPD and the FBI estimate the number of family members at around 890, McCarthy points out, "They're only counting made members. When you count associates, everyone else working for the made men, the number goes up to seven or eight thousand.")

After Cacace took care of the Carini brothers, he then turned around and told Frank Smith to kill the guys who had killed the Carini brothers (this was the Carmine Variale and Frank Santora hit). On May 5, 1988, three weeks before he was sent to prison for a narcotics crime he didn't commit, Frank Smith Jr. shot his last wiseguy.

Before the proffer sessions end, they ask Smith about Ralph Dols, a twenty-eight-year-old police officer who was shot to death in Brooklyn on August 26, 1997. They think Smith might know him because Dols was married to Kym Kennaugh at the time, and there were connections between Kym Kennaugh and Frank Smith. Kym Kennaugh had married two organized-crime guys, including Enrico Carini, and she also had lived with the man who ordered Carini's death and who was the new focus of their investigation, Joel Cacace. (Members of law enforcement sometimes refer to Kym as the "Womb of Doom.") The police believe that Cacace had also ordered the hit on Dols, but Smith can't give them any information about the murder. "They'll never give up on Dols," prosecutors say. Giuliani, who himself may have been a target of the same murderer, pointed to all the men in uniform at Dols's funeral and told Kym,

"They're not just here today. They'll be here five years from now. They'll be here when Gabrielle (their daughter) has to go to college. They'll be there when you need help with the children." Police Commissioner Howard Safir promised, "We will not rest until whoever is responsible for this is brought to justice."

For now, they have another problem. Frank Smith won't sign the cooperation agreement and testify against Cacace until he is cleared on the state's narcotics charge. That's because he knows the state would never parole him once the feds had him on the other murders. The feds, however, might be willing to negotiate his sentence based on the strength of his information about Joel Cacace and others and his willingness to testify. Smith wants the state charge out of the way. Kaplan and everyone else really want Cacace. No one can move forward until the matter is taken care of. Kaplan and everyone else will be forced to do what people in law enforcement do more than anything else: wait.

■

Two weeks before Jean Sanseverino was murdered in her Brooklyn apartment in 1951, a longshoreman named Steve Bove was murdered only a mile away by twenty-one-year-old Alphonse Persico. A DD5 from the Bove case was misfiled with the Sanseverino case by a detective who was working on both. Alphonse's seventeen-year-old brother, Carmine, was also charged, but that charge was later dropped. Alphonse eventually pleaded guilty to second-degree murder and was sentenced to twenty years (he served sixteen). He would murder many more people over the years. His teenage brother Carmine would eventually grow up to be the head of the Colombo crime family. It was this same Carmine Persico, prosecutors believe, who gave the order to Joel Cacace to kill William Aronwald, a retired organized-crime prosecutor who had, among other unforgivable things, unsuccessfully prosecuted Carmine's brother Alphonse in the early seventies. However, it's generally believed that Carmine killed Bove in 1951, not Alphonse. A key prosecution witness in the Bove case moved to California and was gunned down seventeen years later when he took a chance and showed his face in Brooklyn to visit his mother. Apparently, Carmine Persico never lets go of a grudge.

■

Murder in New York is so entwined. When Steve Kaplan first mentioned talking to federal witness Frank Gioia, the Cold Case commanding officer pulled a folder of photographs out of his file cabinet and pointed to one. "Here he is. That's Gioia." Frank Gioia had come up in wiretaps and surveillance photos during a two-year investigation into drug sales in Hell's Kitchen, but they never got enough to arrest him. Years later, Gioia would lead them to Tony Francesehi, then to Frank Smith, who would lead them to Joel Cacace. It later turned out the commanding officer's picture may have been of Gioia's father. Crime is not only entwined, it's forever ongoing. One of the consequences of murder is more murder.

Keeping it all straight is sometimes the hardest part of a Cold Case detective's job. The connections are many and they go back for decades. But if you want to understand the connections you have to know the history. When it comes to murder, and especially organized crime, there's always a backstory. It's all one big low-life network. And from members of this network, the Cold Case guys pick up murderers and information that leads to other murderers.

■

At the end of 2002, a state judge overturns the drug conviction so Frank Smith Jr. can sign the cooperation agreement and testify against Joel Cacace. "He's not guilty of the drug charge, so it's only fair," Kaplan shrugs. In exchange, Smith agrees not to sue them for wrongful imprisonment. Everyone has been waiting a year for this to happen, but that's just how it is with a RICO case. They take years to build. It has already been five years since FBI Special Agent Steve Byrne first called Steve Kaplan with information from Gioia. But they don't give medals for patience in law enforcement.

It all falls into place like this. On December 23, 2002, Frank Smith Jr. accepts a plea of guilty in Kings County State Supreme Court for the murders of Carmine Variale and Frank Santora. Even though Smith is a federal witness now, prosecutor DeMartini has asked that he plead guilty in state court, because they've done so much work on the case. Prosecutors care about numbers, too. Smith is sentenced to twelve to twenty-four, which will run concurrently with the time he has already served. The case is closed, and the case folders are turned over to the feds. Smith is out.

By this time Kaplan has been transferred from Manhattan to the Queens Cold Case Squad, under the command of Lieutenant Phil Panzarella. Detectives in Manhattan are the stars of the police department. The glamour fades the farther you get from 1PP. The Bronx, Brooklyn, and Staten Island are not as prestigious. By the time they get to Queens, detectives often feel they have to justify their post by explaining that it's an easier commute from home. Once, when Panzarella thought a Queens ADA was acting uppity he spat out, "Who are they kidding? If they were any good they'd be in Manhattan." Kaplan started out in Manhattan but he likes it out in Queens. "Queens is really different," he says. He points to the newspaper articles about cases tacked up all over the walls with "Good job, Tommy" or "Great work, Oscar" written by Panzarella in big black Magic Marker. "You ever see anything like that in any other squad room?" he asks.

The problem is, now that he's been transferred to Queens, Kaplan sometimes finds himself caught in the middle of the frequent battles between Lieutenant Phil Panzarella and Deputy Inspector Vito Spano. Panzarella has a thousand years on the job and is long past caring about position or politics. It's almost impossible to tell him what do. And as the boss, Spano quite reasonably wants to tell him what to do, at least from time to time. To complicate matters, Spano, who would rather see his guys solving cases like Christine Diefenbach's, calls Kaplan in for meetings to find out what he's up to, and Panzarella instructs Kaplan not to tell Spano a thing. "Just do your job."

Trying to sort out the truth behind what goes on between Spano and Panzarella and Kaplan is a little like trying to figure out what happened in a marriage after a divorce. All parties have their own take on events. Everyone gathers friends and enemies as they move through the police department and people can be found to support or refute each side. To be fair, Panzarella must be maddening to manage. He sometimes won't provide even a token amount of respect, and as the commanding officer, Spano has a right to know what his detectives have been up to. A now retired Cold Case commander described Panzarella right from the start: "He's a noncompliance guy." Kaplan is a great detective, but he also has a history of being difficult to manage. He complains about Spano being on his back, but others suggest Kaplan brought that on himself. But Vito Spano is a driven commander and sometimes will not let go. About Spano and Kaplan, the same retired commander said, "Vito is in the one-hundred-mile-an-hour zone and Kaplan is in the fifty-mile-an-hour zone." Still, numbers are numbers, and Kaplan and Mike Carrano, the other organized-crime guy in Queens Cold Case, make a lot of arrests, so this is a battle that Panzarella usually wins. And perhaps because they come up with the numbers, it could be argued that Vito could give them more space. It can't be fun for any of them but, unfortunately, they don't give medals for enduring interoffice politics and bickering.

Panzarella sends a memo to the chief of Detectives on January 13, 2003, outlining the plans to arrest crime boss Joel Cacace and listing the murders he will be charged with: Carmine Variale, Frank Santora, George Aronwald, and one other person who came up during his proffer sessions, Carlo Antonino. (Other names that came up in the Frank Smith proffer sessions are still being investigated.) Spano may have felt that this memo should have rightfully come from him.

Next, Frank Smith pleads guilty again, this time in the Eastern District of New York, Federal Supreme Court, on January 17, for the murders of Carmine Variale, Frank Santora, George Aronwald,

Carlo Antonino, and still two more people who came up during the proffer sessions, Joseph Freglette and Gino Longobardi. He is now a cooperating witness. He belongs to the feds.

On January 22, 2003, at six in the morning, six years after Steve Kaplan picked up the Ronald Stapleton case, the FBI, the Cold Case Squad, and members of OCID arrest the then sixty-one-year-old Joel Cacace in Deer Park, Long Island. Someone had tipped off the media, and a bunch of camera crews are already there sitting on the house when the Cold Case detectives and the FBI arrive. (Some members of law enforcement later fix their hair in Cacace's bathroom.) The FBI surrounds the house while Kaplan and Detective Mike Carrano from Queens Cold Case wait inside their car. Kaplan and the FBI go up to the door. Carrano stays at the bottom of the driveway beside the "hospital car" in case something goes wrong. It's all very civilized and professional. They ring the bell. From upstairs, Cacace calls out, "I'll be right down." Kaplan is pleased. "This is what I like about wiseguys," Kaplan says. "No whining. Okay, you got me. What do I gotta do? Then they do their time." No running, no drama. An arrest etiquette has evolved post-RICO, and both sides know the proper arrest code of conduct.

By the time Cacace is finally arrested, he's been living like an indigent, in a starkly furnished house with no phone. He seems weary and sad. "I've been eating like an animal," he says.

The police department has absolute faith that Cacace will take a plea, at which point he will have to confess to every murder he knows about, and that is when they will finally learn who murdered Police Officer Ralph Dols (Dols was married to Kym Kennaugh, who used to live with Cacace). Say what you will, the police department never gives up on cases involving the deaths of children or one of their own.

▪

Stapleton, Schenley, Aronwald. An off-duty cop, a gay pharmacist, and an old man in a laundry who used to make rulings about parking tickets. They had nothing in common beyond the misfortune of getting in the way of men grasping at what remained of a world that better men were dismantling.

"Wiseguys are like what senators are to people," Ken Taub explained in his summation for the Francesehi trial. "They command all the respect and power in the neighborhood." But that power and respect is fading fast.

Frank Gioia Jr., for instance, didn't see any room for advancement in the Genovese family, so he tried to join the Lucheses, whom he later described as the "Microsoft of the mob." Such are their dreams of greatness. From then on it was drugs, murder, and "tit jobs." Today, the Luchese family, like all the families, is in extensive disarray. The NYPD, on the other hand, in spite of all the emotional and political dysfunction, got their act together with CompStat and flourished as organized crime began its decline. Kids from the same neighborhood grew up to be people like Tony Francesehi or Frank Gioia Jr. and now sit in jail or in hiding from everything they once knew. Or they grew up to be like Detective Steve Kaplan, one of the guys who put them there.

Gioia now belongs to the feds. They can keep him on a leash for as long they require. He has to keep coming back to testify. He can't move on.

Mike Cilone, Kaplan's other witness, is out of jail, but he has few friends, and half of his family hate him. At least no one wants him dead anymore. "He's in the clear," Kaplan says. "If anyone went after him at this point, it would put the heat on them." Kaplan maintains a friendly relationship with all his informants. "Cilone's a good guy, he's just trying to get by, he's trying the best he can."

Frank Smith Jr. is out of prison and in the Federal Witness Protection Program. If Kaplan needs to speak to him he has to contact whichever FBI agent is handling him. Smith may be out of prison finally, but he is not a well man. He's disabled from myasthenia gravis and Graves' disease. Both are diseases of the immune system. Symptoms of myasthenia gravis include something called

Cogan's lid twitch, which causes sufferers to repeatedly and uncontrollably look down for ten or twenty seconds, then back up. People with Graves' disease sometimes have protruding eyes or a "staring or frightened expression," along with nervousness, restlessness, weight loss, tremors, sweating, blurred or double vision, redness and swelling in the eyes, increased appetite, frequent bowel movements, depression, and anxiety. "How is he going to make a living like that?" Kaplan asks. "Social Security?"

Additional charges have been added to the original indictment for Joel Cacace, including one involving taking no-show jobs during the recovery operations at the World Trade Center. The feds plan to use Smith to testify against Cacace, who sits in prison waiting for a trial where he could be sentenced to more than a hundred years, with fines exceeding a million dollars. But on August 13, 2004, Joel Cacace pleads guilty and is sentenced to twenty years, which in all likelihood will turn out to be a life sentence for the now sixty-two-year-old mobster.

When given a chance to speak at his sentencing, Cacace has only one point to make, and that is in response to reimbursing the Aronwald family for the funeral expenses for their father. "I'm sure Frank Smith, with the government's help, will be released well before me to make restitution, and at the same time maybe he can find out the real story." William Aronwald's response, in part: "My father was everything that this man has never been and never will be. My father was decent; he's not. My father was law-abiding; he's not. My father worked hard all his life; he's been a thug and hoodlum all his life. . . . On the day he stood here to plead guilty, before Your Honor took the bench, his family was in the courtroom. He came strutting into the courtroom, waving at them, giving them the high five, as if he didn't have a care in the world . . . even up to today he has not demonstrated a scintilla of remorse for what he did."

Tony Francesehi, the murderer who kept trying desperately to break into the doomed organized-crime business, is currently housed in a maximum security prison in Stormville, New York. "It's a tough prison," says a Cold Case commander. "It looks like a castle on the moors, with old brick walls that go up very high. It's claustrophobic."

Francesehi isn't any more well liked in prison than he was out. "They hate the guy in there," Kaplan says. For a while Francesehi enjoyed some perks due to his relationship with Frank Smith, who is at the top of the prison hierarchy. Everyone respects Smith, and Tony was getting a lot of mileage out of the fact that he knew him. But he overdid it. He started abusing his privileges and people complained to Smith. Smith cut him loose. "Do what you gotta do," he said to Francesehi's fellow inmates. Francesehi can't get a foot in the door of organized crime, even in prison.

In letters, Tony Francesehi says he would like help proving his innocence. He wants someone to tell the real story. "Like why that person was at the bar/club," he writes. "That person," the one he won't name, is Ronald Stapleton. "Or why did the police department fabricated the story to cover his were about [sic]." Except we know it wasn't the police department who covered for Stapleton, but Robert Race, Stapleton's attorney. Even if Stapleton wasn't where he should be, or doing something he shouldn't, that doesn't let Francesehi off the hook for murder. "It's going to be a long fight for me but when you are innocent it don't matter how long it will take to prove it."

When pressed for details and an explanation as to why those in his own circle testified against him Francesehi writes, "I can't tell you what I have on hand that will show its [sic] no way that I committed this crime back in 1977. Everything I have on the case is safe with someone on the outside would. Until I need it to prove my case!!"

Francesehi currently advertises himself on a singles Web site called Meet an Inmate. "Hi there ladies," he begins, before lying about everything about himself, starting with the fact that he is not single. He even still claims to be Italian. "Roses are read, sugar is sweet. Please let's take the time to meet," he writes in his ad. "All reply's [*sic*] will be answered." And then he finishes with: "No head games please." Francesehi comes up for parole for the first time on December 11, 2023.

Cops don't spend a lot of time examining their emotional states, so when they're asked to account for how they feel they're usually at a loss. Kaplan, instead, makes jokes. He married a woman with a similar sense of humor. When she heard her husband was to be included in this book she cracked, "It's going to be a boring book." Kaplan beams with pride each time he repeats her remark. Not surprisingly, Kaplan doesn't have a lot to say about Tony Francesehi. "I don't spend a minute thinking about Francesehi; I couldn't care less about that guy." It's as if spending any time thinking about him now that he's in jail accords Francesehi stature and respect. When asked about Francesehi professing his innocence, Kaplan responds, "I couldn't care less." He seemed almost angry that I had even communicated with Francesehi. "Who gives a shit what that guy has to say?"

Meanwhile, the network of crime that stretches back to the fifties continues into the twenty-first century with succeeding generations. The second of Carmine Persico's sons, Lawrence Persico, was indicted on some of the same extortion and no-show charges as Cacace. (Carmine's oldest son, Alphonse, is already in jail for racketeering.) "I am sure you are aware of Larry's mental condition," Carmine wrote the judge about his son. "This condition dates back to 1972 when I received 14 years in prison. Larry took it very hard and his troubles began." As if it wasn't possible for someone with psychological problems to be a mobster. "They're all mentally ill," Kaplan insists. Larry later pleaded guilty.

Kaplan works a lot of organized-crime cases now, even though the cases continue to be a source of problems for him. Spano may not like them, but organized-crime cases get a lot of attention both within the police department and in the media. The courtroom for Linda Leon and Esteban Martinez was almost empty. When an organized-crime case goes to trial, those courtrooms are packed, with signs and arrows directing the public, media, and law enforcement personnel where to sit. As a result, who gets which case can sometimes generate nasty battles. In fact, someone in the police department successfully battled Kaplan for Cacace. Kaplan wasn't concerned about losing attention. He cared because after years of getting everyone to talk and building the case, another investigator got to bring it home. For this reason, Kaplan and his occasional partner, Detective Mike Carrano, prefer organized-crime cases involving Colombians. "You kill a Colombian, no one cares," Carrano explains. "You kill an old Italian guy, and everybody wants to get in on it."

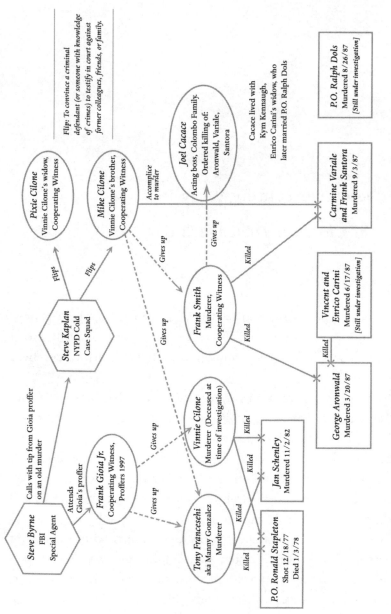

Eight seemingly unrelated murders come together for Detective Steve Kaplan

Steve Byrne
FBI
Special Agent

Calls with tip from Gioia proffer on an old murder

Attends Gioia's proffer

Frank Gioia Jr.
Cooperating Witness,
Proffers 1997

Steve Kaplan
NYPD Cold
Case Squad

Flips

Flips

Pixie Cilone
Vinnie Cilone's widow,
Cooperating Witness

Mike Cilone
Vinnie Cilone's brother,
Cooperating Witness

Flip: To convince a criminal defendant (or someone with knowledge of crimes) to testify in court against former colleagues, friends, or family.

Accomplice to murder

Gives up

Gives up

Frank Smith
Murderer,
Cooperating Witness

Joel Cacace
Acting boss, Colombo Family.
Ordered killing of:
Aronwald, Variale,
Santora

Gives up

Cacace lived with
Kym Kennaugh,
Enrico Carini's widow, who
later married P.O. Ralph Dols

Gives up

Gives up

Gives up

Gives up

Vinnie Cilone
Murderer (Deceased at
time of investigation)

Killed

Killed

Tony Franceschi
aka Manny Gonzalez
Murderer

Killed

Jan Schenley
Murdered 11/2/82

Killed

P.O. Ronald Stapleton
Shot 12/18/77
Died 1/3/78

Killed

Killed

George Aronwald
Murdered 3/20/87

Killed

**Vincent and
Enrico Carini**
Murdered 6/17/87
[Still under investigation]

Killed

**Carmine Variale
and Frank Santora**
Murdered 9/3/87

P.O. Ralph Dols
Murdered 8/26/87
[Still under investigation]

12 Detective Tommy Wray

The Christine Diefenbach Case

The house where Christine Diefenbach lived is boarded up now. Finnegan's Bar is empty, and the area on the Long Island Railroad tracks where Christine was murdered in 1988 is surrounded by a locked fence.

Most cold cases are never solved. A detective's hard work is not always rewarded. The number of cold cases goes up every year, never down. "Every time I come to work," Tommy Wray says, "I see that folder. Her folder. It's there. I formed a mental attachment to it. It eats at me." None of the other 590 unsolved murders from 1988 were solved in 2003. Realistically, the best the Cold Case Squad and all the rest of the NYPD can do is make the inevitable climb of cold cases less steep. The families of murder victims whose cases are never solved will always wonder, why did they die? why in this way? If they were hoping for the elusive sense of closure, they will be forever disappointed. But which is worse? Never knowing and continuing to hope that there is an answer in all the universe that will bring some measure of relief? Or perhaps discovering that a satisfying answer can't possibly exist, and now you have nothing left, not even hope? "My youngest daughter is sixteen," Wray says. "I can't imagine something like this happening to Kaitlyn. Christine's father may never find out why, but he'll find out what happened. He'll feel better."

■

Lieutenant Panzarella brought the Diefenbach case to Cold Case Squad when they first formed in 1996 because he believed her case could be solved. He still believes it. "We have concrete leads. But we're not ready to go to a grand jury right now. We have a possible sixty-forty shot at winning. I don't like to go into court with less than seventy. We work so hard to get to this point, why go into court right now? Especially with a victim/victim (an innocent child as opposed to an adult criminal). There's no time frame for when you're going to get that seventy or ninety percent. It might be next week."

Tommy Wray could retire any day he wants. He's been on the force thirty years. "The only reason I'm still here is once in a while I get to tap a guy on the shoulder and say, 'You thought you got away with it. Guess what?'"

And if he fails? "We're the last frontier for the family," Panzarella explains. "If we don't do it, there isn't anybody else gonna do it. Because once we're finished with it, ninety-nine percent of the time that case is going to be put away. If we don't solve it, it's done."

■

The metal bar that sat for years unexamined, and that Tommy diligently recovered, is determined to be of no value as evidence. But the OCME did find two spots of semen on Christine's clothing. There is hope. "They said she wasn't raped," Tommy says, "but I always believed the killer tried." He can get a profile from the semen. And he still has the single hair. Tommy gets a call from the Police Lab saying that the hair he brought them is not Christine's and is ready to undergo mitochondrial DNA testing. Tommy drives everything down to Mitotyping Technologies in Pennsylvania. Not long after, yet another potential lead dies. The semen DNA sample is unusable. "I was hoping that would tell me who the killer was," he explains. "I feel comfortable that the hair came from the killer also, because it was found in Christine's vaginal area, but the semen is definitely the perp's." It's just another disappointment to add to sixteen years' worth of disappointments. Then a month later Tommy gets the first solid lead he's had since he interviewed bartender John Sanderson two years before—the lab was able to get a mitochondrial DNA profile from the hair. Tommy Wray is as jubilant as you can get when talking about murder. "I'm more confident than ever. It's a piece of physical evidence." Evidence that no one had before. By the beginning of April, he'd driven back down to Pennsylvania five times to drop off still more evidence to be tested. The bill is now up to twenty thousand dollars.

Wray hasn't told Christine's father about the hair yet. "I don't want to give him false hope," he explains. "It could take months or years and then amount to nothing." The National Organization of Parents of Murdered Children, Inc., has a Web site. On it, survivors list tips for law enforcement on how to deal with victims' families:

> Be honest.
> Tell family members everything you know, do not hold back information.
> Answer as many questions as possible and explain why they cannot answer all questions.
> Be truthful.

Those are tips about fresh homicides. It's different with a cold case. Once a detective has reestablished contact with the family, if hope has been extinguished, they've rekindled it. If the family has found peace, they've disturbed it. John Diefenbach remembers what it used to be like. "The worst time is at night. The silence. It makes you think and think and think and think, you drive yourself crazy." I should have been there, I should have been there, I should have been there. Thousands upon thousands of responses in the Parents of Murdered Children's Web site forums echo Diefenbach: "I was supposed to protect her." The anguish is so deep, intense, and unanswerable that if there's even a remote possibility that a family has found some respite, detectives are reluctant to go back with every single development. They prefer to wait until they really have something. "You've seen him on the news," Wray says about Christine's father, John Diefenbach. "He still hasn't forgiven himself for not being there to save her."

Some parents start calling every day for updates once they're contacted, and detectives must reluctantly explain how much time might pass between developments. John Diefenbach is not one of those parents. He calls Tommy Wray every three or four months. He doesn't press for details. Tommy calls him in February 2004, when Joseph Smith is picked up on charges of abducting and murdering eleven-year-old Carlie Brucia in Florida. Wray wants to know if Smith is a relative because Diefenbach's wife's maiden name is Smith, and there are some similarities between the crimes. But no one in the Diefenbach family is related to Joseph Smith.

▪

A month after learning that the DNA from the spots of semen were unusable, Tommy is told that the mitochondrial DNA profile from the hair didn't match their suspects. Tommy's reaction to the news is to keep investigating. "Christine is a complicated case," Wray says. "You could have a team of detectives working her case every day." He just keeps going. He has the lab check the mitochondrial profile of the hair against twelve of the original "people of interest" from the case (these are people detectives are not ready to call suspects). "It was worth a shot." No matches. Fine, he thinks. There are still more things to try. He plans to get DNA samples from every person of interest from the original investigation. He doesn't appear anxious that Christine Diefenbach might be slowly disappearing into a finally unreachable past.

Not long after these setbacks, Tommy is home reading the newspaper when he comes across an article about DNA from an older rape that had been tested and entered into the DNA database. "His DNA popped," Wray says, his voice full of what can only be described as relief. The rapist's DNA was already in the database because he was in jail for another rape. Tommy Wray has another lead to follow because the rape was committed around the same time and place as Christine's murder, by a guy who didn't live far from the Diefenbach family. They haven't reached the end of possibility.

▪

Christine's case is an almost a perfect example of the kind of murder that doesn't get solved. It happened outdoors, she wasn't close to her home, there were no witnesses, and she was likely killed by strangers. It also happened in 1988, when they were just barely beginning to understand the forensic value of DNA. A system for collection and testing wasn't firmly in place.

John Diefenbach is still ambivalent about Wray succeeding. Does he want him to finally catch Christine's murderer? "I do and I don't. I don't want to see someone else go through what me and my wife went through. The first few years are hell. In the very beginning your mind won't accept it. There's a mistake. This didn't happen to me. She's going to walk in the door." He dreads going to court and finally hearing exactly what happened. He's never seen the crime scene photos. He hasn't read the autopsy report.

"But I want to know why," Diefenbach says, longing for answers all the same. "For the life of me, I can't possibly understand what she could have done to deserve that." No one deserves that, but there must be some sort of answer, no matter how unsatisfactory, right? There's got to be an answer.

There doesn't seem to be any part of the whole process that isn't about disappointment. Even if there's an arrest. The Parents of Murdered Children Web site states that "when a suspect is arrested, relief bordering on euphoria is common among survivors, who often believe that now everything is going to be all right." Of course, that's not true. "What they are almost always forced to learn," it continues, "is that arrests do not necessarily result in prosecutions, or prosecutions in convictions, or convictions in stiff sentences, or stiff sentences in stiff sentences served." It just goes on and on.

In the Diefenbach's basement are Christine's *Knight Rider* sleeping bag, boxes of condolence cards, and on a cupboard shelf, her collection of plastic horses. The idea of throwing out her treasures is inconceivable. "When Christine was twelve I took her horseback riding in Sheepshead Bay," her father reminisces. It started to rain. Christine was happy and she didn't want to come in out of the rain, and Diefenbach didn't have the heart to turn around and head back in. So he stayed out with her in the rain, while she rode until she didn't want to ride anymore.

Christine was just beginning to grow into whoever she would have become. She was at that age when girls put their foot down and insist on who they are and her parents were supporting her. They had sent her to art school for a while, because it was her favorite thing, but then she unexpectedly stopped. "They [the teachers] try to change your way of doing things," she told her father. "They're taking away my freedom. They have a bunch of rules." She didn't like being poured in a mold, her father explained. And so that was that. She didn't have to go back.

She also didn't want to be a Jehovah's Witness anymore. "Christine wasn't into it. My wife let her go. She didn't force her and Christine stopped going to meetings when she was twelve. She stopped going door-to-door." They had also begun to address the fact that she was withdrawn and had few friends, and Christine and her family had started therapy. They wanted her to be the person she wanted to be. Like all parents, they wanted her to be happy.

Tommy Wray thinks he has a chance of solving her case. But he says the same thing Panzarella has said. "I could know something any minute, any day, or nothing for years." This is the reality of cold cases. On television, everyone wins. Here, everyone hopes.

"She couldn't run," her father says, haunted. Christine wore corrective shoes that made her walk funny. She couldn't run from the blows and kicks that killed her. He'll be haunted forever. "It's always ongoing," he repeats. "No closure."

And so the detectives wait. Tommy Wray waits. John Diefenbach waits. The families of the 8,894 wait. Almost all of them will wait forever. Most cases will remain cold and unsolved until the very last member of the immediate family is dead, and all the detectives retire, and new detectives stop writing filler 5s, and the cases are put away for good, until the next precinct move, when they will finally be lost forever.

13 Detective Wendell Stradford

The Jean Sanseverino Case

Every year, for the past ten years, the Brooklyn Botanic Garden has held a contest for the Greenest Block in Brooklyn. The block where Jean Sanseverino was murdered won first place in both 1998 and 1999, prompting the contest organizers to make the rule that no block can win two years in a row. "From a horticultural and aesthetic perspective, that block is one of the most beautiful blocks in New York, not just Brooklyn," says Ellen Kirby, from the Brooklyn Botanic Garden. One block west, purple and blue hydrangeas grow in front of suspect Bill Miller's former place. One block east, the building where suspect Joe Moore had a room is listed in the National Registry of Historic Places. To rent a studio apartment anywhere on this stretch of State Street would run you a thousand dollars a month now. But State Street was likely always lovely, even in the worst times. The neighborhood looks elegant in the crime scene photographs taken outside Jean's building. A Native American reminiscing about State Street, which used to have a large Mohawk population, called it the most beautiful place in the world. There is something almost magical about the block where Jean once lived.

All the State Street bars are private residences now, but within walking distance are two drug rehabilitation facilities—a Phoenix House and a Daytop—remnants of a troubled past. The Oxford Theatre, where Bill Miller said Jean walked off and left him before going home to die, is now a parking lot. The Sheridan Bar & Grill where she ate her last meal is now the Brawta Caribbean Cafe. There were only two murders in the 84 precinct last year. Crime has been down for years.

Jean's room is practically unchanged. A wall has been removed so that it's one big room, but the area in the front where she slept and died is the same. It's a pretty room with lots of light, and it looks out onto the same trees and church a few doors down. There's nothing to suggest that someone's life ended brutally here. No taint of death. Everything is all peace and quiet. In the summer, baths can be taken by an open window that looks out onto a garden in the back.

Jean Sanseverino's case would not have gone cold today. The cases that go cold are the ones where the victim is shot, outdoors, by strangers. When someone is murdered in an intimate way by someone she knew, someone she laughed with or shared a steak with, someone who got up close and clamped their hands around her neck and, ignoring her eyes, her fear of dying, squeezed, for perhaps as long as five minutes—those cases get solved. Jean was strangled indoors, and almost assuredly by someone she knew. Vito Spano says men kill to save face or prove their manhood. Jean had a lot of boyfriends. There were plenty of guys who might have been jealous and felt the need to prove themselves. Why wasn't her case cleared?

"The whole investigative process was not as good as it is now," Dr. Robert Shaler, the head of Forensic Biology at the OCME, explains. "Scientists did not go to crime scenes in New York City, so my guess is that they missed a lot of the good evidence. The medical examiners were not as qualified then as they are now. The physicians who did autopsies were not really great forensic pathologists."

Autopsy reports that were only a couple of pages long in 1951 go on for many pages today.

Seasoned homicide detectives and Crime Scene Unit guys in 2004 have the benefit of fifty more years of acquired knowledge and scientific advancement. If Jean were strangled today, the police would try to get the killer's DNA from her neck, where his hands held on until she died. Her body could be exhumed to find the DNA now, but Dr. Robert Shaler doesn't think it's still there. "My guess is during the course of the autopsy they washed it out. They usually washed the bodies. They'll look at the body for something, and then they wash them." They'd also try to get DNA from the cigarettes sitting in the ashtray in the crime scene photographs.

"If the fingerprints are still available there might be some DNA there," Shaler suggests. "When they do a fingerprint lift, it's covered. It's been protected for fifty years." Shaler presses his finger against the desktop. "That's ten cells there," he points out. "If the fingerprints still exist, we could do some LCN work when the lab is ready." LCN, or low copy number, is a DNA test that requires the fewest number of cells. It's done only in Great Britain currently, but the OCME is constructing a high sensitivity and mitochondrial sequencing lab where they'll be able to perform LCN analysis once it's completed. Unfortunately, the fingerprints that were lifted in Jean's apartment are not in the Latent Prints Section's archives.

While the police in 1951 took scrapings from each available suspect, there's no indication in the DD5s that anyone took scrapings from Jean. Today, police still get scrapings from underneath the suspect's fingernails, but they also put brown paper bags over the victim's hands to make sure any trace evidence isn't lost, and the medical examiner removes the scrapings later. In 1951, not only did they not bag victims' hands, they fingerprinted victims at the scene, destroying any hairs or fibers or other trace evidence.

Everyone would pay more attention to hair and fibers today. Spano explains the concept of evidence transfer. "When you enter a room, you leave evidence, and you take away material from where you were in the room when you leave. Even though the concept of evidence transfer has been known to police departments for at least a hundred years, they can do more tests today."

The 1951 police did try to compare the fibers from Jean's sweater to the fibers that were found underneath their suspects' fingernails, but the report they got back from the medical examiner didn't tell them much either way. At the end of his analysis the medical examiner wrote "non-committal." No one at the OCME would take one look under a microscope and write "non-committal" today. They'd begin the same way, with a microscopic comparison, but from there they'd go on to a spectroscopic test, if the fiber was the same type and color, and then they'd do a GC pyrolysis, to get the chemical signature for that fiber type.

"The excrement could be typed if it still exists," Shaler suggests. "They might have been able to get a blood type from the excrement in 1951, but probably not. And if her clothing exists it could be tested."

None of the evidence remains. Two pencils identified as belonging to Bill Miller were left inside the case folder, but they were only collected to see if they were the same as the one left in Jean's bra. They have no value as evidence now. The blood and semen that would be carefully stored at both the OCME and the Property Clerk warehouse today are long gone. Fingernail scrapings were not kept until the late 1970s, when they were sent to NYPD. (Since 1990, they've been kept in the lab at the OCME.) Jean's body could be exhumed to recover the scrapings. Unlike the DNA around her neck that was probably washed away, there is a possibility that trace evidence left underneath her fingernails in 1951 is still there.

Deputy Inspector Vito Spano thinks Jean's case might have gone cold because "no one made a big deal about her. She had no champion." Her family was living all the way down in Alabama in a house without running water. Her husband, a main suspect, wasn't after the police to find her murderer. "Do yout think he gave a shit if they solved the case?" Spano asks. "I don't think her case was deemed that significant. She was on the low level of society; it wasn't a priority case." He says again, "She had no champion."

The four main suspects—Raymond Sanseverino, Bill the Greek, Bill Miller, and Joe Moore—are gone. Bill Miller vanished and was never heard from again. Old Correction records turn up one Bill Miller from Brooklyn who might have been the same guy. This Bill Miller went to jail in 1948 for attempted burglary, third degree, which means he was caught trespassing, possibly trying to break into someone's apartment. And he would have gotten out in time to murder Jean. But there's nothing more on him after that. Joe Moore also disappeared without a trace. The FBI had a warrant for his arrest, but there's no mention in the DD5s of their ever apprehending him, and Spano couldn't find anyone in the FBI who knew where to look for records that old. The FBI in Norfolk, Virginia, who held the original warrant, no longer has any record of it.

A little more is known about Bill the Greek. When he first came to New York he stayed with his sister and her husband in Brooklyn. Phone books from 1951 and today are compared to see if any relatives or neighbors are still around. Two listings are identical. One of Bill the Greek's nephews is living in Bill's sister's house. Bill the Greek left America soon after the murder, the nephew said, and went back to Greece and the sea. He returned only once, in the early sixties, and he didn't leave the ship. He never married, and he died sometime in the early seventies. Bill the Greek's nephew doesn't say much in the end, though. He appears reluctant to speak.

More is learned about Jean's husband, Raymond, from his only surviving sibling, a brother named Patrick. Raymond Sanseverino died of cancer on August 25, 1980, a week after his fifty-fourth birthday. By the time he was diagnosed he had cancer in every vital organ. The doctors didn't know how he lived as long as he did. "He had to have been in a lot of pain but he never told anyone," Patrick says.

"Raymond was not a happy man," his brother remembers. He grew up in institutions. "The nuns were cruel. Some were awfully nice, but the ones who were mean were very, very mean." Once, Raymond broke a nun's chain. According to Patrick, the nun turned around and broke Raymond's arm. "The day the cast came off she hit him again and broke it again." Another time, when Raymond was ten, a prefect beat Patrick with a cane until he bled. Later, in the dining room, Raymond grabbed the cane from the man and broke it in half. "Raymond could be very mean. All the kids in the orphanage were afraid of him. He showed no mercy. I'm sure the orphanage left some scars," Patrick continues. "They left scars on all of us."

Raymond didn't know as a boy that John Sanseverino, who was a morphine addict, wasn't his real father. (Raymond's father was John Blair, who never married his mother.) And no one explained to Raymond why the man he thought was his father refused to see him when he visited his brother Patrick at the orphanage. John Sanseverino was not a kind man. Raymond's mother had to iron John's shirts so he could look nice when he went out to see other women. When he died, Patrick wouldn't kiss his body at the wake. Eleven-year-old Raymond did.

Raymond never finished high school. Instead, he enlisted in the army on July 8, 1944, one month before his eighteenth birthday.

According to his brother, Raymond hated women. "He seemed very charming at first," Patrick continues, "but once you got to know him—scary. When they found out what he was like, the women of any substance would tell him to go away." But in the early stages of their relationship, Raymond was very much in love with Jean. She wasn't particularly educated or articulate, but she was young and pretty and, while immature, fun. They both liked to drink, they liked to drink a lot, but Raymond complained to Patrick that Jean was drunk all the time and called her a tramp. Patrick describes their apartment on State Street as dirty and unkempt, and the one small bed was always unmade at noontime. A woman's housekeeping was a larger reflection of her character in 1951, and since they lived in a single room, an unmade bed in the middle of the only room would have stood out and made a terrible impression on a 1950s visitor.

If Raymond wanted to kill Jean, he could have done it with one punch, Patrick claims. Raymond fought in the Golden Gloves in 1943, at McCarren Park in Greenpoint, Brooklyn. Raymond was also a racist, and he thought Jean had a black boyfriend. That may have been too much for him. "Once you are intimate with a woman, there's some bond there."

Patrick Sanseverino admits that he believes it's possible that Raymond killed Jean. Their mother believed it, he said. Raymond had an explosive temper and she hated and feared her son. She refused to see him for years. When she was dying, Raymond went to the hospital to console her, but she told him to get away from her. "I don't know where she got the strength," Patrick says, "because she was very weak at the end and slept most of the time. But she sat up and said, 'Don't come anywhere near me.'"

"That's a lot of hatred from a mother," Wendell says. "A child can disappoint a mother repeatedly, but for her to reject her child like that, he had to have done something really bad," Wendell believes. "I've known many people who told their parents they murdered someone, because they knew the parents wouldn't give them up. But just because they don't give them up doesn't mean they're okay with it. Raymond may have told his mother that he screwed up. That he had done something wrong. She couldn't turn him in, but she may have been unable to forgive him or have anything to do with him again."

Raymond didn't say a lot to Patrick about Jean's murder, but he told him he wasn't surprised or sorry that she was dead. A few years later, Raymond came to visit Patrick. He was broke and Patrick bought him four tires for his car. In return, Raymond stole Patrick's credit card, took off, and they saw each other only intermittently after that.

Patrick admits his brother had a gentle side. "He was happiest working with kids." Raymond was involved with the Boy Scouts for twenty-one years. He also fought bravely during World War II. Among other medals, including a Purple Heart, Raymond was awarded the Soldier's Medal. The Soldier's Medal is not given to just anyone. "It's a very big deal. It's equivalent to the Distinguished Flying Cross," an army spokesperson explains. "He saved someone's life, it just didn't happen on a battlefield. But it had to be more than reaching out and grabbing someone who was standing in the path of an oncoming car, though. He had to have done something very heroic." It had to involve a risk to his own life. Raymond was stationed for a time at Camp Sibert, just outside of Gadsden, Alabama, which may have presented him with plenty of opportunities for extreme heroism. Camp Sibert was a chemical warfare training facility, and army personnel from Camp Sibert were brought up to Edgewood Arsenal in Maryland to be used as subjects for live mustard gas tests.

Raymond married three more times after Jean and had two sons, three daughters, and three stepchildren. With one exception, Raymond's children met his brother and sisters for the first time at Raymond's funeral, then they never saw any of them again. The only child Raymond ever spoke to about Jean's murder was his oldest son, Ray, when Ray was fourteen or fifteen, and he didn't tell him much beyond the fact that it had happened. None of the other children know.

Raymond's son remembers a completely different man. His father didn't hate women. His father loved his mother, Raymond's third wife, who left him when her first husband got out of prison (on an organized-crime charge, it turns out). Ray tells the story about a long-lost daughter Raymond tried to find, a girl he had with his second wife. He hired a lawyer, but they weren't successful. She found him, though, in the late seventies, a couple of years before he died. Raymond never earned a college degree, but he was one of those solid working-class types who could fix whatever he wanted to fix, build whatever he wanted to build. It wasn't like he wasn't capable of going further. It just didn't happen.

All of the people the detectives questioned are dead or have disappeared. Carrie Boyd, who owned the building at 180 St. John's Place where Raymond was living when Jean was murdered, and who provided Raymond with an alibi, died in 1969.

Marie Rizzo/Russo, Carrie's foster daughter, who was seeing Raymond at the time, apparently never did anything that was noted in any kind of record that could be found today. The same is true for Jean's roommate, Sylvia Krumholz.

Jean's friend Margaret Hunter, whom everyone called Frankie, was put into the Bedford Reformatory a few weeks after Jean died. This was a step up in seriousness from the Villa Loretta Home for Wayward Girls. She got out in October, though, and married John Fiore a few years later, in 1956. They did not have any children. He died in 1975, and she died in February 2003. The only things a relative would say about her was that she was not a pretty girl, she didn't have a happy life, and she died toothless and alone and on welfare in Florida.

Tommy Pennino, the boxer who was questioned because his name was found on a slip of paper in Jean's room, fought four more times (featherweight) in the few months after Jean's murder. He had two wins by decision, one knockout, and one draw. He never showed up in *The Ring Record Book and Boxing Encyclopedias* again.

Eugene McCarthy, the first cop on the scene, went on to become a Youth Patrol Officer and ran Police Athletic League youth programs in the Red Hook section of Brooklyn. Even though his own father died young, McCarthy still figured out how to be a great and loving father to his children, one of whom died fighting in the first Gulf War. He retired in 1969 and died in December 2001. All the detectives who worked the case are dead, as are the ADAs.

The SS *Gulfcrest,* the ship that Johnny Johansson may or may not have boarded the morning Jean died, and which launched on February 27, 1926, was sold sometime in the early 1980s, and the records from the 1950s were gone by the 1960s.

After more than fifty years and without evidence, witnesses, or a confession, what, realistically, could Detective Wendell Stradford do to solve Jean's case?

■

In current cases, as in cold cases, the husband is always a main suspect, and Raymond was a pretty suspicious husband. He was a womanizer. He had a history of getting into fights, and Jean's autopsy report indicates that she was punched. Raymond was a racist, and he thought Jean had a black boyfriend. His mother was frightened of him. His one remaining brother believes he is capable of murder.

But Raymond was already separated from Jean and seeing other women, one of whom, Marie Rizzo/Russo, was living in the same apartment building he was living in at the time. The night Jean was murdered, Raymond and Marie and his landlady, Carrie Boyd, had dinner together, then watched the Charles-Walcott fight, which began at 10:00 p.m. and went fifteen rounds. Ray had to go to work the next morning. If Ray killed Jean, he would have had to leave Marie after dinner and the fight, which went quite late, to walk what would have been considered a fair distance in those days, then hang out waiting somewhere until five in the morning in order to fit the time frame of Jean's death. It isn't a likely scenario.

As far as the detectives were able to determine, Bill Miller was the last person to see Jean alive. He was generally known to everyone as a surly, unpleasant man. Two months before the murder he showed up in a hospital after midnight with a cut on his head that needed stitches. He clearly had been in a fight. Another time, according to friends, one of Jean's boyfriends gave Miller "a licking" when he antagonized her. Jean's former landlady talked about how Jean didn't like him and complained about him. She said his room smelled.

It's a mystery why Jean spent all evening with Miller that night, except we know she was financially strapped. She asked Joe Moore for money. And, even though Miller seemed willing to pay for her, she stole five dollars from him. Miller had to have been hoping to have sex with Jean at the end of the evening, and if she said no, he might have become enraged. Also, he had a leg injury, for which he gave police two stories. In one he said he fell down, in another he said Jean pushed him down. Why would Jean push him down? Instead, could he have been injured while he was murdering her? People in the building said they heard what sounded like someone hitting the floor.

Bill the Greek and Jean were sleeping together. Before walking out the door of the Sheridan Bar & Grill with Bill Miller, Jean told Bill the Greek that she'd come back. As the night wore on without her return, Bill the Greek got more and more drunk and angry and jealous, and he expressed that anger to several people, just one hour before Jean was killed. Bill the Greek finally gave up and went home, at the same time Jean and Bill Miller were walking home. He might have seen them together, drunk. Even though he got on a train and went home to Manhattan, the detectives were able to prove that he had plenty of time to come back before the estimated time of her death.

Joe Moore was a suspect because they found a note from him in Jean's pocketbook asking her to come see him that night. Moore said it was to lend her money. Joe Moore lived a couple of blocks away from Jean and was also heading home at the same time Jean and Miller were walking down State Street. If they were having an affair, he might have been jealous if he saw them. Raymond thought she had a black boyfriend. If she did, was it Moore? Her friends didn't mention that they were a couple when questioned. But Moore was black. "It wasn't acceptable for a white woman to be with a black man in 1951," Wendell says. "Perhaps Jean's friends were being discreet. Perhaps Jean and Joe were discreet and her friends never knew."

There were hints in the DD5s, however, that Moore may have been homosexual. That would have been something a black sailor in the fifties would have wanted to keep very, very quiet.

Then there was Johnny. Three days after Jean died a letter arrived from someone she was having an affair with. It was signed simply "Johnny." Who was Johnny?

Detectives discounted Jean's neighbor Johnny Johansson early on because they believed he boarded a ship at 3:45 in the morning and was on that ship while Jean was dying. Again, the former owners of the ship explained that there is no proof that he boarded the ship at 3:45, as the log said, or even that he got on the ship at all, and the ship didn't sail until 1:15 that afternoon, many hours after Jean was murdered.

According to the DD5s, more than one person questioned said Johansson was having an affair with Jean and that everyone knew but his wife. Johnny and his wife were at the Sheridan Bar & Grill the night Jean was murdered. They left at nine. Then Johnny slept in the front room and his wife slept on the couch, indicating they'd had a fight. His wife woke up at six the next morning and he was gone. She found ten dollars and a note explaining that he was leaving on a ship. It was not a planned trip. Why would he decide in the middle of the night that he had to leave New York immediately? Johnny and his wife lived one block away from Jean.

The night Jean died, two bartenders, Johnny Neary and Richard Heaney, were in the 7 Corners Bar & Grill, Jean and Bill's last stop before walking home. They left and, later, Johnny dropped Heaney off at his home at 410 State Street in a cab, a block away from Jean. Like the others, the timing could have been just right and they may have seen Jean walking home. A couple of days after the murder a note arrived at the police station that read: *Trail Heaney 46 Hoyt Street He knows Sylvia. Friends got Jean 366 State St go slow, cozy. Investigate. This is hot.*

Raymond and Jean stayed with Raymond's brother-in-law John Kraus and his wife, Eleanor, when Jean first came to New York. Jean referred to him as "Johnny" in a letter home. Was he capable of having an affair? "I wouldn't blame him," Patrick Sanseverino said. "It was possible. My sister was a slob. The house was filthy, cockroaches all over the place. It wasn't a warm relationship. He was good to my sister, though, he came home from work, he was never late." Eleanor and John eventually divorced and have since died.

■

Enter a twenty-first-century Cold Case detective. The first thing Wendell does is call the Crime Scene Unit to see if they have all the original crime scene photos. An envelope of photographs is found in the Central Records warehouse, but they are the same as the ones left in the case folder. Wendell doesn't go to the Property Clerk for evidence because none of the original vouchers were in the case files, and Wendell knows full well that the Property Clerk doesn't have anything left in its possession from the fifties. The Property Clerk later confirms that it has nothing from Jean's case at the warehouse or at the Borough Property Clerk office in Brooklyn.

In addition to the photographs, another file of DD5s for Jean's case is found at the Central Records warehouse, and while most are duplicates of those Stradford already has, there are a few DD5s that weren't in the original file. One in particular mentions briefly the results of tests done on a tie and undershirt belonging to Bill the Greek. According to the newly discovered DD5, they tested positive for blood. But whose? The same DD5 says that semen was found on an undershirt that Detective Kelly left with Deputy Chief Medical Examiner Benjamin Morgan Vance. Maddeningly, the DD5 doesn't say whom the undershirt belonged to. "Perhaps because he didn't know," Wendell says. "Maybe it was found at the scene."

There is also a new letter in the DD5s from Jean's mother, which says, among other things, *"Mr. Officer . . . I just wish I could meet you offers and explane sonething he was a man that could tell a lie and you no it. He was mean to Jean he woulden work she made the liven he tore her cloths of hur at my hous and slapped hur down a cross the bed . . . told us he had a 40 day pass and then he brok out of stocakde at Camp Sibert . . . he tryed to posin Jean's youngest sister by putting something in a cold drink."* She asked about her wedding ring one more time. And for Jean's clothes. She closed her letter with, *"We are just farmers and live out of town and I am the mother of 4 other children and please do you best to find the rites ones that murdered Jean."* Jean's family was convinced Raymond murdered Jean. The only surviving member of her immediate family, her sister Joann, believes it to this day. Wendell points out that the fact that the family didn't like Raymond isn't in and of itself an indictment. "Lots of families don't like their sons-in-law. Doesn't make them murderers."

Like Vito, Wendell tries to find the want card that the FBI sent for Joe Moore, but no one at the FBI knows where records of that type from that year would be. There are a number of ways of tracking down an old seaman, but nothing works. The U.S. Coast Guard National Maritime Center has no record of him. If he ever went to prison, no records have survived. The International Longshoremen's Association was contacted for information about all the men of the sea Wendell was looking for, but so far they haven't come up with anything, and historians warn that it isn't likely that they ever will. They look after their own.

A letter is sent to Sailor's Snug Harbor, a retirement home for sailors that used to be in New York and is now in Sea Level, North Carolina. They didn't have any records for either Joe Moore or Johnny Johansson. The sailors could have been there under different names, however. "We have had some characters here," the executive director's office wrote.

Richard Heaney, Johnny Neary's friend, told detectives that he was running for office in the Bartender's Union. The Robert F. Wagner Labor Archives at New York University has a collection of old records for Local 6 of the Hotel Employees Restaurant Employees union (the Bartender's Union was part of Local 6). They list everyone who was running for election in 1951, but Richard Heaney's name does not appear on the list or in any other record.

One of Carrie Boyd's daughters married an NYPD patrolman named Thomas O'Donnell. According to police pension records, O'Donnell died in 1978, but he had a then nineteen-year-old son named Thomas. Perhaps Thomas might be able to say what became of his grandmother's foster daughter, Marie Rizzo/Russo. Wendell can't find him. The only living relative of Carrie Boyd's that could be found has never heard of Marie Rizzo/Russo.

Wendell tries AutoTrack and Accurint searches on everyone still unfound. Accurint is a new service that the police department is looking at as a possible replacement for AutoTrack. The Accurint records go back thirty and forty years, and in some cases fifty, but that's rare. They also have algorithms, which look for crimes in different cities with similar characteristics, to help the detective to find previously undiscovered links. Neither service provides any useful leads.

The DD5s list everyone in Jean's neighborhood that the police talked to in 1951. In 2003, the buzzers on all the doors and the phone books are checked to see if any names match, but not a single match is found. One State Street resident, Katherine Haddad, who is in her eighties and has lived on State Street all her life, can't remember Jean's murder and doesn't recognize the names of any of the suspects or Jean's friends. Churches are checked to see if anyone remembered the crime or any of the suspects, older parishioners are called, newspapers are scanned. Nothing. An on-line network of librarians and academics provides some leads for Jean's New York roommate, Sylvia Krumholz, but none of them lead anywhere. She remains lost to history.

Wendell goes back to the Office of the Chief Medical Examiner. Were any other tests conducted and is there any possibility the results are still there? The OCME has archives out in Brooklyn, too. The criminalists say they will start looking.

Wendell goes next to the BCI (Bureau of Criminal Investigations), where the records of old B numbers are stored (B numbers are the 1950s equivalent of today's NYSID numbers, the number given to everyone arrested in New York for a felony and some misdemeanors). The BCI also stores photographs of everyone with a B number. Suspect Joe Moore had a B number and Wendell is hoping they'll have his records. Nothing is found. Then he checks a database called the Beta System for old arrests for the four main suspects and roommate Sylvia Krumholz. Nothing comes up.

Wendell can't find anything more at the 76, the precinct where Jean's file folder sat untouched in a closet for decades. Wendell had returned to see if there is something else in that closet to help him, something anywhere in the precinct at all, but there is nothing else left from that time period.

It takes a while for the OCME to find Jean's records, and in the end, they don't provide any more information of value. No other tests had been conducted other than the ones already mentioned in the DD5s.

Wendell is back to the same four suspects the detectives had in 1951, and the same problems. He doesn't have enough evidence to either eliminate them or prove beyond a reasonable doubt that any of them was the killer.

■

At first Wendell leans away from the husband, who had a girlfriend, probably more than one, and who was believed to have been sleeping a mile and three quarters away when Jean was murdered. Bill Miller was the last person to have seen Jean alive. He is the more likely suspect, Wendell thinks. Miller probably figured, "What the hell, I'll just take the sex from her," Wendell theorizes. "But then he worried about getting locked up if he left her alive." Bill the Greek is of interest to Wendell, too. Bill the Greek was sleeping with Jean, and he was drunk and jealous that night.

But when Wendell learns that Raymond Sanseverino's mother refused to speak to him on her deathbed, and that his only surviving brother said he wouldn't be surprised to learn that his brother was guilty, Wendell stops and focuses entirely on Raymond. "That's meaningful," he says, amazed. "It's a lot for a family member to admit even that. It's like the first step toward admitting he did it." Jean's younger sister Joann remembers Detective Duffy telling her when he came to Alabama in 1952 that he thought Raymond did it, but he couldn't prove it.

Duffy never was able to prove it, and Detective Wendell Stradford has it even worse. Raymond is dead. "If the shirt with the semen still existed," Wendell explains, "I could get a mitochondrial DNA profile and compare it to the DNA from Raymond's son or brother, and Bill the Greek's nephew, if they were willing to give it to me, or if I could find a way to retrieve it indirectly. I could follow them for a few days and try to get a discarded cigarette or coffee cup." But the shirt is gone. Like Detectives Duffy and Kelly, Wendell goes back to the people who knew his suspects.

He calls Raymond Sanseverino's oldest son, but the son is hostile. "It's the fucking weekend. Call me back." It takes a few more phone calls before Wendell reaches him again, but Raymond's son refuses to cooperate. "This is becoming a nightmare," he says before he hangs up. Wendell says he often gets that. A single phone call is experienced as a nightmare.

He goes to Bill the Greek's nephew's, and when no one answers the doorbell, he leaves his card with a request that the nephew contact him. He goes back a few more times, but the nephew never calls. Wendell searches for other descendants of the four suspects. No luck. He tries to track down Detectives Walter Duffy, Bill Kelly, and any other detective who originally worked on the case, but Duffy is dead and Kelly is missing, as is every other detective he tries to find.

It's almost over. "Unless Patrick admits that his brother confessed to him, there's nothing more I can do," Wendell says. "But if Raymond told his brother he killed Jean, there's a chance I can get Patrick to tell me."

By 2004, Patrick, who lived in the northeast, has moved to another state far from New York and Wendell can't travel and talk to him in person because of the police department's minimum manning requirements (a certain number of cops must be available at all times) and because the detectives have to be available for special details, such as holidays or protests. Patrick has suffered a stroke, and his health is declining. Time is moving indifferently on. Jean's friend Frankie Hunter, one of the youngest people connected with the original investigation, died just last year.

Wendell starts making phone calls. At the end of the week in mid-December, 2004, he reaches Patrick's wife. Patrick and his wife are a refined couple. She is not thrilled to hear from the police about a decades-old murder, but she expresses her reluctance in more polite and cautious tones. She doesn't know Wendell. He could be anyone. Wendell then turns off his phone's call blocking so, if she has caller ID, she'll see that the call is coming from the New York Police Department. She puts Wendell off. Her husband's condition has worsened and she protects him. Wendell is not going to speak to Patrick today. "This happened more than fifty years ago," she says. Wendell keeps talking to her, hoping to establish trust. They reach a compromise. Wendell and Patrick can attempt a conversation the following Monday. If Patrick is unable to speak to him, Wendell will question his wife. People always tell someone. "If Raymond confessed to Patrick, Patrick may have told his wife."

Monday comes and goes. The Sanseverino phone rings and rings. Later that week Wendell reaches Patrick's wife. She again explains that he's very sick. His hearing is shot. In the morning he sits outside and reads his papers, does some physical therapy, and then he sleeps. He sleeps most of the day now, she says. She is never going to let me speak to him, Wendell is starting to conclude. He tries to learn if Patrick told his wife anything that would allow him to exceptionally clear this case, but she says they never really talked about it. He continues to leave messages for Patrick.

Two thousand five arrives. Wendell reaches Patrick Sanseverino on January 5. Patrick tries to help but he insists that Raymond never confessed to him. Yet, "I wouldn't be surprised to find out that he did it," he says more than once. "It's as if he wants to tell me he did it," Wendell says, "but he can't bring himself to say that his brother did it." Patrick tells Wendell that Raymond asked their mother to say that he was in Rochester with her at the time of murder. That makes at least two people who lied on Raymond's behalf. Everything Wendell learns only strengthens his conviction that Raymond is guilty. "He did it," Wendell believes.

Fifty-four years have now passed since Jean's murder. Nothing has been resolved. Wendell goes back to the homicide printouts and the more than 8,000 other unsolved murders. It's over.

14 The Future of the Cold Case Squad

When I first began research for this book, I thought there was going to be a century's worth of evidence, strange and marvelous artifacts of unsolved murder history that could be used to reconstruct the story of cold cases in New York. Well, there wasn't. So much evidence, so much history, is gone forever. When Vito Spano came to the Cold Case Squad he took a more optimistic view. He didn't mourn the loss of all the evidence, he thought about all the barrels and barrels full of evidence they *did* have, mountains of it just sitting there unexamined and untested in the Property Clerk warehouse and their offices all over New York.

One of the first things Spano did when he took command in 2001 was call Deputy Commissioner Maureen Casey in OMAP, the Office of Management Analysis and Planning. Together they came up with the idea for the DNA No Suspect Program. They believed there were a lot of cases among the almost nine thousand unsolved homicides since 1985 with associated DNA evidence that could be solved if they had the money to find the cases and the evidence to conduct the tests. Casey applied to the State Division of Criminal Justice Services, which went to the National Institute of Justice, and received grant money to fund the project. Just under a million dollars was divided out between the Cold Case Squad and the OCME. The grant would cover the cost of finding five hundred homicide cases with DNA evidence, with twenty-one hours of overtime for each, plus the costs of the tests. It was the biggest jolt the squad had received since its inception. They could really get to work now. But the Cold Case Squad was headed for trouble.

The money came through on July 17, 2003. The first thing the NYPD did was take half of the grant money that was to go to the Cold Case Squad and siphon it off for unsolved burglary cases. There had been a lot of attention in the press about the climbing burglary rate, and the NYPD felt they had to do something about it. The Cold Case Squad was left with enough for 271 cases. Fine. They took the hit and moved on.

Not surprisingly, they had trouble finding cases. There isn't one big central location of unsolved homicide case folders. They're kept in the seventy-six different precincts. The detectives in the seventy-six precincts didn't know what they had, they weren't there when the murders happened, and they didn't have any historical reference to guide them. The Cold Case detectives knew they could locate cases prior to 1973 in the Central Records Division warehouse, but they were looking for cases with DNA evidence. Realistically, if evidence with DNA was collected prior to 1973, it was long gone now.

So the Cold Case detectives went back to the homicide sheets, which are printouts from the Homicide Analysis Unit's database of all unsolved murders going back to 1985. They went through the sheets and looked for female victims first, because with a sex crime—often a component of a woman's murder—there is likely to be more evidence. The murderer got closer to his victim, a savage intimacy that provides more serological evidence, fingernail scrapings, hair, and fibers. For this same reason they focused on homicides that took place indoors, involving blunt-force trauma, stabbing, and strangulation rather than shootings that happened outdoors. And there was a better chance that this evidence had been collected. The detectives put together a likely list of candidates and then went back to the precincts.

They couldn't find all the old case folders. It was a familiar story. Some were misfiled. Some were signed out and never properly recorded or returned. Others were just not there. Then there was the usual problem of finding the evidence at the Property Clerk. "Whenever they can't find something they always give one of the same three excuses," one frustrated detective said. "The flood, the fire, or the move." Twice, detectives were told evidence had been destroyed, but they later found the envelopes in the borough Property Clerk offices. In spite of the difficulties, viable cases started to pile up.

Once everything was pulled together they found they couldn't move the evidence quickly enough between the Property Clerk and the Police Lab and the OCME. They had no control. They were not the bosses of the OCME. They weren't in a position to tell anyone when to conduct the tests. But if they tracked the evidence every step of the way, they could at least call up the OCME or the Police Lab, for instance, and say, "Look, you've had that shirt for two months. What's the deal?" They needed yet another form. Lieutenant Bob McHugh designed the "DNA Analysis No Suspect Homicide Case Program Overtime Report." It identified the case, the DNA evidence, and who had the evidence when. It also included how many hours of overtime were used to investigate the case. This last part, it turns out, highlighted many of their current problems.

In September 2003, Inspector Ray Ferrari, the head of the Fugitive Enforcement Division that the Cold Case Squad operates under, was made the commanding officer of the Detective Bureau in Brooklyn. He was replaced by Deputy Chief Joseph J. Reznick. This was an unusual move. The position calls for an inspector, and a deputy chief is a higher rank. It was—in effect—a demotion. "The department sent him a message," says Michael Palladino, the president of the Detective's Endowment Association (the detectives' union). "They put a chief in an inspector's position." Reznick had some problems in his previous commands, and this assignment could be interpreted as a slap on the wrist.

When Reznick arrived at the Fugitive Enforcement Division he was determined to reduce expenditures. He went after overtime first. Every quarter (and annually), the police department generates a report called the Top Overtime Earners Report. The Fugitive Enforcement Division was making way too many appearances on that report. Reznick was going to do something about that. There's nothing wrong with focusing on the bottom line, but there was a problem with Reznick's execution.

Of all the different groups that give the police department a hard time—the public, the press, criminals—the ones that make their life the most difficult, it turns out, come from their own ranks. "Cops aren't worried about the streets," a detective says in frustration. "They can take care of themselves on the street. It's the bosses."

Reznick put a cap on overtime. No one could take an hour over thirty hours in overtime a month, and if they needed more, they had to call Reznick in advance for an okay. Saving the city money was not the problem, although it must have felt like he was reaching into their pockets and pulling out payments for braces for their kids. The problem was Reznick was being kind of a dick about it. He didn't say, "I know it sucks, but we can't keep coming up on this report quarter after quarter. It looks bad." Reznick treated them like they were scamming the city. In addition, he demanded that any overtime over thirty hours be taken in time (days off) rather than pay, and according to union contracts, he can't do that. The Detective's Endowment Association started getting calls. (A letter of grievance was later filed, on behalf of another officer in Warrants.)

Next, Reznick collected all their cell phones. It wasn't a bad move. At least one detective had over a thousand hours of calls that weren't all work related, and one retired detective still had his phone a year later, still paid for by the NYPD. Now cell phones are kept in the office, and detectives must sign them out each day and return them at the end of their shift.

Reznick then took five hundred hours' worth of the overtime money from the squad's DNA No Suspect grant and gave one hundred each to the five borough homicide squads to find cold cases. He did this because those hours would *still* show up on the overtime report once they were used, and Reznick couldn't have anyone in the Fugitive Enforcement Division coming up a high overtime earner. Finally, Cold Case detectives had to call for permission to use the remaining overtime hours that were already granted and allotted to them. What started out as enough for five hundred cases would now cover one hundred. Once again, they absorbed the loss. They went out and gathered 318 viable cases. As of this writing, the Homicide Squads have found a dozen. The National Institute of Justice might not be thrilled to learn that the portion of the money that was granted to fund cases with DNA evidence yielded so little return from the Homicide Squads.

There is a lot to admire about Reznick. "He is very experienced and has a tremendous amount of knowledge to share with new and experienced investigators," Spano points out. "He's an astute investigator," Palladino agrees. He also has a compassionate side. Like his peers, Reznick is haunted by an unsolved case. On July 23, 1991, a little girl was found in a 40-quart, dark blue Igloo cooler off the Henry Hudson Parkway in northern Manhattan, where Reznick was the commanding officer at the time. Someone folded her in half, wrapped a cord from a venetian blind around her neck and behind her knees, and put her in a plastic bag underneath a cheap black tablecloth and a bunch of red Coke cans.

Crime scene pictures show a naked little girl, hog-tied and badly decomposed, her tiny hands peeking out from between her legs. Her skin is black, brown, and pink, and bone is exposed all over. One eye is gone, and the other bulges like a horribly constructed toy. For the roughly four and a half years of her life, someone barely managed to feed her. She was a little over three feet high and weighed twenty pounds. They beat her. They sexually abused her. Finally, they suffocated her. There was almost no forensic evidence of the killers, no fingerprints, and no DNA. She was never identified, and her case was never solved. The detectives nicknamed her Baby Hope. For two years she was stored in the morgue, but that was more than the detectives could bear. They pooled their money, paid for her funeral, and buried her at St. Raymond's Cemetery in the Bronx in a plot donated by the Catholic Archdiocese. Every year, for the past ten years, on the anniversary of the day they found her and the day she was finally buried, Deputy Chief Joe Reznick visits the grave of Baby Hope.

This same man creates workplaces so hostile detectives who once loved their jobs can't wait to leave. "He is extreme," a former commander says. "He can't just set overtime guidelines and monitor them for people to adhere to. To him, everyone is trying to steal."

It's not just the overtime. "Yeah, he's very smart," a retired detective concedes. "But he uses his intelligence to make the detectives feel stupid. He's smug." "He wants to be at the center of the investigation instead of letting the investigators work," a retired commanding officer says. "He is amazed with himself because he is a deputy chief. In reality, who fucking cares? You should be a nurturer for your people and have them walk in the limelight. You should be there to guide and for assistance and to make sure the job gets done, but they should get all the credit and feel that they accomplished the mission. Let the men have the glory," the commander finishes.

Palladino from the detectives' union photocopied the cover of Dale Carnegie's *How to Win Friends and Influence People* and wrote on it, "Hey Chief, My advice would be to invest a few bucks for this book. Love, Michael Palladino." "Give this to him for me," he instructed.

When the Cold Case Squad was first formed in 1996, Reznick was one of the commanders in the Detective Bureau who wanted to see it gone. He didn't think the police department needed a special Cold Case Squad. He thought this was something that could be handled by the detectives in the Homicide Squads in each borough. A year later, he submitted a proposal to implement the change. It was rejected. Now Reznick is in charge. When asked why he wanted to get rid of the Cold Case Squad in the beginning he said it was because of the caliber of the detectives Eddie Norris and Jack Maple put together. What did he mean? "They were Transit guys." It was the old bias. "I would refute that strongly," former police commissioner

William Bratton responded angrily when told of Reznick's comments about the ability of the detectives. "They were all great detectives," he insisted, "most of whom I knew personally." And what did Reznick, the new chief, have to say to the squad when he took over? "You guys don't come up in CompStat, so you don't count." The Cold Case Squad is a special squad, and their arrests are not submitted to CompStat and from there to the FBI. As a result, they're not scrutinized in the weekly CompStat meetings. "He's a good person, as a person," a retired Cold Case detective said, "but as a manager, when it comes down to dealing with the men, he's a horror." "No one wants to be here anymore," another detective lamented.

Saving the city money is a great thing, but not long after Reznick had taken over the Fugitive Enforcement Division, the mood in the squads plummeted. In his last command, a large number of the detectives there requested transfers. In response to the current problems, the detectives' union established a Reznick Committee to monitor his behavior. "Morale is shot," Palladino explained. Over at 1PP the brass was starting to wonder: What the hell is going on over there?

▪

Few cops make it to twenty years without some bitterness. The public is ambivalent, the media jump on their every move, the bosses are not always on their side. "You make a great case, then turn around and get in trouble for something stupid," a Cold Case detective sighs. A detective who works organized-crime cases compares the police department to the mob. "In the mafia they kill you. In the police department they destroy you." As an outsider, it was a shock to see that they weren't all on the same side on the inside, and that they could be as brutal with each other as they are with criminals. And who cares about cold cases? Counterterrorism has been the focus since 9/11, and the Cold Case Squad doesn't have the juice. "The NYPD is strapped for manpower and won't give people to the Cold Case Squad or any other specialty squad other than Counter Terrorism," Panzarella explains. "There should be ten detectives in each Cold Case unit in each borough, plus a sergeant and a lieutenant. Queens hasn't had a sergeant in two years." The Cold Case Squad began with four lieutenants, four sergeants, and thirty-seven detectives, and they grew from there. They now have three lieutenants, two sergeants, and twenty-five detectives. Detectives in the squad continue to retire but they're not replaced. (Although it must be said that the NYPD has given a lot of detectives and support to their Cold Case Squad compared with other cities. Los Angeles, the next largest city in the United States, has seven detectives in their Cold Case Squad.) There was a time when, if Panzarella wasn't happy about something, he could say, "Let's take it to the building," meaning 1PP. But Anemone and Maple aren't there anymore.

Reznick isn't the only one who'd be happy if the Cold Case Squad just went away. It's as hard to prosecute and defend an old case as it is to investigate it, and prosecutors and defense attorneys openly admit they'd be happy if they never had to deal with another cold case again. Defense attorney David Feige lists the reasons. "The police reports are on microfilm and they're illegible. Witnesses are hard to find. It's hard to construct a solid defense, then prove up. Who remembers where they were on a certain night twenty years ago, and if they do, how would they prove it? Unless you have a video of yourself dancing at your daughter's wedding, preferably in Honduras, you're screwed." Being able to account for your whereabouts is crucial, Feige says, "because jurors tend to think if you're there on a case that old, the police must have something."

Lieutenant Panzarella estimates that Cold Case has about eight cases in each borough where they're ready to make an arrest but the DA won't go forward. In a *New York Times* article, the DA's office points out that, like the police department, they are feeling the effects of city budget constraints and don't have the ADAs to pursue all the cases out there—much less cases that are years and decades old. They may also feel that in some instances, the suspect is already in jail for another crime, anyway, so what's the point?

"For the police department, the priority is the twenty-eight-day CompStat period," Spano explains. "That's the CompStat cycle; they're always looking at the past twenty-eight days. And how they compare to the previous twenty-eight days, and last year's twenty-eight days. They live and die by the numbers." The numbers tell them how much crime has gone down. If crime is not rising, that's all they care about. "If you have an unsolved homicide, that's an issue, but if you have seven rapes, robberies, or grand larcenies, that's a bigger issue." The police department's focus is on the FBI's Crime Index; those are the seven crimes that are reported monthly to the FBI: murder and nonnegligent manslaughter, forcible rape, robbery, aggravated assault, burglary, larceny theft, and motor vehicle theft. The FBI gathers this information from police departments all over the country and publishes it in their Uniform Crime Reports.

While it wasn't any way to inspire the detectives under his command, what Reznick said about the Cold Case Squad and CompStat was essentially the cold, hard truth. Cold cases don't figure in any of these reports. "The only way we can establish relevance is if the perpetrator is committing further murder and mayhem and adding to future crime," says Spano.

The NYPD's position is understandable, but the number of people getting away with murder is hard to swallow. Spano goes back to Reznick's response to the DNA No Suspect Program. "Yes, counterterrorism is important, it's all-important, but we got the money. The money is there. Why not give it a try instead of fighting it every step of the way?" he asks. "There are all these unsolved murders. We can clear some of them, and finally give an answer to the families who lost their loved ones. We can enhance the future."

There is also the connection between crimes then and crimes now, and the Cold Case Squad's track record is impressive. As pointed out earlier, from 1996 to 2003, the precinct detectives cleared an average of 2.72 homicide cases per detective. In the same amount of time, the Cold Case Squad detectives cleared an average of 14.8 cases. When looking at where to place limited resources, those numbers seem to suggest that fifteen additional detectives in the Cold Case

Squad would clear more homicide cases than fifteen detectives spread out over the five or ten precincts with the highest rates of unsolved murders (again, precinct detectives are working all cases, not just homicides, and that is why they solved fewer homicides).

It's true that those are numbers isolated from the circumstances that created them. Perhaps the numbers wouldn't continue to expand proportionally. Spano himself points out that the Cold Case detectives got results initially because no one had focused resources in the area before. "You're on the fat end of the curve." He called the cases that were solved "hangers." Like the balls hanging on the edge of a pocket in a pool game, they need only a small tap to sink them. If they were hangers, why didn't the precinct detectives knock them into the pocket? Spano thinks a lot of the hangers were cases with known perps, but they were reluctant to issue warrants because once an accusatory instrument is filed, the suspect has the right to counsel. They would prefer that the detectives get the perp to talk without one, which takes time.

▪

New DNA legislation would certainly help the police department and the Cold Case Squad. In 2003, then New Jersey governor James E. McGreevey signed legislation requiring all newly convicted criminals in New Jersey to submit DNA samples for the state and, ultimately, CODIS, the national DNA data bank. In New York State, DNA collection is more limited, although almost all violent criminals convicted after 1999 must submit DNA. Governor George Pataki proposed legislation in 2004 that would eliminate the statute of limitations for sexual assault, and also allow law enforcement to begin collecting DNA samples for all felonies, misdemeanors, and youthful offenders. Before the end of the legislative session, however, parts of the DNA section of the bill were taken out and reintroduced as a separate bill, adding to the list close to one hundred crimes that would compel convicted criminals to provide DNA. These included all sex crimes and sexually violent crimes. That bill passed later in 2004. The original bill, which includes eliminating the statute of limitations for sexual assault, will be revisited in 2005.

The ACLU has a problem with broadening DNA collection for a number of reasons. In a 1999 speech before the National Commission on the Future of DNA Evidence, ACLU associate director Barry Steinhardt demonstrated that it's not hard to come up with examples of how information initially gathered for one use was eventually used for another. Social Security numbers, for instance. He also pointed out that DNA samples are more than a genetic fingerprint and contain a lot more information, both known and yet to be discovered, about not only the person whose sample was taken but about anyone in their bloodline. "It's not clear," Steinhardt said later about expanding DNA legislation, "that the financial cost and the cost to our civil liberties justifies the expense. In any event," he finished, "once the sample is taken and law enforcement has the thirteen loci they need for forensic identification, the most important step the ACLU would like to see happen is the destruction of the sample. There's no need for them to be warehoused up in Albany." Law enforcement might be reluctant to do that, not knowing what future scientific discoveries might help them solve murders in years to come. Just like they didn't know they'd be able to recover DNA from latent fingerprints when they began storing them.

Forensic technology continues to improve. In addition to the new lab being constructed at the OCME, which will allow them to do low copy number DNA analysis, there now exists a handheld device that can analyze DNA on the spot at crime scenes. However, "there are problems with its integration and reliability with respect to meeting government standards for public forensic DNA laboratories," Dr. Robert Shaler points out. Maybe someday, but it's not in New York's immediate future.

"Every single crime scene should be examined by a scientist," Shaler says. "MEs are not forensic scientists. The medical-legal investigators who go out to crime scenes instead of MEs are not forensic scientists.

They are there to certify that it's an ME case, that the death is a homicide. You need someone who understands all areas of forensic science." If this were standard procedure, perhaps fewer cases would go cold in the first place. "The American Academy of Forensic Sciences has for the first time accredited crime scene analysis," Shaler continues. "It's a first step. That means the people who go to crime scenes have to be accredited as investigators to do this kind of scientific work."

The bottom line is, the Cold Case detectives have a demonstrated history of clearing more murder cases, and the percentage of unsolved homicides is not going down.

"If you put more detectives into Cold Case and you got this whole DNA project humming and you got cooperation from the medical examiner's office and you found the physical evidence, how many more cases do you think you could solve?" Spano asks. "I know we could do much better. But it's not a priority with the police department. The priority is the twenty-eight-day CompStat period."

"There are always going to be people who don't want Cold Case to succeed," Panzarella says. "But no one thinks the Cold Case Squad will go away entirely. It will probably be continually downsized. It might be put under the Special Investigation Division and merged with the Major Case Squad, for instance. There'd be some number of detectives under Major Case whose specialty is cold cases." Or they might do what Reznick always wanted. "They might decentralize it and spread the guys out among the Homicide Squads in the boroughs."

"It's a political issue," Spano points out. "Do you think anyone is going to give a shit about some prostitute or some woman in Bed-Stuy [Bedford-Stuyvesant] besides us and the family, if she has any family? The cases that are not a big deal, those are the cold cases." Those are the people who make up the 8,894 who fill the homicide sheets. They are not a priority. "They don't affect the twenty-eight-day cycle, they don't affect what's going on in the world today. It's why Jean Sanseverino's case didn't get solved."

■

"I feel very lucky," Tommy Wray admits. "I'm working in a squad where I still enjoy what I'm doing." "We got it made," Steve Kaplan agrees. "Anyone in the Cold Case Squad who's complaining hasn't been out there enough." When others bring up all the problems, Kaplan asks, "Isn't that part of the territory of being a cop? You gotta work around it." Things have evened out over at the Cold Case Squad. Reznick has settled down and loosened some of the earlier restrictions on overtime. The squad has gotten used to the changes, and the complaints about Reznick are starting to die out. Mike Palladino thinks it's only because "he's set his predator eyes on the guys in Warrants. He's a wolf in sheep's clothing. He pulls back a little, lures you in, and then he attacks." In any case, arrests are back up. Even though he's not exactly enamored with the guy, Kaplan says, "If I was in charge I'd want Reznick running the show. You gotta pay attention to the bottom line. You may not like the guy, but he's saving the city money." And all the detectives agree, "If I were murdered I'd want him heading the investigation." The highest compliment a detective could possibly give. Reznick's appearance never slowed down Wendell Stradford somehow. While complaints whirled around the squads about cell phones and overtime, Wendell Stradford—a former Transit guy—kept going like he was in another Cold Case universe, arresting as many murderers as ever.

According to an *Atlantic Monthly* article in 1997, "A Grief Like No Other" by Eric Schlosser, the Justice Department did a study that found that "a convicted murderer who has been released from prison is hundreds of times as likely to kill as an ordinary citizen." A fifth of them will commit another violent crime within three years.

As of early 2004 in New York, there are roughly 7,600 murderers in prison, a number of whom will eventually get out on parole, 2,465 are already out on parole, and 964 are awaiting trial. There's no way of knowing how many of those people are responsible for the 8,894 still unsolved murders, and any other skeletons that might turn up.

15 Epilogue

In March 2004, Captain Charles "Butch" Neacy was put in charge of the Cold Case Squad, replacing Vito Spano, who had retired that January. The slot always called for a deputy inspector, so while it was like another downsizing gesture for the Cold Case Squad, it was like a promotion for Neacy, who lobbied to get there. Neacy appears as laid-back as Vito Spano was intense. Before taking over the Cold Case Squad, Neacy was an investigative captain, coordinating between the detectives and narcotics bureaus in the 73 Precinct (261 unsolved murders) and the 75 Precinct (422 unsolved murders). Like Spano, Neacy is less interested in organized-crime cases. "That's business," he says, describing mob killings. "There's a need, but what percentage of our energy should be put into it? We have lots of true homicide victims." This is not the only area of interest he shares with Spano. "I want to expand on the work started by Vito Spano with the DNA No Suspect Grant Project. We have requested an extension for another year." So far they've accumulated fifty-one DNA profiles and expect to get many more. "In the future, a significant portion of the Cold Case Squad's investigations will include DNA evidence," Neacy says. "This technology will be the centerpiece of the cases we present to the district attorneys' offices for prosecution." Neacy has also been successful in adding a few detectives to the squad.

The same month Neacy took command, Eddie Norris, the very first commander of the Cold Case Squad, pleaded guilty to using up to thirty thousand dollars of police funds while he was police commissioner of Baltimore to carry on several simultaneous affairs and to pay for dinner and entertainment for himself and his friends. He also pleaded guilty to filing false tax returns. In the summer of 2004, Norris was sentenced to prison for six months, to be followed by six months of home detention. He was also ordered to pay a ten-thousand-dollar fine and perform five hundred hours of community service. According to all newspaper accounts, Norris cried when he heard his sentence, and his father fled the courtroom, choking back tears.

Anemone, who put the Cold Case Squad into place, was fired from his job as head of security at the Metropolitan Transportation Authority in May 2003 because the MTA's inspector general decided that Anemone had pretended to have an informant while investigating corruption within the MTA. Anemone now has his own law enforcement and counterterrorism consulting company, which is developing software that is expected to accomplish worldwide some of the things that CompStat did for New York City. He lectures around the country about domestic security, most recently at a conference at Northeastern University, which was jointly sponsored by the Police Institute at Rutgers University, the Boston Police Department, and the Massachusetts Public Safety Department. Anemone moderated the Police Leaders Roundtable, and his old boss William Bratton, now the police commissioner in Los Angeles, gave the keynote address. With respect to his firing from the MTA, Anemone maintains his innocence. The inspector general who did not believe him found corruption within the MTA.

Former chief of Department John Timoney has so far stayed out of trouble and is currently the chief of police in Miami. Former chief of Criminal Justice Charles Reuther retired on December 31, 1997. Lieutenant Joseph Pollini, the commanding officer of the Special Projects Unit of the Cold Case Squad, retired and is now an associate professor at John Jay College and an assistant professor at St. Francis College, and runs his own private investigation firm.

It's not such a shock that some of these guys got into trouble. They're risk takers. They have big strengths and, in some cases, big flaws. And whenever you take a risk and put yourself out there, there are going to be people gunning for you, calling you an asshole and looking for proof to back it up. And there will always be proof. These are complicated, imperfect men. It would be interesting to learn why the feds set their sights on Norris. There are a lot of bad guys out there and they can't go after every one. Some feel it was because Norris was openly critical of the FBI. His main complaint was that they didn't share information, something all our leaders now admit regularly on national TV. Still, while it's tragic that such a capable cop fell, the feds are hardly responsible for his mistakes, and it is perhaps better for society and Norris that they did not ignore them.

The best cops loved Norris and continue to defend him. "Eddie was aggressive and he liked aggressive cops," Kaplan says. "He stuck up for us. He was loyal." And he inspired loyalty and hard work in return. "When you made a great case Eddie'd go to the chief and say, 'Look what my guys did,'" Stradford points out. "Not every commander would do that."

Kaplan remembers the very first meeting of the Cold Case Squad. "Eddie got up and said, 'We're all grown-ups here. I'm not going to be checking up on you. Let's not embarrass ourselves. We're a brand-new unit. Let's go out there and do good work.'" Stradford was equally motivated by Norris's speech. "'You are here for a reason,'" he remembers Norris saying. "'You were handpicked. You know how to put a case together. You know how to find someone.'"

Go out and find these guys who thought they were going to get away with murder.

And it was Lou Anemone who made sure that Norris could get up and make that speech and inspire his men in the first place. "Anemone would have made a great police commissioner," Panzarella says. "In Manhattan he was an outstanding street cop. Every place he worked he excelled. His rise to the chief of Department was not unexpected. To this day the chief bleeds police department blue 24-7. [Even though Anemone is no longer with the police department, they'll call him "the chief" until the day he dies.] All the people who worked for him knew that he would always be there for them. The workers miss him."

While no one thinks Norris's criminal actions are excusable, it should be noted that the mayor of Baltimore recently put out a press release touting a 40 percent reduction in crime beginning in 1999, just before Norris was hired, and ending in 2003, when Norris resigned. (Norris resigned as police commissioner in December 2002 and as chief of the State Police in December 2003.) Murder rates have been going up ever since he left.

The Cold Case Squad continues to do good work. On October 7, 2004, the Cold Case Squad made their first arrest as a result of Vito Spano's DNA No Suspect grant. They arrested Richard Jackson on charges of killing his aunt, a maternity nurse, in 1994. The event was covered in the *New York Times* and all the local papers. Deputy Chief Joe Reznick, who now supports the program and speaks of the science of DNA with enthusiasm, is quoted in almost every article. Cold Case detective Steve Berger, who made the case, and retired deputy inspector Vito Spano, who came up with the DNA No Suspect program and helped secure the funding in order to enhance its future, are not mentioned.

In the Queens squad office there's a framed picture of the original members of the Cold Case Squad. As each person retires they put an X over his face. Of the original forty-nine guys from 1996, five remain. "When I joined the police department I died and went to heaven," Vito Spano remembers. "I always wanted this job. I grew up in a neighborhood that was all cops and firemen. I was so disappointed in the seventies when I couldn't join, but I finally got it." After thirty years, first with the Department of Correction and then with the New York Police Department, Spano now works in the office of the New York State Attorney General under Eliot Spitzer, as the chief investigator for the Medicaid Fraud Control Unit.

Lieutenant Phil Panzarella says he won't retire until 2007, when he's sixty-three years old and at which time he will have forty-two years on the force.

Detective Tommy Wray won't retire until Panzarella retires. He'll have thirty-three years.

Detective Steve Kaplan says the same thing. He'll retire when Panzarella retires. At that point, he'll have twenty-two years.

Detective Wendell Stradford could technically have retired on January 4, 2004, when he had twenty years, but he plans to go until 2009, when he hits twenty-five.

In four years, all of the champions in this book will be gone.

■

For more than fifty years, no one from New York made any attempt to contact the only surviving member of Jean Sanseverino's immediate family, her youngest sister, Joann. Joann was just a young girl when the murder happened. By the time she had grown, the case was already long cold. Joann is seventy now. She was excited when the first call came. "Anytime I see a relative or a friend from those days we talk about Jean. 'I still remember your sister getting killed in New York,' they say. It's never been forgotten." When the second call from New York came, Joann was more of a wreck. All the old photographs were out now, everything Joann could find. She'd been crying off and on for days, recalling what she could of the first thirteen years of her life, when her sister was still alive, half-intoxicated and half-tortured by an excess of memories that had been long ago put to uneasy rest. But she was still thrilled that after all these years someone in New York was once again looking into the case. "The only regret I have is my parents and siblings are dead, and they won't see any recognition of the fact that she got killed, they won't see that. Whether they solve it or not. As far as the public is concerned she was just a girl who once lived and got killed in New York." Life went on. The neighbors forgot her. The detectives started working other cases. "But she was my sister who I adored," Joann said. Even if the detective fails, it matters to her that we're not all slumbering peacefully and undisturbed up here in New York, when it was her sister who was violently laid down so many years ago, to join thousands of others in a long and restless sleep.

Appendix

Total Homicides and Unsolved Homicides by Year*
(as of 3/4/04)

Year	Total	Unsolved	Percent Unsolved	Year	Total	Unsolved	Percent Unsolved
1900	140	46	33.0%	1935	370	147	39.9%
1901	112	37	33.0%	1936	364	145	39.9%
1902	127	42	33.0%	1937	331	137	41.3%
1903	136	45	33.0%	1938	272	110	40.8%
1904	176	58	33.0%	1939	291	103	35.4%
1905	165	54	33.0%	1940	275	71	25.8%
1906	255	84	33.0%	1941	268	95	35.4%
1907	285	94	33.0%	1942	265	83	31.3%
1908	251	83	33.0%	1943	201	57	28.3%
1909	182	60	33.0%	1944	228	36	15.7%
1910	286	94	33.0%	1945	292	59	20.2%
1911	281	92	33.0%	1946	346	64	18.4%
1912	275	64	23.2%	1947	333	67	20.1%
1913	326	136	41.7%	1948	315	46	14.6%
1914	299	98	33.0%	1949	301	53	17.6%
1915	261	86	33.0%	1950	294	47	15.9%
1916	256	84	33.0%	1951	243	36	15.0%
1917	236	124	52.5%	1952	309	43	13.9%
1918	223	76	34.0%	1953	350	42	12.0%
1919	224	74	33.0%	1954	342	49	6.9%
1920	215[1]	70	33.0%	1955	306	49	15.8%
1921	237	78	33.0%	1956	315	40	12.6%
1922	266	88	33.0%	1957	314	33	10.8%
1923	262	97	37.0%	1958	354	32	9.0%
1924	310[2]	97	31.2%	1959	390	32	8.2%
1925	308	101	33.0%	1960	390	46	11.7%
1926	289	95	33.0%	1961	483	60	12.4%
1927	278	92	33.0%	1962	508	50	9.8%
1928	339	112	33.0%	1963	549	59	10.7%
1929	357	86	24.0%	1964	637	81	12.7%
1930	421	112[3]	26.6%	1965	634	105	16.7%
1931	489	175	35.9%	1966	654	143	21.8%
1932	478	171	35.9%	1967	746	155	20.8%
1933	431	195	45.2%	1968	986	217	22.1%
1934	400	154	38.5%	1969	1,043	333	32.0%

Total Homicides and Unsolved Homicides by Year* (continued)
(as of 3/4/04)

Year	Total	Unsolved	Percent Unsolved	Year	Total	Unsolved	Percent Unsolved
1970	1,117	344	30.8%	1988	1,896	591	31.1%
1971	1,466	633	43.2%	1989	1,905	652	34.2%
1972	1,691	732	43.3%	1990	2,245	791	35.2%
1973	1,680	514	30.6%	1991	2,154	783	36.3%
1974	1,554	494	31.8%	1992	1,995	770	38.5%
1975	1,645	583	35.5%	1993	1,946	710	36.4%
1976	1,622	702	43.3%	1994	1,561	595	38.1%
1977	1,557	649	41.7%	1995	1,177	358	30.4%
1978	1,504	463	30.8%	1996	983	327	33.2%
1979	1,733	753	43.5%	1997	767	240	31.2%
1980	1,814	558	30.8%	1998	633	185	29.2%
1981	1,826	787	43.0%	1999	667	215	32.2%
1982	1,668	524	31.4%	2000	671	253	37.7%
1983	1,662	416	25.0%	2001	642	235	36.6%
1984	1,450	469	34.2%	2002	586	222	37.8%
1985	1,384	305	22.0%	2003	596	294	49.3%
1986	1,582	477	30.1%	2004	571		
1987	1,672	483	28.8%				

*All figures come from the NYPD annual reports and from the office of the deputy commissioner of Public Information, except for the following.

Totals from 2002 and 2003 come from the NYPD's Homicide Analysis Unit.

The number of total homicides for the years 1900–11 and 1913–16 come from "Population, Births, Notifiable Diseases, and Deaths, Assembled for New York City, NY, 1866–1936 from Official Record," compiled by Haven Emerson, MD, and published by Columbia University. Emerson got his figures from the Department of Health, so his numbers, like those from the Office of the Chief Medical Examiner, are going to be higher because they count all homicides, including justifiable homicides and the like.

The clearance rates for the years 1969–80 and 1983 are based on "crime comparison" figures rather than the FBI Crime Index. Crime comparison is based on the New York State Penal Code, where more deaths are classified as homicides. The NYPD has adopted the FBI Crime Index for reporting purposes, but where those figures were not available, the crime comparison figures were used. Those figures will always be higher.

The clearance rates for the years 1985–2003 come directly from the unsolved-homicide reports provided by the NYPD's Homicide Analysis Unit.

The clearance rates for all other years are based on the NYPD annual reports. When the NYPD did not provide a clearance rate, an estimate was made based on an average for that time period. The years that are based on an average are as follows: 1900–11, 1914–16, 1919–22, 1925–28, 1931–32, and 1935–36.

The total number of homicides for 2004 is the number as of January 3, 2005. The number will likely change.

1. Does not include 39 people killed in the Wall Street explosion.
2. Includes 13 Chinese people killed in the Tong War.
3. 280 were closed with arrests; 29 perpetrators committed suicide.

Total Homicides and Unsolved Homicides Over Three Years

Year	Total	Unsolved as of 3/04		Unsolved as of 5/03		Unsolved as of 5/02*	
1985	1,384	305	22.0%	304	21.9%	298	
1986	1,582	477	30.1%	478	30.2%	467	
1987	1,672	483	28.8%	483	23.8%	489	
1988	1,896	591	31.1%	591	31.1%	594	
1989	1,905	652	34.2%	653	34.2%	663	
1990	2,245	791	35.2%	794	35.3%	796	
1991	2,154	783	36.3%	784	36.3%	783	
1992	1,995	770	38.5%	777	38.9%	756	
1993	1,946	710	36.4%	711	36.5%		
1994	1,561	595	38.1%	601	38.5%	600	
1995	1,177	358	30.4%	364	30.9%	368	
1996	983	327	33.2%	331	33.6%	332	
1997	767	240	31.2%	245	31.9%	247	
1998	633	185	29.2%	185	29.2%	185	
1999	667	215	32.2%	226	33.8%	231	34.6%
2000	671	253	37.7%	256	38.1%	261	38.8%
2001	642	235	36.6%	257	40.0%	270	42.0%
2002	586	222	37.8%	253	43.4%		
2003	596	294	49.3%				

*Raw numbers. The printout for May 2002 is no longer in my possession. The figures cannot be recounted, so their 100 percent accuracy cannot be substantiated. They have been checked once, however, so when numbers appear, they are not far off.

Notes

In each of the cases I had access to the Cold Case Squad detective who worked the case, the commanding officer of their unit, and the commanding officer of the Cold Case Squad. Although not every person listed in the source notes appears in the acknowledgments, I owe everyone here a thank-you for all the information they contributed.

1 Linda Leon and Esteban Martinez | *December 15, 1996*

Interviews with or information supplied from: Detective Sheila L. A. Aparicio, Homicide Analysis Unit, CIRD; retired Chief of Detectives William Allee; Lieutenant Robert McHugh, Cold Case Squad; retired Detective Patrick Lanigan, Cold Case Squad; Detective Oscar Hernandez, Cold Case Squad; Detective Meg Fisher, Cold Case Squad; retired Detective Angelo Cioffi, Cold Case Squad.

911 tape of Esteban Martinez and Linda Leon's son's call, December 16, 1996.

NYPD Homicide Analysis Unit report of all open homicides, 1985–2003.

NYPD Homicide Logbooks, 1964–2002.

Case study prepared by Vito R. Spano for FBI class: Managing Death and Sexually Related Investigations Using Investigative Psychology, March 8, 2002.

Anticipated Arrests in Connection with the Murders of Esteban Martinez and Linda Leon—43 Precinct—December 15, 1996, NYPD Interoffice Memo, June 28, 2001.

Double Homicide of Esteban Martinez and Linda Leon, in the Confines of the 43 Precinct, December 15, 1996, NYPD interoffice memo, December 22, 2001.

Lynette Holloway, "Child Summons Help After His Parents Are Killed at Home," *New York Times*, December 16, 1996.

Virgina Breen and Wendell Jamieson, "Bx. boy knows killer," *Daily News*, December 17, 1996.

Angelica Mosconi, Murray Weiss, and Andy Geller, "'Coke,' Cash & Carnage," *New York Post,* December 17, 1996.

"Three arrests in 1996 torture/murder; one suspect still at large," The Associated Press, August 28, 2001.

Richard Weird, "4th Suspect Is Sought in '96 Slayings" *Daily News,* August 28, 2001.

Louis N. Eliopulos, *Cold Case Investigation, Death Investigators Handbook II* (Boulder, CO: Paladin Press, 2002).

2 A Brief History of the Cold Case Squad

Interviews with or information supplied from: Louis Anemone, former NYPD chief of Department; Edward T. Norris, former deputy commissioner of Operations; William J. Bratton, former police commissioner, NYPD; Inspector Ray Ferrari; all the principals in this book, Sergeant Dennis Bootle, Cold Case Squad; retired Detective Patrick Lanigan, Cold Case Squad; Miami Police Commissioner John Timoney; retired chief of Detectives, William Allee; former chief of Criminal Justice Charles Reuther; Inspector John Gerrish, NYPD Office of Management, Analysis and Planning; Detective Walter Burnes, DCPI.

NYPD Annual Reports, 1862–1990.

NYPD Homicide Analysis Unit report of all open homicides from 1985 to present, run in 2002, 2003, 2004.

NYPD, Office of the Deputy Commissioner of Public Information, "Yearly Homicides Since 1939–2001," chart.

Cold Case Squad Stats Reports, run in 2002, 2003, 2004.

Cold Case Squad Case 494 Sheet, April 28, 2003.

Cold Case Squad Arrest Logs 1997–2003.

Detective Bureau Case Closing and Referral Guidelines, July 1991.

Detective Bureau Personal Audit Cold Case and Apprehension Squad, 2002.

New York State Division of Criminal Justice Services Office of Funding & Program Assistance Quarterly Progress Report, March, June, September, December 2000, March 2001.

FBI Uniform Crime Reports.

United States Census Reports.

Norah Rudin and Keith Inman, "Forensic Science Timeline," from *Principles and Practice of Forensic Science: The Profession of Forensic Science,* February 7, 2002.

A Brief History of NYPD Data Processing and Information Technology, prepared by the NYPD–Management Information Systems Division.

The CompStat Process, prepared by the Office of Management Analysis and Planning (when Howard Safir was the police commissioner).

NYPD interoffice memo announcing the establishment of the Cold Case Squad, February 29, 1996.

NYPD interoffice memo announcing the transfer of jurisdiction of the Cold Case Squad from the Chief of Department to the Detective Bureau, August 9, 1996.

William J. Bratton, "Cutting Crime and Restoring Order: What America Can Learn from New York's Finest" (speech, Heritage Foundation, Washington, D.C., on October 15, 1996).

Address of Police Commissioner Richard E. Enright, September 12, 1923.

International Association of Chiefs of Police, *An Organizational Study of the Police Department, New York City, New York,* July 1967.

Charles L. Regini, "The Cold Case Concept," *FBI Law Enforcement Bulletin* (August 1997).

James Q. Wilson, George L. Kelling, "Broken Windows," *Atlantic Monthly,* March 1982.

William G. Eckert, "Medicolegal Investigation in New York City: History and Activities 1918–1978," *American Journal of Forensic Medicine and Pathology,* 4:1 (March 1983).

Bob Drury, "Stone Cold Cases," *Playboy,* November 1995.

John Marzulli, "New elite cop unit draws fire," *Daily News,* January 1, 1996.

Clifford Krauss, "Police Remove Popular Chief from Position," *New York Times,* July 4, 1996.

"LEN salutes its 1996 People of the Year, the NYPD and its Compstat process," *Law Enforcement News,* December 31, 1996.

Jack Maple, "Betting on Intelligence," *Government Technology,* April 1999.

Kate Sheehy and Kiran Randhawa, "Hoax-Leery Cops Probe Radio Call-In Slay Confess," *New York Post,* May 15, 2002.

Eric H. Monkkonen, *Murder in New York City* (Berkeley and Los Angeles: University of California Press, 2001).

Edwin G. Burrows, and Mike Wallace, *Gotham: A History of New York City to 1898* (New York: Oxford University Press, 1999).

3 Police Officer Ronald Stapleton | *December 18, 1977*

Interviews with or information supplied from: G. R. Blakey, Notre Dame Law School, principal author of the RICO Statute; Deputy District Attorney Kenneth Taub, bureau chief of the Homicide Bureau in Brooklyn; Mark Feldman, section chief of Organized Crime in the United States Attorney's Office, Eastern District; Detective Carl "Chuck" Harrison, Cold Case Squad. In connection with the Latanesha Carmichael case: Detective Daniel D'Alessandro, Cold Case Squad, deputy bureau chief; Frank Urzi, Brooklyn District Attorney.

U.S. Department of Justice, "Genovese and Colombo Families Leadership Targeted in Multi-District Racketeering Prosecutions," press release, February 26, 2003.

Alan Feuer, "Brother's Search for Twin Revealed a 20-Year-Old Killing," *New York Times,* November 19, 1999.

Murray Weiss, "Heat's on Colombo Clan Don," *New York Post,* January 11, 2003.

William Glaberson, "Tangled Tale of Botch Hit Is Detailed in an Indictment," *New York Times,* January 23, 2003.

Kati Cornell Smith, Murray Weiss, William J. Gorta, Rita Delfiner, "Hit Parade: Wiseguy World," *New York Post,* January 23, 2003.

John Marzulli, "Alleged boss faces rap in botched mob slaying," *Daily News,* January 23, 2003.

Al Guart and John Lehman, "No-Show Workers to Show Up in Cuffs," *New York Post,* February 26, 2003.

Jerry Capeci, "Feds Nail Joe Waverly for 1987 Murders," *This Week in Gang Land: The Online Column,* January 23, 2003, http://www.ganglandnews.com.

Jerry Capeci, "Feds Go to the Vault on Joe Waverly," *This Week in Gang Land: The Online Column,* February 6, 2003, http://www.ganglandnews.com.

Jerry Capeci, "Fat Sal Turns On Joe Waverly," *This Week in Gang Land: The Online Column,* October 9, 2003, http://www.ganglandnews.com.

4 Christine Diefenbach | *February 7, 1988*

Interviews with or information supplied from: Louis Anemone; Edward Norris; retired deputy chief Larry Loesch; James Penton, author of *Apocalypse Delayed: The Story of Jehovah's Witnesses;* Marjorie Taylor, author of *Imaginary Companions and the Children Who Create Them;* Scott Laufer, Laufer Media, Inc., publishers of *Tigerbeat* magazine; Yuri Forbin, childhood friend of Christine Diefenbach.

Excerpts from Christine Diefenbach's journal.

Don Terry, "Girl, 14, Slain During Errand to Buy a Paper," *New York Times,* February 8, 1988.

Elaine Rivera and Clara Hemphill, "14-Year-Old Queens Girl Found Slain in Rail Yard," *Newsday*, February 8, 1988.

Sam Rosensohn and Leo Standora, "Queens Teen Raped and Slain," *New York Post*, February 8, 1988.

George James, "Richmond Hill Grieves for Girl Beaten to Death," *New York Times*, February 9, 1988.

Carol Polsky, "Police Scramble for Clues in Slaying of Queen's Girl," *Daily News*, February 9, 1988.

Jehovah's Witnesses, "Jehovah's Witnesses—Who Are They? What Do They Believe?" http://www.watchtower.org.

5 Jean Sanseverino | *March 8, 1951*

Interviews with or information supplied from: Patrick Sanseverino; Raymond Sanseverino Jr.; Joann Sly, Jean's sister; James R. Vice; Richard Alford; Glenda Arther; Lucy Hindman; Mary Johnson; Alan Hayes; Shirley Pruitt; Joy Pruitt Robertson; Charlie Bowman; Lois Mills East; Michael Wade Chapman; Nell Jo Chapman; Oscar Shaw; James Halcomb, former Gadsden, Alabama, resident; Susan Rowe, St. James Catholic Church, Gadsden, Alabama; Rita King, Oak Grove Baptist Church, Gadsden, Alabama; Kevin Graves, Gadsden Public Library; Tom Mullins, Anniston Public Library; Bill Partridge, Calhoun County coroner; Captain Jeff Wright, commander of Professional Standards, Gadsden Police Department; Principal Ronald Chambless, Alexandria High School, Alexandria, Alabama; Debbie Pendleton, assistant director for Public Services, Alabama Department of Archives and History.

In addition to the DD5s, I had access to the original detectives' handwritten notes, Jean's autopsy report, and letters from Jean's family to the police.

FBI Uniform Crime Report, 1951, 1952.

Alabama Official and Statistical Register, 1951.

Spring 3100 (in-house police magazine).

Alabama Criminal Justice Information System, http://www.acjic.state.al.us.

Ancestry.com.

1930 United States Federal Census.

Social Security Death Index.

Faces of the Nation/AutoTrack.

"Girl Found Dead in State St. Flat," *Brooklyn Daily Eagle*, March 8, 1951.

"Woman Found Strangled, Clad in Sweater, Bra," *Daily News*, March 9, 1951.

"Gadsden Woman Is Slain in New York, Mate Sought," *Gadsden Times*, March 9, 1951.

"State Street Strangling: Estranged Mate Exonerated in Death of Brunette," *Brooklyn Eagle*, March 9, 1951.

"Estranged Mate Sheds No Light on Strangulation," *Gadsden Times*, March 10, 1951.

"Service Set Here for Murder Victim," *Gadsden Times*, March 12, 1951.

Obituary, Mrs. Bessie Jean Sanseverino, *Anniston Star*, March 12, 1951.

6 Detective Wendell Stradford | *The Leon-Martinez Double Homicide*

Interviews with or information supplied from: Dr. Robert Shaler, director of Forensic Biology, OCME; John Pickert, Criminalist IV, Department of Forensic Biology, OCME; Monique Samuels, Criminalist II, Department of Forensic Biology, OCME; Detective Daniel Perruzza, Latent Prints unit, Forensic Investigations Division; Julie Pasquini, director of Bureau Justice Partnership, NYS Division of Criminal Justice Services; ADA Sandy Bagget, Bronx District Attorney; Detective Carl "Chuck" Harrison, Cold Case Squad; retired Sergeant Steven Racanelli, Office of Management Analysis and Planning.

NYPD Annual Reports, 1862–1990.

NYPD, Office of the Deputy Commissioner of Public Information, "Yearly Homicides Since 1939–2001," chart.

Homicide Analysis Unit Reports of all open homicides.

"Population, Births, Notifiable Diseases, and Deaths, Assembled for New York City, NY, 1866–1936 from Official Record," compiled by Haven Emerson, MD, Columbia University Press. Emerson got his figures from the Department of Health, so his numbers, like those from the Office of the Chief Medical Examiner, are going to be higher because they count all homicides, including justifiable homicides and the like.

FBI Uniform Crime Reports, 1969–80, 1983.

Cold Case Squad Stats Reports, run in 2002, 2003, 2004.

Cold Case Squad Case 494 Sheet, April 28, 2003.

Cold Case Squad Arrest Logs 1997–2003.

Ed German, Chief of Intelligence for the Army Criminal Investigation Command's worldwide activities, "Cyanoacrylate (Superglue) Fuming Tips," self-published paper, August 1, 2003.

Louis N. Eliopulos, *DNA Procedures, Death Investigators Handbook II* (Boulder, CO: Paladin Press, 2002).

Using DNA to Solve Cold Cases, National Institute of Justice Special Report, July 2002.

Susan Suksuwan, "DNA Finger Printing for Dummies," *SAKSI*, no. 3 (January 1999).

The Combined DNA Index System, Statement on Compliance with Laws and Regulations, U.S. Department of Justice, September 17, 2001.

"The Future of DNA Testing: Predictions of the Research and Development Working Group," *National Criminal Justice* (November 2000).

An outline of qualifying offenses for DNA sampling, NYS Division of Criminal Justice Services, Office of Forensic Services, February 26, 2003.

U.S. Department of Justice, FBI Laboratory Division, *Handbook of Forensic Services*, 1999.

Albert Lugo, "Factors and Characteristics Relating to Solved and Unsolved Murder Cases," doctoral thesis, John Jay College of Criminal Justice, 1994.

John Houde, *Crime Lab: A Guide for Nonscientists* (New York: Calico Press, 1999).

The New York State Division of Criminal Justice Services Web site, DNA Databank Statistics, http://www.criminaljustice.state.ny.us.

Searching for a Known Perp, NYPD, April 12, 2000.

Lona Manning, "New York Detective Promotes New Method of Crime Detection," *Old News* 15, no. 7 (April 2004).

John Persinos, "NYPD Aviation Unit to Replace Helicopter Fleet," *Rotor & Wing*, August 2002.

7 Detective Steve Kaplan | *The Ronald Stapleton Case*

Interviews with or information supplied from: G. R. Blakey; Paul DeMartini, former bureau chief of the Trial Division in the Rackets Bureau, Brooklyn District Attorney; Jay Shapiro, former head of the Rackets Division, Brooklyn District Attorney; Tom Frongillo, former AUSA, District of Massachusetts; Kenneth Taub, bureau chief of the Homicide Bureau in Brooklyn; Mark Feldman, section chief of Organized Crime, in the United States Attorney's Office, Eastern District; Laureen Schenley; Dennis Graf; Duncan Osbourne, LGNY; Ron Stapleton Jr.; retired Detective Glenn Whelpley; Special Agent Steve Byrne; William Aronwald; Detective Mike Carrano, Cold Case Squad; Director John Simon, Central Records Division; Deputy Director Judith Laffey, Central Records Division; David Wertheimer, mental health and criminal justice consultant; John Buettner, Pension Fund, NYPD; retired Detective Ron Cadieux; attorney Robert Race.

302 ■ *Notes*

The People of the State of New York v. Tony Francesehi, Trial Proceedings Summations, Brooklyn Supreme Court, September 28, 1999.

Before the Departmental Disciplinary Committee Appellate Division: First Judicial Department, In the Matter of Robert R. Race, Esq., Respondent, RP No. 7031/00, July 11, 2001.

Amy Zelson Mundorff, "Hard Evidence: Case Studies in Forensic Anthropology," in *Urban Anthropology: Case Studies from the New York City Medical Examiner's Office* (Englewood Cliffs, NJ: Prentice Hall, 2002), chap. 4.

Duncan Osbourne, "Gay Cold Case Gets Colder as NYPD Fumbles," *lgny News,* March 23, 1996.

Duncan Osbourne, "Will Death Bed Confession Yield Justice for Murdered Gay Man?" *lgny News,* February 11, 1998.

Duncan Osbourne, "Evidence Lost in Gay Slaying," *lgny News,* February 25, 1999.

Duncan Osbourne, "Police Investigation of Brooklyn Gay Murder Faulted," *lgny News,* October 7, 1999.

Duncan Osbourne, "Gonzalez Sentenced in Cop Slaying, Fate of Jan Schenley Murder Unresolved," *lgny News,* November 4, 1999.

Duncan Osbourne, "Suspect in Murder of Gay Brooklyn Man Convicted in Cop Killing," *lgny News,* October 1, 1999.

Duncan Osbourne, "Brooklyn Gay Murder Solved 18 Years Later, But Does the Penalty Fit the Crime?" *lgny News,* October 19, 2000.

Duncan Osbourne, "Laureen Schenley Speaks Out at Sentencing of Brother's Killer," *lgny News,* November 2, 2000.

Peter A. Michaels, *The Detectives: Their Toughest Cases in Their Own Words* (New York: St. Martin's Press, 1994).

8 Detective Tommy Wray | *The Christine Diefenbach Case*

Interviews with or information supplied from: John Diefenbach; Dr. Robert Shaler, director of Forensic Biology, OCME; Stuart W. Pyhrr, curator in charge of Department of Arms and Armor, The Metropolitan Museum of Art; Peter Finer, antique arms and armor dealer, The Old Rectory, Warwickshire, England; Inspector Jack Trabitz and Lieutenant Kevin Serpico from the Property Clerk Division; and retired Property Clerk personnel (who asked not to be named); Police Officer Robert Schnelle, K-9 Unit, handler of Atlas and Zeus; Lisa Dzegliewski, Criminalist II, Department of Forensic Biology, OCME; Lisa Faber, Criminalist III, Hair and Fiber Section, Trace Evidence Analysis Unit, NYPD Police Laboratory, Forensics Investigations Division; Ron LaBarca, US Radar Inc.; Detective Mike Carrano, Cold Case Squad; Detective Mike Solomeno, Cold Case Squad.

Fire Incident Reports from the FDNY Public Records Unit, Metro Tech Center.

NYPD Annual Reports, 1862–1965.

William Lenson, "An Appraisal of the Operations and Management of the Property Clerk's Office, Police Department, City of New York" (master's thesis, Baruch College, The City University of New York, June 1963).

"Auction of Unclaimed Property," *New York Times,* April 20, 1858.

"Action Against Police Commissioners," *New York Times,* January 19, 1860.

"Old Crime Relics Ordered Burned," *New York Times,* June 29, 1924.

John Walker Harrington, "Police Force Expands as Its Duties Increase," *New York Times,* November 9, 1924.

"Seized Drugs Worth $1,500,000 to Be Burned Today as Sequel to 2,732 Arrests," *New York Times,* June 15, 1925.

"Police Auction Yields $10,000 for Pensions," *New York Times*, July 6, 1932.

"3,816 Weapons Seized in Year to Be Cast in Sea by Police," *New York Times*, June 8, 1933.

"1,200 Serenaded at Police Auction," *New York Times*, May 8, 1935.

"1,575 Slugs Defraud City Subway Daily: Two Tons of Them to Be Dumped in Sound," *New York Times*, June 6, 1935.

"Bay Gets Long Drink of Bootleg Liquor," *New York Times*, November 18, 1937.

"$125,000 in Marijuana Will Be Burned Today," *New York Times*, July 29, 1938.

"Burning Narcotics Seized by the City Police Department," *New York Times*, January 23, 1952.

Paul Crowell, "Big Changes Urged in Police Program," *New York Times*, October 21, 1952.

Guy Passant, "$20,000 in Police Safe Vanishes at Headquarters Property Office," *New York Times*, June 12, 1958.

"Honor Policeman Admits to Thefts," *New York Times*, June 27, 1958.

"1.35 million in Narcotics Burned," *New York Times*, July 18, 1962.

"2 Tons of Obscene Material Seized by Police Is Burned," *New York Times*, November 21, 1963.

Eric Pace, "Police Dump Confiscated Weapons into Atlantic," *New York Times*, June 7, 1972.

David Burnham, "$10-Million Heroin Stolen from a Police Office Vault," *New York Times*, December 15, 1972.

Alfred E. Clark, "Egan Linked 'Slipshod' Practices in Police Office to Heroin Theft," *New York Times*, December 16, 1972.

Christopher S. Wren, "Police-Held Drugs Guarded by Tighter Security System," *New York Times*, August 13, 1973.

Deirdre Carmody, "Police Auction Produces Bargains—Some Good, Some Bad," *New York Times*, April 17, 1974.

"Ex-Detective Gets 3 Years," *New York Times*, April 1, 1977.

Robert D. McFadden, "Orsini, 'French Connection' Figure, Is Found Slain at Atlanta Prison," *New York Times*, April 11, 1978.

Nicholas Pileggi, "How to Retire at 29 with $20 Million," *New York Times*, May 28, 1978.

Constance L. Hays, "Police Store 'One of Everything Ever Made' (Well, Nearly)," *New York Times*, September 5, 1988.

Larry Celona and Linda Masserella, "8-year-old murder cracked: Police dog finds body," *New York Post*, August 21, 1995.

"M'Alpin Murder Victim a Soldier," *New York Times*, August 16, 1919.

"Follow Two Clues to Girl's Slayer," *New York Times*, February 22, 1920.

"Seek Caller Seen at Hoxsie Home in Murder Hour," *New York Times*, February 4, 1920.

"Man's Head Found in a Bag in Woods," *New York Times*, October 2, 1922.

Sherwin B. Nuland, *How We Die: Reflections on Life's Final Chapter* (New York: Knopf, 1994).

NYPD Web site section for the Property Clerk Division: http://www.nyc.gov/html/nypd/html/ssb/pcdindex.html.

9 Detectives Walter Duffy, William Kelly, et al. | *The Jean Sanseverino Case*

Interviews with or information supplied from: Katherine Haddad, Anne Vaterlaus, David Fitzpatrick, Dave Caplan, and Kate Perry, all residents of State Street; retired Captain Harry Exarchakis; retired Detective William Hahn; retired Lieutenant Harold McCauley; Dennis McCarthy (Patrolman Eugene McCarthy's son); retired Detective John Cornicello; retired Detective Mike Bosak; retired Detective John Reilly; Ellen Borakove; director of Public Affairs; OCME; Dr. Jonathan Hayes, Senior Medical Examiner, OCME; Dr. Robert Shaler, director of Forensic Biology, OCME; Sister Winifred, Sisters of the Good Shepherd; Barbara

304 ▪ *Notes*

Lima; retired Detective Mike Cronin, curator, The New York City Police Museum; the former INS, Department of Homeland Security; Seamens Church Institute; Wilson Hulme, curator of Philately, National Postal Museum.

Ancestry.com.

1930 United States Federal Census.

Social Security Death Index.

MapQuest.com.

"Burlesque Shows of City Are Shut as Public Menace," *New York Times*, May 2, 1937.

"On Television," *New York Times*, March 7, 1951.

Judge Peter M. Horn as told to Hartzell Spence, "We Don't Call Them Criminals," *Saturday Evening Post*, June 24, 1961.

10 Detective Wendell Stradford | *The Leon-Martinez Double Homicide*

Interviews with or information supplied from: Tom Antenen, deputy commissioner for Public Information, NYPD; Correction Officer Sean Jones and Captain Fred Sporrer from the City of New York Department of Correction; attorney Jay Shapiro; Detective Carl "Chuck" Harrison, Cold Case Squad.

An Overview of NYC DOC Facilities, City of New York Department of Correction, 2003.

NYPD interoffice memo, Chief of Department's Cold Case and Apprehension Squad, January 31, 1996.

NYPD interoffice memo, Cold Case Squad Protocol, February 24, 1998.

NYPD interoffice memo, Cold Case Squad Protocol, April 14, 1998.

The City of New York Department of Correction Operations Order: Processing and Monitoring New Admissions, 1989.

Josh Barbanel, "Still a Beacon, Parkchester Climbs Back," *New York Times*, March 14, 2004.

"Baltimore Man Convicted of Murdering Parkchester Couple 'Execution Style' in Drug Related Dispute," Bronx District Attorney press release, March 26, 2004.

11 Detective Steve Kaplan | *The Ronald Stapleton Case*

Interviews with or information supplied from: Joseph Ponzi, chief investigator, Brooklyn District Attorney; Emilio Ponzi, retired Detective Sergeant, NYPD; Detective Mike Carrano, Cold Case Squad; Sergeant Dennis Bootle, Cold Case Squad; correspondence with Tony Francesehi; Andrea Coleman, MD, Forensic Pathology, OCME; Amy Zelson Mundorff, Forensic Anthropologist, OCME; Mark Feldman, section chief of Organized Crime; FBI Special Agent Steve Byrne; Detective Lynn McCarthy; Meet an Inmate Web site.

The People of the State of New York v. Tony Francesehi, Trial Proceedings Summations, Brooklyn Supreme Court, September 28, 1999.

NYPD interoffice memo, Anticipated Arrest, January 13, 2003.

"Brooklyn Ex-Felon Slain," *New York Times*, February 24, 1951.

"Surrenders in Slaying," *New York Times*, March 17, 1951.

"Man Held in Dockworker Slaying," *New York Times*, March 18, 1951.

"Brooklyn Slayer Pleads Guilty," *New York Times*, August 8, 1951.

"Ex-Jockey Is Slain in a Brooklyn Club," *New York Times*, December 20, 1968.

M. A. Farber, "City Parking Aide Is Shot to Death in Queens Laundry," *New York Times*, March 21, 1987.

Selwyn Raab, "Slain Man's Son Wants U.S. Inquiry," *New York Times*, March 22, 1987.

"Victim's Son: Ex-Prosecutor of the Mafia," *New York Times*, March 22, 1987.

"Alphonse Persico, 61, Is Dead; Leader of Colombo Crime Family," *New York Times*, September 13, 1989.

Elisabeth Bumiller, "Slain Officer Is Mourned as Mob Inquiry Proceeds," *New York Times*, August 30, 1997.

Tom Robbins, "A Deadly Mobster's Pleading Letter for His Son," *Village Voice*, January 28–February 3, 2004.

John Marzulli, "Oh, the agita of being a mob boss!" *Daily News*, May, 4, 2004.

12 Detective Tommy Wray | *The Christine Diefenbach Case*

Interviews with or information supplied from: John Diefenbach, Christine Diefenbach's father.

National Organization of Parents of Murdered Children Web site, "Survivors of Homicide Victims," http://www.pomc.com.

National Organization of Parents of Murdered Children Web site, "Tips from Survivors," http://www.pomc.com.

Eric Schlosser, "A Grief Like No Other," *Atlantic Monthly*, September 1997.

13 Detective Wendell Stradford | *The Jean Sanseverino Case*

Interviews with or information supplied from: Ellen Kirby, Brooklyn Botanic Garden; David Fitzpatrick, 366 State Street; Dr. Robert Shaler; FBI Special Agent Phil Mann, Norfolk, Virginia; John Paganitsa, Bill the Greek's nephew; Patrick Sanseverino; Raymond Sanseverino Jr.; Michael Krasne; correspondence with Harry Boyd; Sergeant Joseph Blozis, Crime Scene Unit, Forensic Investigations Division; Jean Ellis, Passaic (New Jersey) Local Library; Jeff Smart, command historian for the Army Research Development Engineering Command; Dr. Michael Baden, former chief medical examiner, New York City, currently chief forensic pathologist for the New York State Police; Bob Sekac, St. Charles Borromeo; Joan Wojcik, St. Rose of Lima; St. John's Church; Dick Ingalls, ChevronTexaco Shipping Company; Pat Ausband, Sailors Snug Harbor; William Gorman, New York State Archives, New York Department of Education Cultural Education Center; John Mohan, director of Media Services, New York City Department of Correction; Cathy DeMarco, Seisint, Inc.; Daniel Martuscello, State of New York Department of Correctional Services.

State of New York Department of Correctional Services.

NYPD Office of the Chief of Personnel.

National Archives and Records Administration, New York, New York.

National Personal Records Center/Military Personnel Records.

International Boxing Hall of Fame.

NYSA-ILAGAI Fund.

Robert F. Wagner Labor Archives, Bobst Library, New York University.

Obituary, Leonidas Verona, *New York Times*, April 13, 1949.

Obituary, Mrs. Lillie East, *Gadsden Times*, January 19, 1978.

Obituary, Raymond Sanseverino, *Poughkeepsie Journal*, August 27, 1980.

Randy Kennedy, "Mohawk Memories," *New York Times*, December 28, 1996.

Katherine E. Finkelstein, "Plant Thieves Plaque a Block in Brooklyn," *New York Times*, May 28, 1999.

Peter Duffy, "Remembering Mohawk Ironworkers' Urban Heaven," *New York Times*, July 18, 1999.

"Mustard Gas Exposure and Long-Term Health Effects," Department of Veterans Affairs, Office of Public Affairs, fact sheet, April 1999, http://www.va.gov/pressrel/99mustd.htm.

14 The Future of the Cold Case Squad

Interviews with or information supplied from: Los Angeles Police Commissioner William J. Bratton; Lieutenant Robert McHugh, Cold Case Squad; Deputy Chief Joseph J. Reznick, Fugitive Enforcement Division; retired Detective Jerry Giorgio, now senior investigator, New York County District Attorney's Office; Detective Michael Palladino, president of the Detective's Endowment Association; Detective Richard Bengston, Los Angeles Police Department Cold Case Squad; attorneys David Feiga and Scott Tulman; Barry Steinhardt, director of Technology and Liberty Program, ACLU; Tom Antenen, deputy commissioner for Public Information, the City of New York Department of Correction; Carole Claren-Weaver, confidential assistant, Intergovernmental Relations, New York State Division of Parole; Carla Wilson, Federal Bureau of Prisons; Linda Foglia, New York State Department of Correctional Services; Andrew Bobbe; Mark Rosenthal, United States Eastern and Southern District Courts, Probation Departments; Sergeant Julia Collins, U.S. Army.

NYPD Organization Guide, Procedure Number 101-20, February 18, 2000.

FBI Uniform Crime Report, 2002.

William Plummer, "A Child Called Hope: The long, desolate hunt for the killer of a little girl," *People,* December 9, 1972.

Sean Gardiner, "Murder, They Solved: Retirements Diminish NYPD Squad," *Newsday,* March 31, 2002.

Michele McPhee, "Remembering Baby Hope: Detective Still Determined to Solve Child's Killing," *Daily News,* July 24, 2002.

Eric Schlosser, "A Grief Like No Other," *Atlantic Monthly,* September 1997.

15 Epilogue

Jayne Miller, WBAL Baltimore, NBC News Channel 11, Thursday, October 28, 2004.

Office of the Mayor, "Baltimore Once Again Posts Dramatic Reductions in Violent Crime Rate," press release, October 28, 2004.

Web Sites

Ancestry.com
http://www.ancestry.com

Proquest Historical Newspapers
http://www.il.proquest.com/proquest

MapQuest
http://www.mapquest.com

Classmates.com
http://www.classmates.com

New York State Department of Correctional Services Inmate Lookup
http://www.nysdocslookup.docs.state.ny.us/GCA00P00/WIQ3/WINQ130

National Archives and Records Administration
http://www.archives.gov/

NYPD, Official New York City Police Department Web Site
http://www.nyc.gov/html/nypd/home.html

New York State Division of Criminal Justice Services, Office of Forensic Services
http://www.criminaljustice.state.ny.us/forensic/index.htm

New York City Department of Finance, Office of the City Register
http://www.nyc.gov/html/dof/home.html

Federal Bureau of Investigation
http://www.fbi.gov

Federal Bureau of Prisons, National Institute of Corrections
http://www.bop.gov

DNAResource.com
http://www.dnaresource.com/bill_tracking_list.htm

New York City Department of Records
http://www.nyc.gov/html/records/home.html

New York City Criminal Justice Agency
http://www.nycja.org

Survivors of Homicide Victims, National Organization of Parents of Murdered Children
http://www.pomc.com

United States Department of Justice
http://www.usdoj.gov

New York Correction History Society
http://www.correctionhistory.org

New York State Department of Correctional Services
http://www.docs.state.ny.us/

American Family Immigration History Center
http://www.ellisisland.org/

The New York Genealogical and Biographical Society
http://www.newyorkfamilyhistory.org/

Locations of Major Research

New York City Municipal Archives
Archive of the New York County Clerk
City Hall Library
New York Public Library
John Jay College of Criminal Justice, Lloyd Sealy Library, New York
National Archives and Records Administration, New York, New York
National Maritime Center, Arlington, Virginia
The New York Genealogical and Biographical Society, New York

Glossary

Acknowledgments

Now that I know something about how law enforcement works, I'm amazed that anyone in the NYPD ever spoke to me in the first place. Not that the cops have anything to hide—but with the constant potential for things to go terribly wrong, usually through no fault of their own, inviting someone to witness everything they do was an incredibly vulnerable choice. I didn't understand the risk when I started, but they did.

I would like to especially thank the following people for repeatedly taking that risk: Vito Spano, Phil Panzarella, Robert McHugh, Wendell Stradford, Tommy Wray, and Steve Kaplan. When I first contacted the squad after 9/11, I said, "Books take years. Before we decide yes or no about doing this book, let's meet and see if we want to spend the next few years together." Thank you all for saying yes, and for doing everything you did to help me, and thank you, too, for three years I will never forget.

Knowing what I do now, I also can't believe the miracles Walter Burnes from the Office of the Deputy Commissioner of Public Information regularly came up with for me. I am in your debt.

I'm grateful to everyone listed in my source notes. Each of them supplied a critical piece of information, particularly Dr. Robert Shaler from the Office of the Chief Medical Examiner, who contributed more than his fair share.

I would also like to thank now retired Chief of Detectives William Allee and the former commissioner of Public Information Michael Looney for graciously allowing me to write this book in the first place. And to Chief Allee, thank you for your kind assistance in the beginning, when I needed it most.

Among those who go to work without guns, cuffs, and printed copies of the Miranda warning, I would like to thank my agent, Betsy Lerner; my editor, Molly Stern; her assistant, Alessandra Lusardi; and my friend Howard Mittelmark. Betsy, I know this book was a lot more work than the last one, but thank you for it all, and for being more than an agent when I needed it. Molly, thanks for giving me the chance to do something different with the subject, and then helping me pull it off. Alessandra, your help at the end was invaluable, thank you. Howard, I'm sorry for making you read that same chapter seventeen times.

To John Diefenbach, Joann Sly, Ronald Stapleton, Laureen Schenley, William Aronwald, Dennis Graf, and all the relatives, friends, and associates of the murder victims that I spoke to, your cooperation involved something even more valuable than your time. You have my deepest gratitude for opening up about something that is surely more painful than anything anyone should ever have to endure. To Patrick Sanseverino, Raymond Sanseverino, John Paganitsa, and all the relatives, friends, and associates of the people of interest that I spoke to, I appreciate the grace with which you transcended a difficult situation in order to contribute to our understanding of a most difficult subject.

Finally, thank you to all my friends for helping me day and night. You know who you are, you know what you did, and there wouldn't be a book without you.

Index